English with a Difference

A SEASONAL COOKERY BOOK

To Jane
1 Corinthians 2:9

ENGLISH WITH A DIFFERENCE
A SEASONAL COOKERY BOOK

STEVEN WHEELER

PHOTOGRAPHS BY SIMON WHEELER
ILLUSTRATIONS BY LORRAINE HARRISON

SALEM HOUSE PUBLISHERS
TOPSFIELD, MASSACHUSETTS

First published in the United States by
Salem House Publishers, 1989,
462 Boston Street, Topsfield,
Massachusetts 01983

Library of Congress Cataloguing in Publication Data

Wheeler, Steven,
  English with a difference

  Includes index.
  1. Cookery, English. 2. Cookery, International.
I. Title
IX717.W46   1989   647.5947   88-24011

ISBN 0 88162 399 7

Typeset by SX Composing Ltd, Rayleigh, Essex
Colour separation by York House Graphics, London
Printed and bound in Spain by Graficas Estella, Navarra

Designed by Carol McCleeve

Contents

INTRODUCTION
7

JANUARY
11

FEBRUARY
23

MARCH
39

APRIL
55

MAY
71

JUNE
87

JULY
103

AUGUST
123

SEPTEMBER
143

OCTOBER
159

NOVEMBER
179

DECEMBER
199

INDEX
218

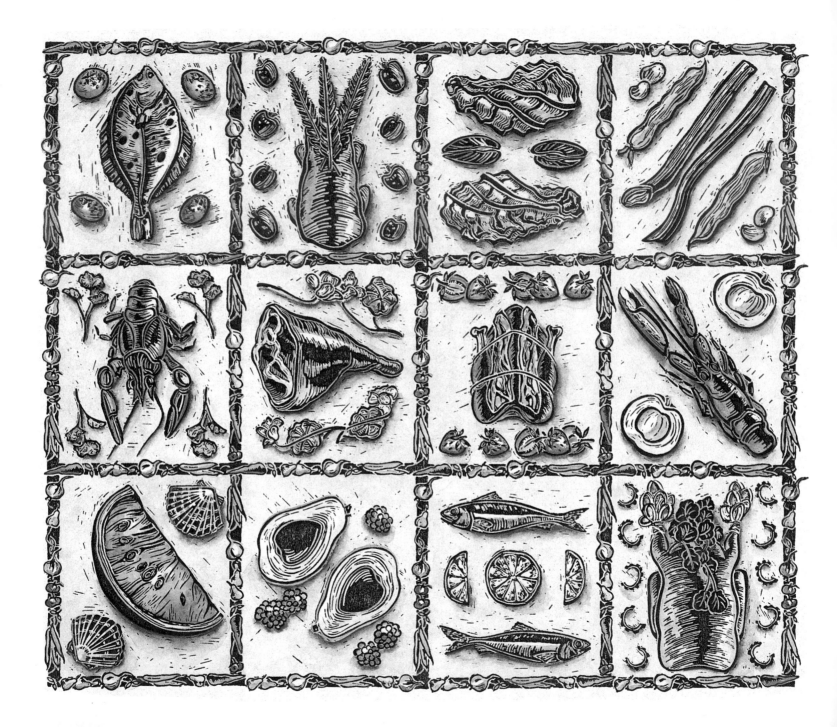

Introduction

Only one thing has inhibited the development of English cookery and that is the Englishman and his unwillingness to accept English food as anything more than overcooked vegetables, thick sauces, starchy puddings and mountains of bland meat. Fortunately we are living in a new age when we are able to leave behind the worst of our eating habits and turn to a fresh, exciting approach to English cooking: a style of cooking that relies entirely on fresh ingredients as they appear in season. English food no longer carries with it the stigma of the past and is at last beginning to appeal to modern changes in diet. At last, we are coming to realize that English pastures are indeed green and can provide us with more than we need to establish our own style of cooking.

Walk into any market in England at any time of the year, choose the very best of what you can find and you will have the makings of the finest cooking. *English with a Difference* is a detailed account of what I managed to find in my market and how I have chosen to prepare those ingredients throughout the year. It is the result of the experiences of a year during which, month by month, I set out down the high street with a family budget to find out how much I could buy that was in season. I discovered that not only were fruit, vegetables, fish and meat less expensive in season, but also that they were bursting with flavor and freshness. I became friendly with my greengrocer, fishmonger, butcher and game dealer and quizzed them at every opportunity. Where did their produce come from? When was it at its best? How long are various items in season? At times I must have been an absolute nuisance to them, but asking questions was the only way for me to stay reliably informed.

Buying only what I saw to be in prime condition, there were times when my shopping was limited to only a few items. As a rule I have preferred to do without rather than to settle for poor quality. If more of us refused to buy rubbish, gradually our markets would stop selling it. Arriving home and putting everything out on the kitchen table, I began to find that, providing I bought seasonally, the ingredients that I had chosen were inclined to work well together: ingredients that belonged to the same season were often complementary in smell and taste. It has been my intention to allow the contents of my shopping basket to represent the seasons' best. In turn, as I have cooked through the year, my intention has been to display the seasonal qualities of food as intimately as possible at the table.

From the moment we wake up in the morning, we are aware of the time of year and the weather; even our moods are altered by gray skies or sunshine. We are sensitive to changes in climate that occur during the year. The weather has much to do with our appetite, and our changing moods seem to accord with the natural order of the seasons. Summer is a time of relaxation and abundance when we like to be pampered with colorful salads, fruits and vegetables. Autumn is when we prepare for the winter and are attracted to the woodland associations of log fires, feathered game and wild mushrooms. The winter mood is warm and homely: our appetites grow for thick soups, rich stews, root vegetables and steamed puddings. By the spring we welcome all that is new, young and tender: the first lamb of the season, new potatoes, baby carrots and asparagus, followed by strawberries and cream.

The more I cook the more I realize that, essentially, there is nothing new in cooking. Everything we learn is founded on the knowledge and expertise of previous generations. Success depends entirely on our ability to draw on that knowledge and apply it in the kitchen. The French, for instance, started their culinary tradition by adapting and improving on seventeenth-century Italian cooking. Gradually, French chefs began to make use of their own resources, not least their abundance of good wine. To this day, the French are still able to adapt new ideas to fit in with what has become their own style of eating, exploring in great detail as many tastes, textures and smells as possible in a single meal – pure indulgence for most of us, but a way of life for the French.

The English also are keen to travel in search of new ideas, but tend to idolize new discoveries, often reconstructing them and giving them fancy foreign names, thus distinguishing them from common English food. It is this element of snobbery that has, until recently, made English food seem inferior. The progress that we have made in recent years in establishing our own style of cooking has indeed resulted from our curiosity and willingness to learn from other countries. While on vacation we are encouraged to try new dishes, many of which lead us to experiment with English ingredients. Television and magazines have also had much to contribute to our interest in good food, but where is this all leading us? Are we going to continue labeling our new-found creations with foreign names for the sake of snobbery, or are we prepared, as I am, to be proud of what is English?

In the past it has been fashionable, not to mention lucrative, for young chefs to set up restaurants in this country and to announce that their style of cooking is French. However, the French would not recognize it as anything but English. After all, it has been prepared by the English for the English from English ingredients. So who are we trying to fool? Gradually both we and the proprietors of such restaurants are coming to realize that what is English really ought to be called English. The finest English cooking may well be influenced by other styles of cuisine, but one should never ignore the fact that, when the food is on the table, it is as English as the land in which both we and the ingredients were raised.

Notes

All recipes serve 4 people unless otherwise stated.
In the monthly charts giving ingredients in season, the American
term is given in parenthesis, where appropriate.

January

*J*anuary is a time not only for looking forward into the new year, but for making the most of the moment, and using the winter vegetables which are in abundance just now, in warming soups, stews and casseroles. Traditional English beef stew would not be nearly as delicious without the usual helping of buttered rutabaga, mashed and ready to soak up the rich brown gravy. Carrots and turnips are at their best early in the year and are delicious served tossed in melted butter and chopped parsley. Other root vegetables – parsnips, celeriac, beet and salsify – are also worth experimenting with, providing they are firm and fresh. Parsnips are excellent roasted like potatoes around a piece of meat. Beets are good in winter salads and for a variety of substantial soups.

In January the vegetable stalls seem to have been taken over by mountains of full-blown cabbages as beautiful as they are huge. Savoy varieties with their tracery of veins, designed to trap buttery juices, offer the best flavor. Red winter cabbage is traditionally braised with apples and vinegar. Brussels sprouts are a good buy and stay fresher if you can buy them on the stem from the farm gate.

Greengrocers who have over-ordered for the Christmas period are often keen to sell their produce at reduced prices, and although quality is not always what it should be, there are usually bargains to be had. Potatoes are in good condition for boiling, baking and roasting, although it is always advisable to consult your greengrocer on the variety which will best suit your needs.

The fruit market has been invaded by an army of brightly colored citrus fruits, many of which have acquired a much improved flavor. Navel oranges are the easiest to peel, although for my money, the smaller Valencias have a sharper, more refreshing flavor. Seville oranges, best suited for marmalade making, usually appear toward the end of the month, along with varieties of blood oranges for squeezing. Pink grapefruit make a welcome appearance at this time of the year, offering a refreshing, healthy start to the day and looking most attrac-tive in winter fruit salads. Lemons and limes are at their best when they feel heavy for their size, indicating a greater proportion of juice. There are still plenty of exotic fruits on the market. Pineapples, bananas, mangoes and kiwi fruits can be specially good buys. Look out, too, for papayas, passion fruits and guavas to combine in an unforgettable fruit salad, or to make a sparkling sorbet. Home-grown apples and pears continue to provide a source of inspiration for many sweet and savory dishes. Early varieties of forced rhubarb are beginning to appear, although their season will not begin in earnest until February.

Providing the weather is favorable at sea for the fishermen, fish-mongers are able to offer the usual variety of flat fish – lemon and Dover sole, flounder, brill, halibut and turbot – many of which are now carrying their roe. Fresh sardines become more widely available in the new year and join other oily fish such as mackerel, herring and sprats for their winter season. Cod, haddock, pollock and whiting are in good condition this month and provide inspiration for tasty pies and other dishes for the midweek menu. One of the best buys for January is wings of skate, pearly white and full of flavor. The flesh parts easily from a central bone making it one of the easiest fish to eat. Skate knobs, cut from the tail, are popular in some parts of the country and are delicious fried simply in a little butter with a squeeze of lemon juice. Supplies of shellfish remain plentiful throughout the winter with oysters and scal-lops, despite their price, as popular as ever. A little less damaging to the family budget are pink and brown shrimp, mussels, cockles, win-kles and whelks, all brimming with the flavor of the sea.

The game season thins out quite considerably during January when pheasants, partridges, woodcock and snipe enjoy the relative peace of the closed season. Those birds that are available at this time of the year are usually too old for roasting and are better suited to soups and casseroles. The season for hare, venison, teal, mallard and pigeon continues.

FRUIT & NUTS

British at their best:
Apples
Chestnuts
Cooking Apples
Hazelnuts (Filberts)
Pears
Quinces
Rhubarb, forced
Walnuts

Imported in season:
Almonds
Bananas
Brazil Nuts
Clementines
Cranberries
Dates
Grapefruit
Grapes
Kiwi Fruit
Lemons
Limes
Lychees (Litchis)
Mangoes
Melons
Oranges
Papaya
Passion Fruit
Peanuts
Pecans
Pineapples
Pistachio Nuts
Pomegranates
Satsumas

VEGETABLES & HERBS

British at their best:
Beets, Broccoli
Cabbages
Cauliflowers
Celeriac
Celery
Chicory (Belgian Endive)
Kohlrabi
Leeks
Onions
Parsley
Parsnips
Potatoes
Rosemary
Sage
Salsify
Savory
Shallots
Spring Greens
Sprouts
Swedes (Rutabaga)
Thyme
Turnips
Watercress

Also available:
Carrots
Cucumbers
Fennel
Mustard and Cress
Spring Onions (Scallions)

Imported in season:
Aubergines (Eggplant)
Avocados
Courgettes (Zucchini)
Garlic
Lettuce
Sweet Peppers
Tomatoes

FISH & SHELLFISH

British at their best:
Cod
Coley (Pollock)
Gray Mullet
Haddock
Hake
Mussels
Oysters
Scallops
Sea Bass
Skate
Sprats
Whiting

Also available:
Brill
Cockles
Conger Eel
Dabs
Dover Sole
Halibut
Herring
Huss
Lemon Sole
Mackerel
Monkfish
Plaice
Prawns
Salmon
Sea Trout
Shrimp
Trout
Turbot
Winkles

Imported in season:
John Dory
Red Mullet
Sardines
Squid

POULTRY & GAME

British at their best:
Goose
Hare
Partridge
Pheasant
Snipe
Turkey
Venison
Wild Duck
Woodcock

Also available:
Chicken
Duck
Guinea Fowl
Pigeon
Quail
Rabbit

MEAT

Beef
Lamb
Offal
Pork
Veal

Starters

AN OLD ENGLISH GAME SOUP

There could be no finer dish to warm the cockles of the heart on a cold winter's day than a soup of English game, finished with a measure of sherry or brandy and served with chunks of crusty bread. If you have access to a game dealer, he may let you have one or two older birds, which provide the best flavor for soups and stews.

ingredients

one 2½lb old pheasant, partridge or grouse, cut up
1lb boneless venison or beef for stew, diced
¼lb unsmoked bacon, diced
½cup full-bodied red wine
1 beet or veal bone, sawn
1 large onion, quartered
I white of leek, split, washed and chopped
1 small carrot, roughly chopped
1 celery stalk, roughly chopped

2oz button mushrooms, quartered
1 bay leaf
10 juniper berries
1 large rosemary sprig

To finish
4tbsp butter
¼cup flour
salt and pepper
⅓cup dry sherry or brandy

Brown the game pieces, the venison or beef and the bacon in a large saucepan to bring out the flavor. You shouldn't need any extra oil since the birds and bacon will produce their own cooking fat. Add the wine and enough water to cover. Add the bone, vegetables and herbs and bring to a boil, then simmer for 2 hours.

Strain the bouillon into a bowl and allow to cool completely, then remove the fat from the surface. Remove the meat from the game birds and set aside. To finish the soup, melt the butter in a clean saucepan, add the flour and brown over a steady heat, stirring all the time. Remove from the heat and add the bouillon a little at a time, stirring until smooth. Add the game meat and bring to a boil, then season and simmer for 10-15 minutes. Add the sherry or brandy and serve with hot crispy bread.

WINTER PEA AND HAM SOUP

For those of us who settled for a ham over the Christmas period, finding ways of using up endless quantities of meat can become a bit of a problem. This year I suggest turning the leftover ham into a delicious pea and ham soup.

ingredients

2tbsp butter
1 onion, roughly chopped
1 small carrot, roughly chopped
½lb potatoes, sliced
6oz cooked ham, roughly chopped (1 heaping cup)
1 ham bone

7½cups water or ham bouillon
1 bouquet garni, consisting of 1 leek leaf, 1 thyme sprig, 1 bay leaf
1lb frozen peas (3cups)
salt and pepper

Melt the butter in a large saucepan, add the onion, carrot, potatoes and ham, cover and soften over a gentle heat for 3-4 minutes. Add the ham bone and the water or bouillon. To prepare the bouquet garni, wrap the thyme and the bay leaf in the leek leaf and tie with fine string. Add the bouquet garni to the saucepan, cover and simmer for 30 minutes. Add the peas, season to taste and simmer for 15 minutes.

Remove the ham bone and the bouquet garni from the soup and liquidize in a blender or food processor until smooth. Reheat the soup, taste for seasoning and serve with hot crusty bread or croûtons.

Pea and ham soup will freeze for up to 6 months.

CARROT AND HAZELNUT SOUFFLÉ

or those of us who are not vegetarians, the prospect of inviting friends who are to supper can be a little daunting. It is essential to choose very carefully dishes that will please everyone. Leafing through vegetarian cook books, it would appear that most recipes are written by and for vegetarians and rarely stir the interest of those who prefer meat. Throughout this book you will find vegetarian dishes created according to my own tastes, with the intention of keeping everyone happy. This light soufflé can be served either as a starter or as a main course for lunch.

ingredients . . . .

3tbsp butter
1½cups grated carrot, squeezed
  dry
1 onion, finely chopped
3tbsp flour

1cup milk
½cup ground hazelnuts (filberts),
  toasted
5 eggs, separated
salt and pepper

Grease a 7inch soufflé dish well with 1tbsp of the butter and set aside. Melt the remaining butter in a saucepan, add the carrot and onion and soften, uncovered, to allow the moisture from the carrot to evaporate. Add the flour and remove the pan from the heat. Add the milk a little at a time, stirring until evenly blended. Return to the heat to thicken. Add the ground hazelnuts, egg yolks and seasoning, cook for 30 seconds or so, then remove from the heat. If you are planning ahead, this mixture can be prepared well in advance.

Preheat the oven to 400°F. To finish: beat the egg whites until they are smooth and firm. Stir a quarter of the beaten whites into the hot mixture until evenly blended, then fold in the remainder with a large metal spoon or spatula. Turn the mixture into the prepared soufflé dish and spread the top level.

If you are well practiced in your soufflé making, the uncooked soufflé should be able to stand in a warm place for up to 30 minutes before baking. Otherwise the soufflé is best cooked immediately in the center of the oven for 20-25 minutes, until puffed up and set on top, but still creamy in the center. Serve immediately.

A CHICKEN LIVER, APPLE AND WALNUT PÂTÉ

or a starter to be a success from the cook's point of view, it must be quick and easy to prepare as well as delicious. Perhaps another element of success is for your guests to be convinced that the dish took a long time to prepare. The truth of the matter is that this pâté can be prepared from start to finish in 20 minutes.

ingredients . . . .

½lb frozen chicken livers,
  thawed
1 stick unsalted butter
1 onion, chopped
2 firm sweet apples, peeled,
  cored and chopped

½cup coarsely broken walnuts
1tsp English mustard powder
1 pinch freshly grated nutmeg
salt

Place the chicken livers in a saucepan, cover with water and simmer for 10-12 minutes. Meanwhile, melt 2tbsp butter in another saucepan, add the onion together with the apple, cover and soften over a gentle heat for 3-4 minutes.

Drain the chicken livers of their cooking liquid. Place the livers in a blender or food processor with the onion and the apple. Add the remaining butter, walnut pieces, mustard and nutmeg. Blend the ingredients until smooth. Taste and season with salt. Spoon the pâté into an attractive dish and refrigerate before serving.

If you need to keep the pâté for longer than 2 days, pour a layer of clarified butter over the surface and leave to set. Covered in this way, the pâté will keep in the refrigerator for up to 10 days. Serve the pâté with a small green salad together with slices of apple to garnish. Offer a basket of hot toast at the table.

Main Courses

GRANDAD'S GUDGEONS OF SOLE WITH BANANAS AND ALMONDS

 y grandfather, George Wheeler, has been the proprietor and one-time chef of the King's Arms Hotel, Pembroke, for over thirty years. During his time in the kitchens he established this most delicious way of preparing sole: breadcrumbed and fried until golden with bananas and toasted almonds, an unusual combination of flavors which makes a change from traditional ways of cooking this fish. If sole is not available, fillets of flounder can be used in its stead.

ingredients . . . .

2lb sole or flounder, skinned, filleted and cut into fingers	½cup peanut oil
salt and pepper	2tbsp butter
3tbsp flour	2 bananas, sliced diagonally
2 eggs	½cup sliced almonds
2cups dried bread crumbs	1 lemon, cut into wedges, for garnish

Season the sole with salt and pepper and dust with the flour. Break the eggs into a shallow dish and spread the bread crumbs out on a small pan. Dip the fingers of fish first into the egg, then into the bread crumbs, pressing them onto coat thoroughly. If you are planning ahead, the gudgeons can be spread out on a pan and kept in the refrigerator for up to 3 hours.

To cook the gudgeons, heat the oil and butter together in a large skillet. (The oil will prevent the butter from burning.) When the mixture is hot, fry the gudgeons one handful at a time for 3-4 minutes or until golden. Drain the gudgeons on paper towels and keep warm while you fry the remainder.

Fry the banana slices together with the almonds until the almonds are brown. Serve the gudgeons with the bananas and almonds sprinkled over the top, accompanied by lemon wedges. Broccoli, turnips or shallow-fried potatoes sprinkled with parsley are best suited to this dish.

AN ENGLISH FISH STEW WITH PARSLEY DUMPLINGS

 lmost every country with a coastline is able to boast at least one dish that combines the fruits of its own particular sea. Every country, that is, except England! Surely it is time we realized the potential that awaits us beneath our own waters. This delicious fish concoction is bejeweled with tiny parsley dumplings.

ingredients . . . .

3tbsp olive oil	skinned and diced
2 onions, roughly chopped	½lb squid, cleaned and cut into rings
2 garlic cloves, minced	1 thyme sprig
1 leek, split, washed and roughly chopped	¼lb peeled small shrimp
2 celery stalks, cut into 1inch batons	Parsley Dumplings
2 carrots, cut into 1inch batons	1¼cups self-rising flour
¼lb bacon, cut into strips	⅓cup shredded beef suet
½lb potatoes, peeled and diced	2tbsp chopped parsley
½lb boneless monkfish, diced	Garnish
½lb eel, preferably conger eel,	freshly chopped parsley

Heat the oil in a flameproof casserole, add the onions, garlic, leek, celery, carrots and bacon, cover and soften over a gentle heat for 6-8 minutes. Add 2 pints water, the potatoes, monkfish, eel, squid and thyme. Cover once again and bring to a boil, then simmer for 20 minutes.

Meanwhile, prepare the dumplings: sift the flour into a mixing bowl, add the remaining dumpling ingredients with 3 tbsp cold water and mix to an even dough. Shape the dough into a long sausage and cut into pieces no larger than a grape.

Add the dumplings to the casserole with the shrimp, cover and simmer for a further 15-20 minutes or until the dumplings are floating and risen. Season with salt and pepper, sprinkle with parsley and serve in heated soup plates.

STILTON AND CELERY SOUFFLÉ

After the initial sense of relief that Christmas has come and gone for another year, we are often faced with the problem of how to use up the leftovers. Leftover pieces of Stilton seem to pose the biggest problem as they sit at the back of the refrigerator waiting for a sudden flash of inspiration. For this recipe I have crumbled the Stilton into a basic soufflé mixture with crispy celery and a hint of fresh sage.

ingredients ....

1tbsp butter, softened
1¼cups milk
3tbsp flour
5 eggs, separated
2 pinches salt

1 pinch cayenne
¾cup crumbled or grated Stilton
  cheese
1 celery stalk, chopped
1tbsp chopped fresh sage

Grease a 6inch soufflé dish generously with the butter and set aside. Preheat the oven to 400°F.

Measure 4tbsp of the milk into a mixing bowl, add the flour, egg yolks, half the salt and the cayenne and whisk until thoroughly blended. Bring the remaining milk to a boil and whisk into the bowl. Return to the pan, bring to a boil and simmer until thickened. Add the Stilton, celery and sage. The mixture should drop from a spoon in thick blobs. If you are planning ahead, this mixture can be left to stand at room temperature for up to 3 hours, then reheated 30 minutes before you are ready to serve the soufflé.

Place the egg whites in a mixing bowl with the remaining salt and beat until they hold a soft peak on the end of the beater. It is important that the egg whites are smooth when they are folded into the cheese mixture. Egg whites can become grainy if they are over-beaten or if they are left to stand even briefly before folding in. If this happens, let them stand for a few minutes, then beat again.

Stir about a quarter of the smooth beaten egg whites into the hot cheese mixture until evenly mixed, then fold in the remainder with a rubber spatula. Turn the soufflé mixture into the prepared dish, spread the top level and bake in the center of the oven for 20 minutes. To test whether the soufflé is cooked, pierce the side with a wooden skewer. It is cooked when it is still a little soft in the middle. Serve the soufflé as soon as it comes out of the oven, with a crisp green salad.

WINGS OF SKATE WITH NUT BROWN BUTTER AND CAPERS

The price at which fish is sold in the market is largely determined by the quality of its flavor and texture. Skate, however, is an exception to this rule and remains, for my money, one of the best buys, especially during the winter months when its flesh is pearly-white. When a fish has such an excellent flavor, it is often best to cook it as simply as possible; in this case shallow-fried in nut-brown butter and finished with a handful of chopped capers in vinegar.

ingredients ....

four 7oz skate wings
salt and pepper
flour, for dusting
2tbsp peanut oil
6tbsp unsalted butter
3tbsp capers, roughly chopped

1tbsp caper vinegar

Garnish
wedges of lemon
parsley sprigs

Season the skate on both sides with salt and pepper and dust with flour. Heat the oil and 2tbsp of the butter in a large skillet and fry the skate for 5 minutes on each side. Transfer to a warm plate.

Heat the remaining butter in the skillet until it bubbles and begins to brown. Add the capers and vinegar, then pour over the skate wings and serve garnished with lemon wedges and parsley sprigs.

SLOW BEEF CASSEROLE COOKED WITH GUINNESS

---

*T*he French have a wonderfully romantic phrase to describe what we in England call a stew: *les petits plats qui mijotent au coin du feu,* referring to a dish that cooks gracefully over a very low heat. The phrase reveals one of the great secrets of how to treat cuts of meat suitable for stewing and braising. We all know that less tender cuts of meat need longer cooking, but one thing we can learn from the French is that the heat that surrounds the casserole must be so gentle as merely to caress the meat with the slightest simmer. In this way the meat can relax, absorb its surrounding juices and cook to perfection.

ingredients . . . .

¼cup beef drippings or peanut oil	2tbsp flour
3oz slab bacon, cut into strips	¾cup Guinness or stout
1 onion, sliced	1¼cups hot beef stock
1 small carrot, sliced	1tsp tomato paste
1½lb lean beef chuck, cut into 1inch cubes	1tsp dried marjoram or oregano
	1 bay leaf
	salt and pepper

Heat 2tbsp of the drippings or oil in a large heavy skillet. Add the bacon and fry until crisp. Add the onion and carrot and brown evenly over a steady heat. Transfer the bacon and the vegetables to a heavy casserole.

Heat the remaining drippings or oil in the skillet and brown the beef cubes to seal in the flavor. Add the meat to the casserole and sprinkle with the flour. Stir until the flour is absorbed by the cooking juices.

Pour off the remaining fat from the skillet, leaving the sediment in the bottom. Return the pan to the heat, add the Guinness or stout and stir with a flat wooden spoon in order to loosen the sediment. Pour the contents of the skillet over the meat and add the hot bouillon, tomato paste, herbs and seasoning. It is important that the liquid in which the beef is cooked is hot before the casserole goes into the oven since the beef will not start to cook until just below boiling.

The most effective way to cook the beef is to allow it to simmer very gently on top of an Aga for 2½-3 hours (in which case you must use a flameproof casserole). If you do not have an Aga, cook the beef for the same length of time in the oven preheated to 300°F. Serve the beef with creamed potatoes and leeks.

A LANCASHIRE HOT POT OF LAMB

---

*T*he traditional Lancashire Hot Pot became popular during the last century in the northern counties of England as an inexpensive meal that both warmed and satisfied during the bitterly cold winters.

ingredients . . . .

2lb lamb shoulder blade or arm chops	2lb potatoes, peeled and cut into ¼inch slices
3tbsp drippings or oil	2tbsp flour
2 onions, sliced	salt and pepper
3 carrots, peeled and cut into short fingers	1tbsp Worcestershire sauce
3 celery stalks, cut into short lengths	1 thyme sprig
	1 rosemary sprig

Preheat the oven to 350°F. Trim the lamb chops. Heat the drippings or oil in a large skillet and brown the lamb on both sides to seal in the goodness. (Browning will also give a better flavor to the meat.) Remove the lamb and set aside while you brown the onions, carrots and celery in the same way.

Arrange a layer of lamb chops in the bottom of a casserole. Add a layer of onion, carrot and celery, followed by a layer of potatoes. Continue with another layer of lamb and mixed vegetables, finishing with a final layer of potatoes to cover.

Stir the flour into the skillet to absorb the remaining fat. Off the heat, gradually stir in 2½cups of boiling water until smooth and thoroughly blended. Add the seasoning and Worcestershire sauce and pour the mixture over the potatoes. Push a sprig of thyme and rosemary down the side of the casserole, cover and bake in the center of the oven for 2 hours. To finish, remove the lid from the casserole, increase the oven temperature to 400°F and cook for a further 15 minutes until the potato topping is browned.

ROAST DUCK WITH CARDAMOM AND ORANGE

O ne duck recipe that has stood the test of time is that old favorite, Duck with Orange. At this time of the year I cannot resist making use of the new season's oranges, so sharp and full of flavor. However, when I entertain, my guests have come to expect a little more than standard fare, so for this recipe I chose to add a hint of cardamom to the sauce to lift the flavor of the orange.

ingredients . . . .

one 5lb duck with giblets	1tbsp wine vinegar
1 small onion, roughly chopped	5 cardamom pods, crushed
1 small carrot, roughly chopped	2tbsp butter, softened
1 thyme sprig	2tbsp flour
1 bay leaf	salt and pepper
2 oranges	1 bunch of watercress, for
1 lemon	garnish
3tbsp sugar	

Remove the wings from the duck at the second joint and place them in a saucepan ready for a simple bouillon. Remove the liver from the giblets. Add the remaining giblets, the onion, carrot, thyme and bay leaf to the pan. Cover with cold water and bring to a boil, then let simmer for 1 hour.

Preheat the oven to 425°F. Pierce the duck skin several times to enable the fat to flow while cooking. Rub the skin with fine salt and place the duck breast side down on a trivet in a roasting pan. Roast in center of the oven for 20-30 minutes, then reduce the oven temperature to 350°F, turn the duck breast side uppermost and continue to roast for a further 1¼ hours, until cooked through.

To prepare the sauce: remove the outer zest from one of the oranges with a vegetable peeler and cut into fine shreds as if making marmalade. Cover the shredded zest with cold water and bring to a boil, then simmer for 2-3 minutes. Squeeze the juice of both oranges and the lemon into a small bowl and set aside. Measure the sugar into a small heavy-bottomed saucepan and stir over a moderate heat until the sugar has caramelized. Remove from the heat, stand well back and add the orange and lemon juices. Add the vinegar, cardamom pods and 1cup of the strained duck bouillon. Bring to a boil, then simmer for 10-12 minutes.

To thicken the sauce, combine the soft butter with the flour to form a well blended paste. Remove the sauce from the heat and gradually beat in the paste until the butter has melted. Return to a boil to thicken. Strain and add the shredded orange zest. Taste and season with salt and pepper.

Remove the cooked duck to a heated serving dish, saving the drippings for roast or fried potatoes. Garnish the duck with the watercress and serve with roast potatoes, carrots, turnips and peas, with the sauce handed separately in a sauce-boat.

The duck carcass can be made into An Old-fashioned Duck Broth with Port Wine (see October).

TURKEY GRATIN WITH LEEKS AND GARLIC

A long with the post-Christmas blues and the New Year hangover comes the perennial problem of how to get just one more meal out of the leftover turkey. Here is a recipe which is also delicious made with cooked ham or a combination of ham and turkey.

ingredients . . . .

4tbsp butter	1¼cups milk
2 large leeks, split, washed and	salt and pepper
shredded	1lb cooked turkey and/or ham,
2 garlic cloves, minced	diced (3-4cups)
3oz slab bacon, cut into strips	3tbsp dry sherry (optional)
¼cup flour	1½lb potatoes, sliced

Preheat the oven to 400°F.

Melt the butter in a saucepan, add the leeks, garlic and bacon, cover and soften over a gentle heat for 6-7 minutes. Stir in the flour, remove from the heat and gradually add the milk, until smooth. Return to the heat, season and simmer until thickened. Add the turkey and/or the ham and stir in the sherry.

Spread the mixture in the bottom of a large gratin dish and cover the top with overlapping slices of potato. Cook near the top of the oven for 45-50 minutes. Finish by browning the potatoes under the broiler.

*Winter Pea and Ham Soup; English Fish Stew with Parsley Dumplings;
Butterscotch Meringue Tart.*

Puddings

AN UPSIDE-DOWN APPLE SPONGE CAKE

The idea for this recipe came some years ago when I was having lunch with some friends and was asked if I could rustle up a quick dessert. Inspiration came from some apples on the kitchen table. Before long they and some eggs, flour, butter and sugar became this upside-down apple sponge cake. For the benefit of my host, here is the recipe.

ingredients . . . .

butter for greasing
4tbsp unsalted butter
2lb firm sweet apples, peeled, quartered and cored

3 eggs, at room temperature
6tbsp sugar
9tbsp flour

Lightly grease an 8inch cake pan with butter and set aside. Preheat the oven to 400°F.

Melt the butter in a large skillet and toss the apples in the butter for 6-8 minutes until they are golden. Place the eggs and the sugar in a mixing bowl and beat for 3-4 minutes, until the mixture will leave a trail across the surface. Sift the flour over the beaten eggs and fold in with a large metal spoon or spatula.

Place the apples in the bottom of the cake tin, pour the cake batter over the top and bake in the center of the oven for 30-35 minutes, until the cake is risen and golden, and the apples are tender. Place a serving plate over the pan and unmold the cake so that the apples are on the top. Serve with softly whipped cream or custard sauce.

Pears or a mixture of apples and pears can be used as variations. If you have some ground almonds left over from the Christmas cake they will add extra richness to the cake combined half and half with the flour.

MANCHESTER PUDDING WITH BANANAS AND LIME

It is a fact that many of our most popular desserts were created not by clever pastry cooks in fancy hotels and restaurants, but by equally clever mums at home with time-consuming children. This is just such a recipe, wonderfully simple and most effective in the way it works.

ingredients . . . .

6tbsp butter, softened
6tbsp sugar
1 egg, beaten
6tbsp self-rising flour
3tbsp ground almonds
3 bananas, sliced

grated zest and juice of 1 lime

Custard
2½cups milk
3 eggs
2tbsp sugar

Preheat the oven to 375°F. Place the butter and sugar in a mixing bowl and beat together until light and fluffy. Add the egg a little at a time and stir in the flour and ground almonds until thoroughly blended. Scatter the bananas over the bottom of a 2-quart soufflé dish or casserole. Add the lime zest and juice. Spread the creamed cake batter over the top and set aside.

To prepare the custard: bring the milk to a boil and pour over the beaten eggs and sugar in a bowl. Strain over the batter. Stand the dish in a roasting pan, pour in boiling water to come halfway up the sides of the dish and bake in oven for 40-45 minutes. Serve the pudding warm or cold.

BUTTERSCOTCH MERINGUE TART

*D*eciding on a dessert that will appeal to everyone's taste can be a tricky business, especially when there are children at the table. From past experience I have found that virtually anything that contains custard, pastry or meringue is bound to be a great success. This recipe features all three.

ingredients..........................

Pastry
1²/₃cups flour
2tbsp sugar
1 stick firm butter
4-5tbsp cold water

Butterscotch custard
2tbsp butter
3tbsp heavy cream

¼cup sugar
1cup milk
3 egg yolks
3tbsp flour

Topping
3 egg whites
2tbsp sugar

To make the pastry: sift the flour and sugar into a mixing bowl or food processor, add the butter and cut together or process until the mixture resembles large bread crumbs. Add enough water to make an even dough. Do not work more than you have to. Cover and rest in the refrigerator for 15-20 minutes.

Preheat the oven to 375°F. Lightly grease an 8inch tart pan with butter. Roll out the pastry on a floured work surface and use to line the tart pan. Place a circle of parchment paper in the pastry case, fill with dry beans or rice and bake the case unfilled in the oven for 25-30 minutes.

To prepare the custard: measure the butter and cream and put to one side. Measure 1tbsp of the sugar into a small heavy saucepan and melt over a steady heat. Before the sugar caramelizes, stir in the remaining sugar a little at a time. Allow the sugar to color to a reddish-brown, then remove from the heat and stir in the butter and cream.

Measure 2tbsp of the milk into a mixing bowl, add the egg yolks and stir in the flour. Add the remaining milk to the butterscotch mixture in the pan and bring to a boil, stirring. Pour the butterscotch-flavored milk over the egg and flour mixture, then return to the pan and thicken over a gentle heat. Spread the butterscotch custard in the baked pastry case.

To make the topping: beat the egg whites in a clean bowl, adding the sugar gradually until firm. Spread the meringue over the tart, sprinkle with extra sugar and brown under the broiler.

ORANGE AND LEMON CHEESECAKE

*O*ne of the most effective ways of capturing the special tang of oranges and lemons this month is to combine their zest and juice with soft cheese and eggs in a delicate, tempting cheesecake.

ingredients..........................

Crumb base
4tbsp butter
1cup packed graham cracker
  crumbs

Filling
1cup packed pot cheese
²/₃cup plain yogurt
finely grated zest and juice of 2
  oranges
finely grated zest and juice of 1
  lemon

²/₃cup whipping cream
1 envelope unflavored gelatin
2 eggs
3tbsp sugar

Decoration
2 oranges
1 kiwi fruit
²/₃cup black grapes

Lightly grease an 8inch springform cake pan and line with wax paper. To make the base: melt the butter in a saucepan, stir in the crumbs and press into the bottom of the cake pan.

To prepare the filling: blend the pot cheese and yogurt together in a bowl with the orange and lemon zests and juice. Softly whip the cream and fold in evenly. Soften the gelatin with 2tbsp cold water in a small heatproof bowl and melt by standing the bowl over a saucepan of boiling water.

Place the eggs and sugar in a mixing bowl and beat for 3-4 minutes until a ribbon of the mixture can be drawn across the surface. Add the liquid gelatin to the beaten eggs and sugar and fold into the cheese mixture. Turn into the prepared cake pan and refrigerate for 2-3 hours until set. Decorate with segments of orange, kiwi fruit and grapes.

February

With the bleakest month of the year now behind us, the days are becoming noticeably longer. Brave little snowdrops and crocuses make a first appearance, seemingly impervious to the bitterly cold winter, perhaps protected by their glow of color. To provide our own inner glow for the twenty-eight days of February, we can look forward to a variety of thick, warming stews and steamed sponge puddings accompanied by piping hot custard sauce.

The vegetable markets have plenty on offer during February with several varieties of cabbage. Brussels sprouts and spring greens are still in good condition and seem to do well in the colder weather. Root vegetables — carrots, turnips, rutabaga and parsnips — are still full of flavor and are at their best cooked in winter stews and casseroles. Mushrooms, an essential ingredient for a good steak and kidney pudding, are often in good supply early in the year. Broccoli and cauliflower are often well priced during February although some varieties are in poor conditon. Avocados are good value for money at the moment and are delicious in a variety of starters and salads, or served hot, as in the gratin recipe on page 30. Look out for seedless cocktail avocados. These make an attractive garnish and look pretty sliced into a green salad.

The fruit stalls are becoming more colorful now with varieties of forced rhubarb, mainly from Yorkshire, taking pride of place among mountains of imported oranges. In fact, the two flavors marry well together; try this combination in a pie, crumble or compote. February has long been the month of marmalade-making, with the arrival of the bumpy-skinned Seville bitters from Spain. Blood oranges make a special appearance in February and are delicious squeezed at the breakfast table. Don't be surprised when you cut into one: they really are the most shocking red color. Lemons make an extra effort to provide juice enough for Shrove Tuesday, while pink grapefruits are also in good supply. Passion fruit seems to have formed a special association with St Valentine's Day on the 14th and can inspire a number of exotically scented desserts for the occasion.

At the fishmonger's there are usually good supplies of codling, large cod, haddock and whiting, all of which are reasonably priced. Herring, mackerel and sea bass seem to fatten up in the cold weather along with sprats and sardines which also have a good flavor. Skate wings are still widely available at most fishmongers and remain one of the best buys of the month. Flat fish, although still available, are not doing so well at the moment. Those that are carrying their roe tend to sacrifice much of their flavor and texture and remain in poor condition until April. The rod and line salmon season has opened on the River Tey, although supplies of wild salmon will be limited until netting is allowed later in the year. Shellfish remain plentiful throughout the winter months with mussels, oysters, scallops, cockles, clams, winkles and shrimp all in good supply.

The feathered game season nears its end in February with pheasant finishing on the 1st and wild duck on the 20th. If you are offered any feathered game late in the season, take it gladly: older birds make a wonderful casserole. Rabbit and hare continue to be good value.

FEBRUARY INGREDIENTS IN SEASON

FRUIT AND NUTS

British at their best:
Apples
Chestnuts
Cooking Apples
Pears
Rhubarb, forced
Hazelnuts (Filberts)
Walnuts

Imported in season:
Almonds
Bananas
Brazil Nuts
Clementines
Dates
Grapefruit
Grapes
Kiwi Fruit
Kumquats
Lemons
Limes
Lychees (Litchis)
Melons
Oranges
Passion Fruit
Peanuts
Pecans
Pineapple
Pistachio Nuts
Pomegranates
Satsumas

VEGETABLES & HERBS

British at their best:
Cabbages
Cauliflowers
Celeriac
Celery
Chicory (Belgian Endive)
Broccoli
Kohlrabi
Leeks
Onions
Parsley
Parsnips
Potatoes
Rosemary
Sage
Salsify
Savory
Shallots
Spring Greens
Sprouts
Swedes (Rutabaga)
Thyme
Turnips
Watercress

Also available:
Beets

Carrots
Cucumbers
Fennel
Mustard and Cress
Spring Onions (Scallions)

Imported in season:
Aubergines (Eggplants)
Avocados
Courgettes (Zucchini)
Garlic
Lettuce
Sweet Peppers
Tomatoes

FISH & SHELLFISH

British at their best:
Cod
Coley (Pollock)
Gray Mullet
Haddock
Hake
Mussels
Oysters
Prawns
Scallops
Sea Bass
Shrimp
Skate
Sprats
Whiting

Also available:
Brill
Cockles
Conger Eel
Dabs
Dover Sole
Halibut
Herring
Huss
Lemon Sole
Mackerel
Monkfish
Plaice
Red Mullet
Salmon
Sea Trout
Turbot
Trout
Winkles

Imported in season:
John Dory
Sardines
Squid

POULTRY & GAME

British at their best:
Hare
Venison
Wild Duck until the 20th

Also available:
Chicken
Duck
Goose
Guinea Fowl
Pigeon
Quail
Rabbit
Turkey

MEAT

Beef
Lamb
Offal
Pork
Veal

Starters

AN ENGLISH ONION SOUP WITH A TOASTED CHEESE TOPPING

When the weather is bitterly cold, there are few things as welcoming as a warming homemade soup. This soup is made very simply from sliced onions and a well-flavored beef bouillon and finished under the broiler with a delicious arrangement of toasted cheese.

ingredients

2tbsp butter	5cups good beef bouillon
2 onions, thinly sliced	1 slice of stale bread, quartered
1tsp sugar	½cup grated Cheddar cheese
salt and pepper	1 pinch paprika

Melt the butter in a shallow, heavy-based pan, add the onions, sugar and salt and cook the onions over a steady heat for 15-20 minutes until they are well browned but not burnt. (Browning the onions will give the soup its delicate flavor and color.)

Transfer the onions to a larger saucepan, add the bouillon and simmer for 25-30 minutes. Season the soup with freshly ground black pepper and divide among 4 flameproof bowls. Float a piece of bread on the surface of each bowl, sprinkle with the grated cheese and paprika and finish under the broiler until golden brown.

LITTLE SEAFOOD HOT POTS

The increasing variety of seafood available during the winter months has inspired me to put together these little hot pots, finished under the broiler and served as a starter or light main course with hot crusty bread.

ingredients

2½pints mussels	1tbsp flour
2 parsley sprigs	½lb small cooked peeled shrimp
⅓cup dry white wine	salt and pepper
½lb squid, cleaned and cut into rings	⅓cup heavy cream
½lb cod or haddock fillet, skinned and diced	2 egg yolks
4tbsp butter	Garnish
1 onion, chopped	parsley sprigs
1 carrot, cut into short batons	
1 celery stalk, cut into short batons	

Wash the mussels in plenty of cold water and scrub them to remove any beards or barnacles. Discard any that are open. Place the mussels in a large saucepan with the parsley, wine and ⅓cup water. Cover and cook for 6-8 minutes or until the mussels have opened. Strain the mussel juice into a saucepan and leave the mussels to cool, then shuck them. Discard any that have not opened.

Cook the squid in the mussel juices for 5 minutes, add the cod or haddock and cook for a further 10 minutes. Meanwhile, melt the butter in another saucepan, add the onion, carrot and celery and soften over a gentle heat. Stir in the flour until absorbed. Strain the well-flavored juices from the cooked fish over the vegetables and allow to thicken.

Add the shucked mussels, the cod or haddock, squid and shrimp and season with salt and pepper. Combine the cream and egg yolks in a cup and stir into the seafood mixture. Divide among 4 gratin dishes and finish under the broiler for 8-10 minutes, until browned. Garnish with parsley sprigs.

KIPPER PÂTÉ WITH LEMON AND PARSLEY

It is still possible to buy properly kippered herrings, smoked as they should be over oak chippings. Kippers from the Isle of Man, Loch Fyne and Great Yarmouth are considered to be among the finest, while factory-produced alternatives are not really worth bothering with. One of my favorite ways of preparing kippers, apart from the usual breakfast treat, is to turn them into a delicious pâté sharpened with lemon juice. Serve as a starter or for an informal lunch with Melba toast or whole-grain bread.

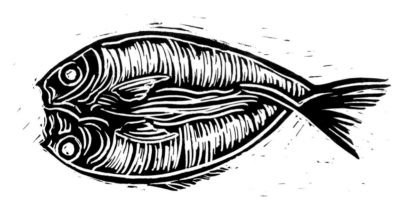

ingredients . . . .

½lb finest kippers
heaping ⅓cup packed pot
  cheese
4tbsp butter, softened
2 lemons

freshly ground black pepper

Garnish
parsley sprigs
lemon wedges

Place the kippers in a large pitcher, cover with boiling water and leave to stand for 10-12 minutes. This process will cook the kippers as well as removing any saltiness.

Drain the kippers, remove the backbones and as many of the smaller bones as you can, and flake the flesh into a blender or food processor, discarding the skin. Add the cheese, butter, the finely grated zest of one lemon and the juice of both. Season with freshly ground black pepper and process until smooth.

Pack the pâté into 4 individual dishes or one large one and refrigerate. If you need to keep the pâté for longer than 3 days, it will be necessary to seal it with a layer of melted butter. This way, the pâté will keep for up to 10 days. To serve, decorate with parsley sprigs and lemon wedges and offer melba toast or whole-grain bread.

CREAMY LEEK AND MUSHROOM TARTLETS

Both leeks and mushrooms are plentiful during February and combine beautifully with eggs and cream to make these delicious little tarts.

ingredients . . . .

3tbsp butter
basic pie pastry, made with
  1½cups flour
2 thick bacon slices, cut into
  strips
½lb leeks, split, washed and
  shredded

¼lb button mushrooms, sliced
1 thyme sprig
⅔cup light cream
2 eggs
salt and pepper

Lightly grease four 4inch tartlet pans with 1tbsp of the butter. Roll out the pastry as thinly as you can on a floured work surface and line the pans without stretching the pastry. (If the pastry is too thick, there will be no room for the filling.) Allow the tartlet cases to rest for 30 minutes to prevent them from shrinking.

Preheat the oven to 375°F. Place a square of foil in each tartlet case and bake unfilled for 20-25 minutes. Meanwhile, melt the remaining butter in a shallow saucepan, add the bacon, leeks, mushrooms and thyme, cover and cook over a gentle heat for 8-10 minutes, until soft.

Divide the mixture among the tartlet cases. Combine the cream, eggs and seasoning in a measuring cup, pour into the cases and bake near the top of the oven for a further 20-25 minutes or until just set.

If you are planning ahead, the pastry cases and the filling can be prepared well in advance and baked nearer the time of serving.

Main Courses

CRISPY FISH CAKES WITH A PARSLEY AND LEMON SAUCE

❦

he Victorians popularized the idea of fish cakes, but today the fish cake seems to have suffered from factory production and has been reduced both in flavor and texture to that of wet cardboard. The salvation of this tasty and easy dish is in the hands of the home cook who, with a little loving care, can restore it to its former glory.

ingredients ....

1lb cod or haddock, fresh or smoked, or a mixture
1¼cups milk
1lb potatoes, cooked and mashed
3 eggs
1tbsp chopped parsley
salt and pepper
3tbsp flour

1⅓cups dried bread crumbs
5tbsp peanut oil

Sauce
2tbsp butter
2tbsp flour
finely grated zest and juice of 1 lemon
2tbsp chopped parsley

Place the fish in a saucepan with the milk, cover and simmer for 6-8 minutes. Lift the fish out of the milk and leave to cool. Save the milk for the parsley and lemon sauce.

When the fish is cool enough to handle, flake it through your fingers to remove any small bones. Combine the fish together with the mashed potato, 1 egg, parsley and seasoning. If the mixture seems dry, add a little milk to moisten. Divide the mixture into 8 portions, dust with flour and shape into neat little patties.

Beat the remaining 2 eggs in a shallow dish. Spread out the bread crumbs on another plate. Coat the fish cakes in beaten egg, then press them into the bread crumbs, to cover completely.

To make the sauce, melt the butter in a small saucepan and stir in the flour. Remove from the heat and gradually stir in the milk in which the fish was cooked, until smooth. Bring to a boil, then simmer for 10 minutes. Add the lemon zest and juice, the parsley and the seasoning just before serving.

To cook the fish cakes, heat the oil with a pat of butter in a large skillet, add the fish cakes and fry for 5-7 minutes on each side or until the cakes are golden. Drain on paper towels and serve with the sauce poured over.

Fish cakes can be frozen between sheets of freezer paper for up to 8 weeks. Allow to thaw completely before cooking.

FRESH SARDINES WITH RHUBARB, GINGER AND SOY

❦

resh sardines become more widely available early in the year and are well worth trying. Here I have blended the sharpness of fresh rhubarb with the Eastern flavors of ginger root and soy sauce.

ingredients ....

12 fresh sardines, scaled and cleaned, heads removed
½lb pink rhubarb, cut into 1½inch matchsticks
1inch piece of ginger root, bruised

juice of 1 lemon
3tbsp light soy sauce
1tsp sugar
1tbsp chopped coriander (cilantro) leaves

Place the sardines on a heatproof plate and toss together with the rhubarb, ginger, lemon juice, soy sauce and sugar. Cover and leave to marinate for 6-8 hours, or overnight if possible.

Arrange the plate in a large oriental steamer, cover and steam over a gentle heat for 20-25 minutes. (If you do not have a large enough steamer, you can improvise with a wide shallow saucepan or a roasting pan. Bring an inch or so of water to a boil in the pan on top of the stove. Position an upturned saucer in the bottom of the pan and rest the plate of sardines on top, keeping them out of the water. Cover the whole with foil and steam.)

Sprinkle with coriander and serve, either as a starter with rye bread or as a main course with rice, broccoli and cauliflower.

NORTH ATLANTIC CRÊPES IN A WHITE WINE AND MUSHROOM SAUCE

*W*ith Shrove Tuesday in mind, I have prepared these delicious seafood crêpes, stuffed with a variety of fish in a creamy mushroom sauce. If you are planning ahead, the dish can be prepared in advance and reheated in the oven.

ingredients..................

¾lb cod or haddock
salt and pepper
1¼cups milk
1 thyme sprig
2tbsp butter
½lb leeks, split, washed and
   shredded
⅓cup dry white wine

2tbsp flour
¼lb button mushrooms,
   quartered
6oz small cooked peeled shrimp
eight 6inch crêpes (see Basic
   Crêpes, page 34)
a little extra butter for greasing

Season the cod or haddock with salt and pepper and place in a saucepan. Cover with the milk, add the thyme and simmer over a gentle heat for 6-8 minutes. Lift the fish out onto a plate and leave to cool.

To prepare the sauce: melt the butter in a clean saucepan, add the leeks and wine, cover and soften for 3-4 minutes. Stir in the flour until absorbed and remove from the heat. Gradually add the milk in which the fish was cooked, stirring until smooth. Flake the cooked fish into the sauce, discarding the skin and any bones. Add the mushrooms and shrimp and simmer briefly.

Preheat the oven to 375°F. Lay the crêpes 4 at a time on a work surface, divide the fishy mixture among them and roll up into cigar shapes. Lightly butter an ovenproof baking dish and line the crêpes up in a row. (If you are planning ahead, the crêpes will keep in the refrigerator for up to 24 hours.) Cover the dish with foil and bake in the oven for 35-40 minutes, until heated through.

STUFFED SAVOY CABBAGE

ingredients..................

1 Savoy cabbage
½cup long-grain rice
2tbsp olive oil
1 onion, chopped
1 small carrot, chopped
1 garlic clove, minced

14oz can flageolet or lima beans,
   drained
¾cup packed pot cheese
1 egg
½tsp dried thyme
salt and pepper

Bring a large saucepan of salted water to a boil and blanch 10 of the cabbage leaves for 3-4 minutes, then plunge into cold water and drain. Place the rice in a small saucepan, cover with ⅞cup water, add a pinch of salt and simmer for 20 minutes, until the rice is tender and the water absorbed.

Heat the oil in a skillet, add the onion, carrot and garlic and soften without coloring over a gentle heat for 2-3 minutes. Stir the cooked rice into the softened vegetables, then stir in the flageolet beans and cheese, followed by the egg, thyme and seasoning. Mix well to combine.

To reassemble the cabbage: line a colander with a double layer of cheesecloth and then with the blanched outer leaves. Place the filling in the center, draw the corners of the cheesecloth together and tie securely with string. Place the cabbage in a steamer basket, stand in a saucepan containing an inch or so of boiling water, cover and steam for 30 minutes, until tender. Unwrap the cheesecloth and serve the cabbage cut into wedges.

STEAK AND KIDNEY PUDDING WITH MUSHROOMS

———————— ❧ ————————

*A*sk me which is my favorite meal on a cold winter's day and I am bound to settle for a good old-fashioned steak and kidney pudding made with a proper suet crust to soak up the rich brown gravy. The Victorians, who were very fond of their steak and kidney pudding, used to add a quantity of oysters to make the meat go a little further. Today, however, we prefer to add a handful of button mushrooms since they taste good and are much less expensive.

ingredients . . . .

Suet pastry
2½cups self-rising flour
½tsp salt
¾cup shredded beef suet
a little butter or oil for greasing

Filling
1½lb chuck steak, diced
½lb beef kidney, diced

salt and pepper
1 onion, roughly chopped
¼lb button mushrooms,
  quartered
2tbsp flour
1tbsp Worcestershire sauce
2tsp anchovy extract
1¼cups beef stock

To make the suet pastry: sift the flour and salt into a mixing bowl, add the suet, then ¾cup cold water and mix to an even dough. Dust the pastry with flour and roll out to a 9inch circle.

Lightly grease a 5-cup pudding basin or steaming mold with butter or oil. Cut a quarter out of the pastry circle and reserve for the lid. Line the basin with the remaining three-quarters of the pastry and seal the join with a little water. Trim the edges of the pastry level with the basin rim and roll out the remaining quarter of pastry to form a lid.

To prepare the filling: season the steak and kidney with salt and pepper, add the onion and the mushrooms and sprinkle with the flour. Add the Worcestershire sauce and anchovy extract and turn into the pastry-lined basin. Pour in enough of the bouillon to barely cover the meat. Moisten the edges of the suet pastry with water and place the lid over the top. Seal the edges firmly. Cover the pudding with parchment paper or foil, pleated in the middle to allow for expansion, and secure with string to form a handle.

Place the pudding in a large saucepan containing 2-3inches boiling water. Cover and steam for 3½ hours, replenishing the water level from time to time. To serve, remove the foil or paper from the top and cover the sides of the basin with a folded white napkin. Serve with mashed potatoes, peas and buttered rutabaga.

A CASSEROLE OF HARE WITH SOUR CREAM AND CAPERS

———————— ❧ ————————

*A*t this time of the year farmers trying to start their crops of wheat and barley often fight a losing battle with hares, for whom the tender shoots are a delicacy. Fortunately for the farmer, there is no closed season in England for the hare, although game dealers may only sell it from August to the end of February. Young hares up to one year old are known as leverets and should weigh between 6-7lb before they are dressed. The flesh of the leveret can be as tender as chicken and has a mild, gamey flavor.

ingredients . . . .

one 6lb hare or rabbit, cut up
salt and pepper
3tbsp olive oil
2 thick bacon slices, roughly
  chopped
1 onion, sliced
1 carrot, halved and sliced
1 celery stalk, sliced

2tbsp/30ml plain flour
2cups boiling chicken bouillon
⅓cup dry white wine
1tsp dried marjoram or oregano
1 bay leaf
⅔cup sour cream
2tbsp capers, roughly chopped

Preheat the oven to 350°F. Season the hare with salt and pepper. Heat the oil in a flameproof casserole on top of the stove, add the hare, bacon and all the vegetables and brown evenly for 6-8 minutes over a steady heat.

Remove from the heat and stir in the flour. Add the chicken bouillon a little at a time and stir until thoroughly blended. Add the wine and herbs, cover and cook in the oven for 2 hours, until the hare is tender.

To finish the sauce: place the sour cream in a small bowl and stir in ⅔cup of the liquid from the casserole. Stir the contents of the bowl into the casserole, add the capers and serve with buttered noodles sprinkled with poppy seeds.

A CHICKEN CASSEROLE WITH MUSSELS AND ROOT VEGETABLES

*T*here is nothing new about the idea of combining shellfish with butchers' meats to make them go further. At one time, when oysters were cheap and plentiful in England, they were combined with beef into stews and casseroles both for flavor and economy. Here is a variation on this theme combining fresh mussels with chicken in a creamy casserole flavored with root vegetables, to make a pleasant change.

ingredients . . . .

3tbsp peanut oil	1 thyme sprig
1 onion, sliced	1 bay leaf
2 carrots, sliced	salt and pepper
2 turnips, diced	2½pints mussels
2 celery stalks, sliced	⅓cup dry white wine
2tbsp flour	½cup heavy cream
4 chicken pieces	2 egg yolks
2cups chicken stock	chopped parsley for garnish

Preheat the oven to 325°F. Heat the oil in a large skillet, add the vegetables and brown over a steady heat. Transfer to a casserole and stir in the flour until absorbed. Brown the chicken pieces in the skillet, adding a little more oil if necessary. Add the chicken to the casserole together with the bouillon, thyme and bay leaf. Season with salt and pepper, cover and cook in the oven for 1¼ hours, until cooked through.

Meanwhile, scrub the mussels, discarding any that are open. Place the mussels in a large stainless steel or enamel saucepan with the wine, cover and steam the mussels open over a fast heat for 8 minutes. Drain the mussels in a colander set over a bowl to collect the juices. When the mussels are cool enough to handle, remove them from their shells and set aside. Discard any that are not open.

Fifteen minutes before the chicken is cooked, add the mussels to the casserole together with the juices that have collected in the bowl and continue cooking.

To finish, combine the cream and the egg yolks in a small bowl and stir in a little of the hot sauce from the chicken. Stir the contents of the bowl into the casserole, season to taste, sprinkle with chopped parsley and serve with rice or noodles.

HOT AVOCADO, CHICKEN, BACON AND POTATO GRATIN

*A*vocados are in plentiful supply early in the year and provide a source of inspiration for both hot and cold dishes. For this recipe, suitable for a midweek menu, I have incorporated pieces of ripe avocado into a creamy sauce with chicken, crispy bacon and celery. This simple concoction is then covered with a layer of sliced potatoes and finished in a hot oven until crisp and golden.

ingredients . . . .

2tbsp peanut oil	3 celery stalks, roughly chopped
6oz Canadian bacon, cut into strips	3tbsp flour
3 chicken breast halves, skin and bone removed and cut into strips	1¼cups milk
	3 shakes of hot pepper sauce
salt and pepper	1 large ripe avocado, halved, peeled and diced
1 onion, roughly chopped	juice of 1 lemon
	1½lb potatoes, sliced

Preheat the oven to 400°F. Heat the oil in a skillet and brown the bacon until crisp. Transfer the bacon to a small plate. Season the chicken strips and cook them quickly in the fat left in the skillet. Transfer to the small plate with the bacon.

Add the onion and the celery to the skillet and soften over a gentle heat without letting the vegetables color. Stir in the flour until absorbed, remove from the heat and gradually stir in the milk. Season with salt and hot pepper sauce and return to the heat to thicken. Add the avocado, lemon juice, chicken and crispy bacon and spread out in a shallow gratin dish. Top with overlapping slices of potato and bake in the oven for 45-50 minutes, until the topping is lightly browned.

Creamy Leek and Mushroom Tartlets; Fresh Sardines with Rhubarb, Ginger and Soy;
Rolled Crêpes with a Moist Almond and Orange Filling.

Puddings

RHUBARB AND GINGER SPONGE PUDDING

There is something very special about the sticky moistness of a steamed ginger pudding, evoking as it does so many wonderful memories of childhood. When I was a lad my curiosity and excitement would often mount long before the pudding had reached the table, since I had learned to identify the aroma of the warm, syrupy spices that came from the familiar cloth-bound basin steaming away at the back of the stove. The slightly tart flavor of rhubarb and the mellow ginger combine beautifully in this traditional English pudding.

ingredients . . . .

a little butter for greasing
3tbsp stem ginger syrup
6oz rhubarb, peeled and
  chopped
1 stick butter, softened
⅔cup soft light brown sugar

finely grated zest of 1 orange
2 eggs, beaten
¾cup self-rising flour
1tsp ground ginger
2-3tbsp chopped preserved
  stem ginger

Lightly grease a 5-cup pudding basin or steaming mold with butter, place the ginger syrup and rhubarb in the bottom and set aside. To prepare the filling: beat together the butter, sugar and orange zest until pale in color. Add the eggs, a little at a time, and beat until smooth. Sift the flour with the ground ginger and stir into the mixture until evenly blended. Add the stem ginger and turn the mixture into the prepared pudding basin.

Cut a circle of parchment paper to fit inside the top of the basin, cover with two layers of cheesecloth, secure with string and tie the corners of the cheesecloth into a granny knot. (If you are planning ahead, the pudding will keep in the refrigerator for 2 days prior to cooking.) To steam the pudding: stand the basin in a large saucepan, add 2-3inches boiling water and bring to a boil, then cover and steam for 1 hour. To serve: remove the cheesecloth, run a table knife around the edge of the basin and invert the pudding onto a serving dish. Serve with plenty of hot custard sauce.

CARAMELIZED APPLE WAFERS

During a busy week it is all most of us can do to get a basic meal on the table, let alone find time to prepare a dessert to go with it. However, I have one or two tricks up my sleeve that I often rely on when time is short. My favorite involves a circle of uncooked pastry (of which I keep a plentiful supply in my freezer, layered between sheets of freezer paper), an apple, a pat of butter and a sprinkling of sugar. Fifteen minutes in a hot oven and the apples will caramelize into one of the most delicious desserts I know.

ingredients . . . .

one 7-inch circle of puff or pie
  pastry
2 firm sweet apples

2tbsp butter
2tbsp sugar

Preheat the oven to 425°F.
  Place the pastry circle on a baking sheet.
  Peel the apple, cut in half from top to bottom and remove the core.

Slice the apple thinly using a vegetable slicer and arrange the slices to cover the pastry completely. Dot the butter over the top, sprinkle with sugar and bake near the top of the oven for 15 minutes. (It is best to put the tart in the oven as you are sitting down to the main course.) Serve with vanilla ice cream.

will come cleanly out of the center. Allow the custard to cool completely, then chill before serving. To serve: invert the soufflé dish onto a serving plate and gently shake the custard from side to side to release it from its dish.

BAKED CARAMEL CUSTARDS SCENTED WITH ORANGE

aked egg custard topped with a layer of dark caramel has become a popular dessert in many of our finest restaurants, for the soothing way it disappears even after an enormous meal and for its gentle flavor that merely caresses the palate with the subtle taste of caramel. Baked egg custards are just as delicious made at home and rarely fail to impress even the most discerning gourmet.

ingredients . . . .

Caramel
⅔cup sugar

Custard
2½cups milk

finely grated zest of 1 orange
4 eggs
⅓cup sugar

Preheat the oven to 375°F.

To prepare the caramel: measure 2tbsp cold water into a small bowl and set aside. Measure 2tbsp of the sugar into a heavy saucepan and melt over a steady heat, stirring all the time. As the sugar begins to brown, stir in the remaining sugar a little at a time. Allow the sugar to caramelize to a mahogany brown, remove from the heat and stir in the measured water. Return the caramel to a boil and stir until evenly disolved. Pour the caramel into the bottom of a 1-quart straight sided soufflé dish and set aside.

To prepare the custard, bring the milk to a boil with the orange zest. Beat the eggs with the sugar in a bowl. Pour the boiling milk over the eggs and strain into the soufflé dish. Place the dish in a roasting pan, pour in boiling water to come halfway up the sides of the dish, cover and bake the custard in the oven for 25-30 minutes or until a skewer

A PASSION FRUIT MERINGUE SOUFFLÉ FOR YOU AND YOUR VALENTINE

t Valentine's Day on February 14 is an ideal opportunity to prepare a special candle-lit dinner for your loved one. To finish, I often put together this most delicious concoction, which serves two.

ingredients . . . .

a little soft butter for greasing
4 passion fruits
4 egg whites
¼cup sugar

Sauce
⅞cup milk
4 egg yolks
1tsp cornstarch
1tbsp sugar
2 drops vanilla extract

Preheat the oven to 400°F. Grease a 6inch soufflé dish with butter and set aside.

Cut the passion fruits open and scoop out the juice and the edible black seeds. Beat the egg whites, adding the sugar gradually, until the meringue is firm. Stir in the passion fruit juices and seeds and turn into the prepared soufflé dish. Stand the dish in a roasting pan, pour in boiling water to come halfway up the sides of the dish and bake in the oven for 25-30 minutes. (Unlike other soufflés, this one will stand without collapsing even when it has cooled.)

To prepare the sauce: measure 2tbsp of the milk into a bowl and bring the remainder to a boil. Place the egg yolks, cornstarch, sugar and vanilla in the bowl and stir together with a wooden spoon. When the milk has boiled, pour it over the eggs, return to the saucepan and stir until the custard has reached the consistency of heavy cream. (The small amount of cornstarch in the recipe will enable the custard to boil briefly without it curdling.)

Bring the soufflé to the table and serve the sauce separately.

EASY ORANGES WITH DARK CARAMEL AT THE DROP OF A HAT

find increasingly when invited out to supper with friends that I am asked on arrival to produce a dessert at the drop of a hat. I came up with this recipe on one such occasion: to everyone's amazement it was made with only three ingredients.

ingredients......................

4 navel oranges
¾cup sugar

1cup thick plain yogurt or heavy cream

Scrub the oranges under warm running water to remove the waxy veneer. Remove the outer zest from 2 of the oranges with a vegetable peeler, avoiding the bitter white pith. Cut the zest into thin shreds and place in a saucepan of cold water.

Bring to a boil, then simmer for 3-4 minutes until soft. Drain

Cut the top and bottom from each orange with a serrated knife. Stand the oranges on one end and cut away the peel from top to bottom. Slice the oranges evenly into rounds and arrange them in an attractive serving dish.

To prepare the caramel: melt 2tbsp of the sugar in the bottom of a heavy saucepan, stirring all the time with a long-handled wooden spoon. As the sugar begins to brown, continue to add the remaining sugar a little at a time. When the sugar has reached a mahogany-brown color, remove from the heat and add 2 tbsp water. The caramel will bubble furiously, so stand well back. Add the shreds of orange zest to the diluted caramel and simmer briefly. Pour the caramel over the sliced oranges and serve with yogurt or cream. (If you have time it is best to allow the oranges to mingle for an hour or so in their caramel juices.)

Crêpes

n the past, certain foods proscribed by the church were not to be eaten during Lent, so on the day before the start of Lent perishable items such as eggs, milk and butter were made into crêpes, while other leftovers were often used as fillings to make the crêpes more interesting. Although the shriving of sins in preparation for Lent is no longer such an important event for many people, it is still customary to remember Shrove Tuesday by making and tossing crêpes. I confess that for the fillings in the following recipes I have looked a little further than my pantry for inspiration, although I can testify that the best crêpes are still made using the original basic ingredients.

BASIC CRÊPES WITH SUGAR AND LEMON

ingredients......................

1tbsp butter
¾cup flour
1¼cups milk

2 eggs
1tbsp sugar
juice of 2 lemons

Melt the butter in a non-stick skillet until it bubbles. Allow the butter to brown, remove from the heat and cool. (The French call this preparation *beurre noisette* because of its nutty aroma.)

To make the batter: sift the flour into a mixing bowl and make a well in the center. Add one-third of the milk and stir into a lump-free paste. Add the remaining milk, the eggs and sugar to make a smooth batter. Stir in the nut-brown butter and leave the batter to stand for 20 minutes before using.

To make the crêpes: heat a 7inch non-stick skillet or crêpe pan over a steady heat. (It will not be necessary to oil a non-stick pan.) Pour enough crêpe batter into the heated pan to coat the bottom, tilting until even. Allow 30 seconds for the crêpe to brown on the underside, then turn over and cook briefly until lightly colored.

If you have ever tried to make crêpes for a line of hungry people, you will know that it is virtually impossible to make them fast enough. The best way around this problem is to make the crêpes well in advance and stack them interleaved with parchment paper, then reheat them in a warm oven when they are needed. Serve with a sprinkling of sugar and a squeeze of lemon. If you are feeling a little more adventurous, you may like to try your hand at one or two fillings to make the crêpes even more inviting.

Makes about 12

CRÊPE PARCELS WITH FRESH PINEAPPLE AND ORANGE CUSTARD

ingredients . . . .

eight 7inch basic crêpes

Filling
2 egg yolks
7/8cup milk
2tbsp flour

1tbsp sugar
finely grated zest of 1 orange
1 small pineapple, cut into small
  chunks
3tbsp Cointreau or Grand
  Marnier (1 miniature bottle)

Preheat the oven to 350°F. Place the egg yolks in a bowl, add 2tbsp of the milk and beat in the flour and the sugar. Bring the remaining milk to a boil with the orange zest, then strain over the egg mixture. Return to the saucepan and stir over a gentle heat until the mixture boils and thickens. Add the pineapple and Cointreau or Grand Marnier.

Distribute the filling among the crêpes and fold into neat parcels.

Lightly butter an ovenproof dish, arrange the parcels neatly in the bottom, cover with foil and warm through in the oven for 15-20 minutes.

ROLLED CRÊPES WITH A MOIST ALMOND AND ORANGE FILLING

ingredients . . . .

eight 7inch basic crêpes

Filling
6tbsp butter, softened
6tbsp sugar
2 eggs, beaten
1⅓cups ground almonds

2 drops almond extract
finely grated zest and juice of 1
  orange

To finish
2tbsp butter
½cup sliced almonds

Preheat the oven to 375°F. Blend the butter and the sugar together until pale. Add the eggs a little at a time followed by the ground almonds, almond extract and orange zest, and beat until thoroughly combined. Divide the almond filling among the crêpes and roll up into cigar shapes.

Lightly butter an ovenproof dish and arrange the crêpes neatly in the bottom. (If you are planning ahead, the crêpes will keep in the refrigerator for up to a day before baking.) To finish the crêpes, cover the dish with foil and bake in the oven for 25-30 minutes. Meanwhile, melt the butter in a skillet and brown the sliced almonds evenly. Add the orange juice and pour the mixture over the crêpes when they are ready. Serve with softly whipped cream.

Marmalade

At this time of the year, when citrus fruits are so abundant and full of flavor, it would be a mistake to ignore the possibilities of preserving this flavor in delicious marmalades and curds. Marmalade-making is a time-consuming business, but at the end of the day it is always well worth being the proud owner of several jars of glistening homemade marmalade. The flavor of marmalade varies according to which fruits are used. Best of all are the Seville bitter oranges which have a short season between January and the end of February. Other citrus fruits, such as lemons, limes, tangerines and grapefruit, also have a good flavor, but tend to make the marmalade go cloudy.

The most common fault with many marmalade recipes is the inclusion of too much water, resulting in an unnecessarily long boiling time. Another mistake is not boiling the marmalade to jell point. In the following recipes I have attempted to iron out these problems to ensure that your marmalade-making will be a great success.

SEVILLE ORANGE MARMALADE

ingredients

2lb Seville oranges
juice of 2 lemons

7½cups water
4lb (9cups) sugar

Give the oranges a good scrub under running water and remove any loose stalk ends. Remove the outer zest from the oranges with a vegetable peeler or a small knife and cut the zest into matchstick strips with a pair of scissors or a chopping knife.

Halve the oranges and squeeze the juice through a strainer into a large, shallow preserving kettle. Reserve the seeds and tie them up with the squeezed orange halves in a 10inch square piece of cheesecloth. (Both the pith and the seeds contain the pectin that is necessary for the marmalade to set.) Add the lemon juice, orange zest, water and cheesecloth bag to the preserving pan, bring to the boil and simmer for 2 hours.

Thoroughly wash six 1-lb canning jars in hot, soapy water and sterilize in boiling water. Keep hot until ready to fill. Remove the cheesecloth bag from the kettle and squeeze out any liquid through a colander into

the pan. Add the sugar to the pan, dissolve over a low heat and remove any visible scum from the surface. Increase the heat to a fast boil until the temperature reaches 220°F on a candy thermometer (about 25-30 minutes). An alternative test is to cool a little of the marmalade on a saucer in the refrigerator. Jell point is reached when the surface has set and will wrinkle when pushed with a finger.

Allow the marmalade to cool for 15-20 minutes to prevent the orange shreds from floating to the surface, then pour into the hot jars. Cover the jars, process in a boiling water bath, allow to cool, then complete seals if necessary and label.

Makes about 6lb

STEM GINGER AND ORANGE MARMALADE

ingredients

2lb navel oranges
2 lemons
7½cups water

4lb (9cups) sugar
1 cup preserved stem ginger in
syrup

Follow the recipe for Seville Orange Marmalade as far as the point when the sugar is added. Cut the ginger into matchstick-size pieces, add the ginger and syrup and boil as described, until set.

Makes about 6lb

THREE-FRUIT MARMALADE

ingredients.....................

2lb mixed citrus fruits: about 2
    small grapefruit, 2 navel oranges
    and 2 lemons

4lb (9cups) preserving sugar

Wash the fruit thoroughly under running water, remove the outer zest with a vegetable peeler or a small knife and cut into matchstick-size pieces. Squeeze and measure the juice from the fruit, strain into a large preserving kettle and add three times as much water.

Tie up the seeds and the squeezed fruit halves in a 10inch square of cheesecloth, add to the pan with the zest and simmer for 2 hours.

Remove the cheesecloth bag, add the sugar, bring to a boil and continue as directed in the recipe for Seville Orange Marmalade. Mixed fruit marmalades are rarely as clear as those made from pure oranges.

Makes about 6lb

VALENCIA ORANGE CURD

ingredients.....................

4 Valencia oranges
1 lemon
1¾cups sugar

5 eggs
1 stick unsalted butter

Wash the fruit thoroughly under running water and remove any loose stalk ends. Finely grate the outer zest, taking care to avoid the bitter white pith. Squeeze the juice into a stainless steel or glass bowl large enough to stand over a saucepan of boiling water without touching the water.

Add the zests, sugar, eggs and butter and stir over the boiling water for about 15-20 minutes, until the curd has thickened to the consistency of softly whipped cream. Strain the curd into two 1lb jars, cover and allow to set completely. Valencia orange curd will keep unopened in the refrigerator for up to 8 weeks.

Makes about 2lb

March

March heralds the arrival of spring, often accompanied by very changeable weather, which means that supplies of early vegetables cannot be guaranteed until late March or April. Baby carrots, snow peas or mange-tout, and broad beans are worth looking out for. Winter root vegetables, however, remain in good supply. Celery-scented celeriac is still available and is worth trying boiled half and half with potatoes and mashed with butter and freshly ground white pepper. English cabbages are full of flavor during March as are spring greens providing they are not overcooked. I enjoy them shredded, lightly steamed and buttered and served topped with toasted cashew nuts. Brussels sprouts tend to suffer as the weather turns warmer when they lose much of their flavor. English cauliflower is no longer at its best, but broccoli continues to be in good condition throughout the month. Leeks, onions and garlic remain good value for money and provide plenty of inspiration for midweek menus. Home-grown red and white potatoes compete in both price and flavor with several imported varieties now available. The herb garden often shows signs of recovery during March and it may be worth placing a cloche or a large jam jar over a few chives and a root of parsley to bring them on.

On the fruit stalls citrus fruit continues to provide a colorful display. Fresh pineapples, too, are often good value at this time. To test a pineapple for ripeness, tug at one of the central leaves at the top of the fruit. If it comes away easily, the pineapple is ready to eat. The most tender of our forced rhubarb continues to be available throughout the month, with outdoor varieties taking over nearer April. English cooking apples remain in good supply together with many dessert varieties. English pears are nearing the end of their season.

The fish markets have plenty on offer during March, depending on the weather. Supplies of cod, haddock and whiting remain plentiful throughout the month. Fishmongers who smoke their own fish usually have smoked cod roe on offer, since a good proportion of cod at this time of the year is landed with its roe intact. Generally speaking, March is not a month when fish is at its best, since many species, notably the flat fish such as sole, flounder, brill, halibut and turbot, surrender much of their flavor and texture to their roe. Herring in roe, however, seem to be unaffected. Soft herring roes are a great delicacy in many parts of the country, gently fried in butter and served on slices of toast. Toward the end of the month, mackerel return to shallow waters in search of new feeding grounds and usually appear at reasonable prices. Sea bass, the king of the oily fish, although expensive, offers excellent flavor at the moment and is very suitable for a main course if you are planning a dinner party.

Fresh sardines are still good value for money and full of flavor, as are sprats, especially when smoked. Skate continues to be a good buy throughout March and for my money continues to offer the best value. Supplies of shellfish – mussels, oysters, scallops, cockles, clams, winkles and shrimp – remain plentiful and full of flavor.

If the weather has been mild during March, many farmers will have started lambing in preparation for the new season, although one must wait at least until April for the first taste of spring lamb. Free-range duckling, guinea fowl, quail and pigeon remain popular at many butchers and game dealers, while farmers who are keen to clear their land of hungry rabbits are able to provide an inexhaustible supply for butchers and supermarkets.

MARCH INGREDIENTS IN SEASON

FRUIT & NUTS

British at their best:
Apples
Chestnuts
Cooking Apples
Rhubarb, outdoor
Pears
Walnuts

Imported in season:
Almonds
Bananas
Brazil Nuts
Clementines
Dates
Grapefruit
Grapes
Hazelnuts (Filberts)
Kiwi Fruit
Kumquats
Lemons
Limes
Melons
Oranges
Passion Fruit
Peanuts
Pecans
Pineapples
Pistachio Nuts
Satsumas
Strawberries

VEGETABLES & HERBS

British at their best:
Cabbages
Cauliflowers
Celeriac
Celery
Chicory (Belgian Endive)
Broccoli
Jerusalem Artichokes
Leeks
Onions
Parsley
Potatoes
Rosemary
Sage
Salsify
Savory
Shallots
Spring Greens
Thyme
Turnips
Watercress

Parsnips
Spinach
Spring Onions (Scallions)
Sprouts
Swedes (Rutabaga)

Imported in season:
Aubergines (Eggplants)
Avocados
Courgettes (Zucchini)
French (Green) Beans
Garlic
Lettuces
Sweet Peppers
Tomatoes

Also available:
Beets
Carrots
Cucumbers
Fennel
Kohlrabi
Mustard and Cress

FISH & SHELLFISH

British at their best:
Cod
Coley (Pollock)
Gray Mullet
Haddock
Hake
Mussels
Oysters
Prawns
Scallops
Sea Bass
Shrimp
Skate
Sprats
Trout
Turbot
Whiting

Also available:
Brill
Cockles
Conger Eel
Dabs
Dover Sole
Halibut
Herring
Huss
Lemon Sole
Mackerel
Monkfish
Plaice
Salmon
Sea Trout
Winkles

Imported in season:
John Dory
Red Mullet
Sardines
Squid

POULTRY & GAME

British at their best:
Goose
Turkey

Also available:
Chicken
Duck
Guinea Fowl
Pigeon
Quail
Rabbit
Venison

MEAT
Beef
Lamb
Offal
Pork
Veal

Starters

POTTED TROUT WITH LEMON AND TOASTED ALMONDS

❧

This delicious starter of potted trout, sharpened with lemon and rounded off with toasted sliced almonds, should be garnished with a few lettuce leaves and accompanied by a basket of toasted brown bread.

ingredients ....

two ½lb trout, cleaned
2 tbsp unsalted butter
finely grated zest and juice of ½ lemon

1 thyme sprig
salt and pepper
½cup sliced almonds, toasted

Preheat the oven to 350°F. Place the two trout on a large square of foil and add the butter, lemon zest and juice, thyme and seasoning. Wrap up to form a parcel, place in a shallow dish and bake in the oven for 25-30 minutes.

Unwrap the parcel and allow the trout to cool, reserving the cooking juices, then remove the skin and lift the flesh from the bone. Crumble the flesh between your fingers, removing any small bones, and press lightly into 4 ramekin dishes. Sprinkle with almonds, strain the cooking juices into each of the dishes and chill. If you need to keep the potted trout for longer than 2 days, it should be sealed with a layer of clarified butter when it will keep in the refrigerator for up to a week.

A PÂTÉ OF SMOKED COD ROE

❧

Smoked cod roe is a common sight at many fishmongers at this time of the year and has remained popular with the English for generations, especially for high tea. In this recipe I have combined the smoked roe with soft butter, mustard and mace to be spread on fingers of hot toast as a delicious starter. Infinitely preferable to the lurid pink concoction sold under the name Taramasalata in shops up and down the country.

ingredients ....

2tbsp red wine vinegar
2 shallots or 1 onion, chopped
½lb smoked cod roe

1 stick soft unsalted butter
1tsp dry mustard
1 pinch ground mace

Place the vinegar and shallot or onion in a stainless steel or enamel saucepan and soften over a steady heat.

Scrape the cod roe from its skin into a blender or food processor. Add the shallot or onion, the butter, mustard and mace and blend until smooth. Turn the pâté into an attractive pot and refrigerate until ready to serve.

If you intend keeping the pâté for longer than 2 days, it should be covered with a layer of clarified butter when it will keep for up to 3 weeks. Serve with hot buttered toast, a small salad and wedges of lemon.

A LENTIL AND MUSHROOM PÂTÉ WITH GARLIC AND THYME

Although strictly a vegetarian starter, this pâté has a wonderfully rich, almost meaty flavor that will appeal both to vegetarians and to those who enjoy meat.

ingredients . . . .

1¼cups brown lentils
1 vegetable bouillon cube
3tbsp peanut oil
2 onions, finely chopped
1 garlic clove, minced
¼lb button mushrooms, finely
  chopped

1tsp dried thyme
1½cups fresh whole wheat
  breadcrumbs
1 egg
salt and pepper

Place the lentils in a saucepan with the bouillon cube, cover with water and simmer for 45-50 minutes until the lentils are soft (and the bouillon absorbed). Preheat the oven to 350°F. Heat the oil in a skillet, add the onions, garlic, mushrooms and thyme, and soften over a gentle heat without letting them color. Drain the lentils and mix them with the contents of the skillet and the bread crumbs. Add the egg and seasoning and blend together in a food processor.

Lightly grease a small loaf pan, press the mixture in lightly, cover with foil and bake in the oven for 25 minutes, until firm. Allow to cool in the pan, then unmold and serve cold with fingers of toast.

If you are planning ahead, the pâté can be made 3 days in advance.

A SOUFFLÉ OF GOAT'S CHEESE WITH LEEKS AND WALNUTS

English goat's cheeses are becoming a common sight on many cheese-boards with dairy farmers up and down the country turning their hand to small-scale cheese-making. They are usually milder than French varieties.

ingredients . . . .

soft butter for greasing
½cup finely chopped and
  toasted walnuts
2tbsp butter
1½cups shredded white of
  leek

1tsp dried thyme
3tbsp flour
1cup milk
¼lb goat's cheese
5 eggs, separated
salt and pepper

Preheat the oven to 400°F. Grease a 7inch soufflé dish with butter and coat the inside of the dish with the toasted walnuts. Melt the butter in a saucepan, add the leeks and thyme, cover and soften for 3-4 minutes. Stir in the flour, remove from the heat, add the milk a little at a time and stir until evenly blended.

Crumble the cheese into the saucepan and bring to a boil to melt and thicken. Stir in the egg yolks, then season with salt and pepper and set aside.

Beat the egg whites until they hold a peak on the end of the beater. Beaten egg whites have a tendency to become grainy if they are left even for a few seconds, so it is best to give them a final beating just before folding them in. To do this, stir about a quarter of the egg whites into the mixture and fold in the remainder with a large metal spoon or spatula. Turn the mixture into the prepared soufflé dish and spread the top level. Bake in the center of the oven for about 25 minutes until the soufflé is risen and golden but still slightly creamy in the center.

GARLIC-STUFFED MUSHROOMS IN THEIR BUTTERY JUICES

*T*ender mushrooms stuffed with a melting garlic butter make a simple but delicious starter with plenty of hot crispy bread to soak up the juices. To mince the garlic, I use an upturned heavy chopping knife as if I am chopping. The result is far quicker and less messy that with a garlic press.

ingredients . . . .

½lb button mushrooms
2-3 garlic cloves, minced,

6tbsp butter, softened
2tbsp chopped parsley

Preheat the oven to 375°F.

Wipe the mushrooms clean with a dry cloth and trim the stems level with the bases. Combine the garlic with the butter and parsley and stuff the mushrooms with the mixture.

Arrange the mushrooms on a baking sheet with a rim, cover with foil and bake in the center of the oven for 20-25 minutes. Serve with hot crispy bread.

CODDLED EGGS ON A BED OF SPINACH, POTATO AND MUSHROOMS

*G*ood-quality meat, of the sort carnivorous cooks are given to dreaming about, is becoming an increasingly rare sight in the weekly shopping cart. As a result, we are left searching for recipe ideas that make use of other sources of protein. Eggs are always a good stand-by and one dish that I have come to enjoy during the week relies on eggs, baked or coddled in a bed of creamy mashed potato, spinach and mushrooms. I have suggested in the recipe that small eggs be used. If yours happen to be large, it may be necessary to discard a little of the egg white so that the eggs will fit snugly into the filling. If spinach is not available, this recipe is equally delicious prepared with shredded leeks softened in butter.

ingredients . . . .

2lb potatoes
salt and pepper
⅔cup milk
1lb fresh bulk spinach or
  ½lb frozen leaf spinach
4tbsp butter

1 onion, chopped
¼lb button mushrooms,
  chopped
1tsp chopped fresh thyme or
  ½tsp dried
4 eggs

Bring the potatoes to a boil in salted water and simmer for 20 minutes, or until tender. Drain and mash the potatoes, stirring in enough milk to make them creamy.

If you are using fresh spinach, break off the thick stems and wash in plenty of cold water. Place the wet spinach in a large saucepan, cover and allow it to steam in its own moisture for 6-8 minutes. Immerse the cooked spinach in cold water and squeeze dry, then chop finely. If using frozen spinach, thaw and squeeze dry in the same way.

Heat the butter in a shallow saucepan, add the onion, mushrooms and thyme, cover and soften over a gentle heat for 3-4 minutes. Preheat the oven to 400°F.

To assemble the dish: spread the spinach and mushroom mixture in the bottom of a 9inch gratin dish and cover with a layer of creamy mashed potato. Make 4 indentations in the top of the potato, deep enough to accommodate the eggs. Break an egg into each indentation and bake in the oven for 20-25 minutes or until the eggs have set and the potato is golden.

Main Courses

HALIBUT STEAKS WITH A SAUCE OF LEEKS AND PEARS

*H*alibut is one of the largest and most striking flat fish that you are likely to see at the fishmonger's since they can measure up to 5 feet in length. Smaller beasts, known as chicken halibut, are less common and resemble more their relatives sole and flounder. Halibut is fast becoming one of the most expensive fish on the market, being much sought after for its firm white flesh. If the price is just too much for the purse strings, substitute some cod steaks from the tail end.

ingredients......................

four 5oz halibut steaks

Simple fish bouillon
1lb flat fish bones
1 small onion, chopped
1 small carrot, chopped
½ celery stalk, chopped
1 thyme sprig
2 parsley stalks

Sauce
1cup fish bouillon
tbsp unsalted butter
1 ripe pear, peeled, cored and
    finely chopped

3-inch piece white of leek, cut
    into 1½inch matchsticks
1 carrot, cut into 1½inch
    matchsticks
1tbsp flour
¼cup dry vermouth or dry white
    wine
¼cup heavy cream
2tsp lemon juice
salt and pepper

Garnish
1 ripe pear, peeled, cored and
    sliced
1 bunch of watercress

To prepare the fish bouillon: place the bones in a large saucepan together with the remaining bouillon ingredients. Cover with cold water and bring to a boil as slowly as possible, then simmer for 20 minutes.

For this recipe I find it best to cook the fish at the last minute since halibut has a tendency to become dry if kept warm. To prepare the sauce, place the butter and pear in a stainless steel or enamel saucepan, cover and soften over a gentle heat for about 5 minutes, until the pears have fallen apart. Meanwhile, strain 1cup of the fish bouillon into another saucepan, bring to a boil and cook the leek and carrot match-

sticks briefly. Remove with a slotted spoon and set aside.

When the pears have softened, stir in the flour until absorbed. Remove the saucepan from the heat and stir in the measured fish bouillon a little at a time. Return to the heat and simmer until thickened. At this stage allow 15 minutes before serving.

Preheat the oven to 375°F. Season the halibut steaks with salt and pepper and arrange in an ovenproof dish. Pour over the remaining strained fish bouillon and cover. Cook in the center of the oven for 12 minutes.

While the fish is cooking, add the vermouth or white wine and the cream to the pear sauce together with the leek and carrot matchsticks and the lemon juice. Taste for seasoning.

Arrange the sliced pear garnish on a buttered plate and warm briefly in the oven. Lift the halibut steaks out of the bouillon and arrange on a heated serving dish. Pour over the sauce and garnish each halibut steak with slices of pear and a sprig of watercress. Serve with buttered noodles and broccoli.

A GRATIN OF HADDOCK WITH CREAMY LEEKS AND MUSHROOMS

*M*aking the best of what I can find at my local food store, where the choice is fairly limited, often results in my discovering one or two quick and easy weekday meals. I had the idea for this recipe when faced with a rather dull packet of frozen haddock, some milk, 2 leeks and a few button mushrooms. It is nicest made with fresh fish.

ingredients......................

1½lb fresh haddock or cod,
    skinned
salt and pepper
2cups milk
1 thyme sprig
4tbsp butter

¾lb leeks, split, washed and
    finely sliced
1 garlic clove, minced
3tbsp flour
¼lb button mushrooms, sliced

Season the fish with salt and pepper and place in a shallow saucepan with the milk and the thyme. Bring to a boil, then simmer for 6-8 minutes. Meanwhile, melt the butter in another saucepan, add the leeks and garlic, cover and soften over a gentle heat for 3-4 minutes. Stir in the flour until absorbed, then remove from the heat and stir in the hot milk from the fish a little at a time until evenly absorbed. Add the mushrooms and simmer to thicken.

Place the fish in a large gratin dish, cover with the sauce and finish under the broiler until golden. Serve the gratin with rice and a simple green salad.

FLAKY COD FILLETS IN A MILD CURRY SAUCE

*C*od remains one of our most popular fish during the winter months and accounts for nearly half the total weight of fish landed in England. This is hardly surprising since a mature cod can weigh up to 80lb! Cod is not regarded as one of our most delicate fish, although it has always provided an inexpensive source of protein. To make the most of the robust flavor of cod I like to introduce one or two mild curry spices.

ingredients . . . .

1½lb cod fillets, skinned	1tbsp creamed coconut
salt and pepper	3tbsp flour
2cups milk	3oz button mushrooms,
4tbsp butter	quartered
1 onion, finely chopped	flat-leaved parsley sprigs, for
2tsp mild curry paste	garnish

Season the cod with salt and pepper and place in a shallow saucepan with the milk. Bring to a boil, then simmer for 6-8 minutes. Meanwhile, melt the butter in another saucepan, add the onion, the curry paste and coconut and soften over a gentle heat without coloring. Add the flour and stir until absorbed. Remove the pan from the heat and add the milk from the fish a little at a time, stirring. Add the mushrooms, return to the heat and simmer for 10-12 minutes.

Arrange the cod fillets on a serving dish, season the sauce with salt and pepper and spoon over the fish. Decorate with sprigs of flat-leaved parsley and serve with rice and broccoli.

BEEF OLIVES WITH A MUSTARD AND HERB STUFFING

*T*he next time you arrive at your butcher's in search of an interesting supper idea, ask him to cut you a few thin slices of beef round for you to roll into a dish of beef olives.

ingredients . . . .

1½lb beef round, thinly sliced into 8 pieces	2tbsp brandy or dry sherry
salt and pepper	Sauce
1tbsp/15ml spicy brown mustard	2tbsp vegetable oil
	1 onion, sliced
Stuffing	1 carrot, sliced
½lb pork or beef link sausages, skinned	2 celery stalks, sliced
	⅔cup red wine
2oz unsmoked bacon, chopped	2cups beef bouillon
1 onion, chopped	2tsp tomato paste
1tsp dried mixed herbs	4tbsp butter, softened
	6tbsp flour

Season the beef slices with salt and pepper, spread one side with mustard and set aside. To prepare the stuffing: combine the sausage meat with the bacon, onion, herbs and brandy. Season well and spread onto the beef slices, then roll up and secure each with a wooden toothpick. Preheat the oven to 325°F.

To prepare the sauce: heat the oil in a flameproof casserole, add all the vegetables and brown over a steady heat, stirring occasionally. Stir in the wine, bouillon and tomato paste. Add the beef olives, cover and cook in the oven for 1½-2 hours or until the meat is tender.

To thicken the sauce, combine the soft butter and the flour into a paste and beat gradually into the sauce, then bring to a boil and simmer briefly. Serve with buttered noodles and shredded cabbage.

OXTAIL STEW WITH FLAGEOLET BEANS

Many of our best-known English dishes were created when farmers relied on the ox to pull their heavy farm machinery. The ox was a much-prized animal because at the end of its working life it became a plentiful source of nourishment: although the meat was often very tough, the offal, namely the kidney, tongue and tail, were made into many dishes. Since the tractor has replaced the ox, beef cattle now provide the ever-popular tail for soups and stews. Oxtail should be cooked slowly for a long time, when it will have a beautifully rich flavor with a sauce to match. It is a good idea to prepare a large batch of oxtail stew for the freezer.

ingredients . . . .

2½lb oxtail, cut up	1cup red wine
salt and pepper	3¾cups beef bouillon, boiling
2tbsp vegetable oil	1lb (2½cups) dried flageolet or
2 onions, sliced	lima beans, soaked overnight,
2 carrots, sliced	then drained
2 celery stalks, sliced	1tbsp Worcestershire sauce
1tbsp tomato paste	1 bay leaf
½ garlic clove, minced	1 thyme sprig
2tbsp flour	

Season the oxtail with salt and pepper. Heat the oil in a heavy skillet and brown the oxtail evenly to seal in the flavor. Transfer the oxtail to a casserole. Add the vegetables to the skillet and brown evenly. Add the tomato paste and garlic, then stir in the flour to absorb the cooking juices. Remove the pan from the heat and stir in the wine and bouillon.

Pour the contents of the pan over the oxtail and add the flageolet beans, Worcestershire sauce and herbs. Cover and cook in the oven for 3½-4 hours, until the oxtail is very tender. (In this recipe I have intended for there to be too much sauce so that the remainder can be saved for a delicious soup.) Serve the oxtail with plain boiled potatoes, cabbage and buttered rutabaga.

LAMB'S LIVER WITH FRESH CORIANDER AND ORANGE

Put aside, if you can, the memories of school lunch liver, cooked to death in a sea of brown gravy, and let me introduce you to this simple dish where beautifully tender lamb's liver is tossed in butter for no longer than 6 minutes. The sauce is then prepared from fresh orange juice and finished with chopped coriander leaves. Serve with plain boiled potatoes and Savoy cabbage for the perfect midweek meal.

ingredients . . . .

3 oranges	1tbsp ground coriander
1lb lamb's liver, thinly sliced	4tbsp butter
salt and pepper	1 onion, sliced
2tbsp flour	3tbsp chopped coriander
	(cilantro) leaves

Remove the outer zest from one of the oranges with a citrus zester or a vegetable peeler and cut into thin strips. Place the orange zest in a saucepan of cold water and bring to a boil, then simmer for 5 minutes. Drain. Squeeze the juice from all 3 oranges into a bowl and set aside. Season the liver with salt and pepper and dust evenly with the flour and ground coriander. Heat the butter in a non-stick skillet until bubbling, then add the liver and cook over a fast heat for 3 minutes on each side.

Transfer the liver to a hot plate, cover and keep warm. Add the sliced onion to the cooking juices in the pan and brown evenly. Add the orange juice, and zest, return the liver to the sauce to heat through, sprinkle with chopped coriander and serve.

Potted Trout with Lemon and Toasted Almonds;
Beef Olives with a Mustard and Herb Stuffing; Old English Syllabub.

AN ENGLISH-STYLE PORK AND BEAN STEW

ork and beans is one of our oldest dishes in England and was at one time the farmworkers' staple diet during the cold winter months. Although some of the ingredients have changed since the dish was first made, its essential character remains the same.

ingredients . . . .

¼cup lard or drippings
¼lb slab bacon, roughly
  chopped
2 onions, sliced
2 celery stalks, sliced
2 carrots, sliced
1½cups dried pea beans,
  soaked for 12 hours, then
  drained and rinsed

14oz can tomatoes
2tsp English mustard
1 garlic clove, minced
1 thyme sprig
1½lb boneless pork shoulder
  butt or leg (fresh ham), diced
1tbsp sugar
salt and pepper

Preheat the oven to 325°F.
   Melt the lard or drippings in a large skillet, add the bacon, onions, celery and carrots and soften over a gentle heat for 3-4 minutes. Transfer the contents of the skillet to a casserole, add the remaining ingredients and top up with boiling water.
   Cover the casserole and cook in the oven for 2½-3 hours or until the beans are beginning to fall apart and have become creamy. Taste for seasoning and serve from the casserole with hot crispy bread.

A CHICKEN CASSEROLE WITH LEMON, GINGER AND YOGURT

he increased demand for chicken as an inexpensive white meat has done little to improve its flavor. In fact most of the chicken that we buy in the supermarket is relatively tasteless. To make the best of these rather bland beasts, I like to experiment with stronger accompanying flavors, in this case lemon, ginger root and yogurt.

ingredients . . . .

3lb chicken, cut up
salt and pepper
2tbsp vegetable oil
1 onion, sliced
2 small red chili peppers, finely
  chopped
½inch ginger root, grated

1¼cups chicken bouillon, boiling
finely grated zest and juice of ½
  lemon
2tbsp cornstarch
⅔cup plain yogurt

Preheat the oven to 325°F.
Season the chicken with salt and pepper. Heat the oil in a heavy skillet and brown the chicken evenly. Transfer the chicken to a casserole. Add the onion, chilies and ginger to the skillet, cover and soften without coloring for 2-3 minutes. Add the contents of the pan to the casserole with the chicken bouillon and lemon zest and juice. Cover and cook in the oven for 1½ hours.
   To finish the sauce, mix the cornstarch with 3tbsp cold water and stir into the yogurt. Stir the yogurt into the cooking juices in the casserole and return to the oven for a further 15 minutes to thicken. Serve the casserole with Basmati rice and lightly steamed and buttered Savoy cabbage.

Puddings

AN EXOTIC FRUIT SALAD

ingredients . . . .

2/3cup orange juice
1 small pineapple, peeled, cored
and cut into chunks
1 ripe mango, peeled and sliced

3 oranges, segmented
2 kiwi fruit, peeled and sliced
2 bananas, peeled and sliced
1cup black grapes

Place the orange juice in a bowl, add the fruit and refrigerate, to allow the flavors to mingle. Serve with plain whole-milk yogurt.

FLUFFY WHITE MERINGUES FLOATING IN A POOL OF CUSTARD

The popularity of this stunningly simple dessert is based on two equally pleasing features: a soft white meringue and a deliciously smooth custard sauce flavored with vanilla.

ingredients . . . .

2½cups milk
4 eggs, separated
¾cup superfine sugar

½ fresh vanilla bean or 2 drops
vanilla extract
1tbsp cornstarch

Measure the milk into a large shallow saucepan and bring to a simmer. Put the egg whites into a clean mixing bowl, making sure there are no traces of yolk. Beat the egg whites until they hold their weight on the beater. Add 6tbsp of the sugar a little at a time, beating continually until the meringue forms stiff peaks.

Shape ovals of meringue between two large spoons dipped into warm water and float them on the surface of the simmering milk. Cook for 2 minutes, turning once. Lift the soft meringues out of the milk and place on a pan lined with a damp dish towel.

To prepare the custard sauce: split the vanilla bean in half to reveal the tiny black seeds and add to the milk, or add the vanilla extract. Place the egg yolks in a mixing bowl with the remaining sugar and the cornstarch and stir until evenly mixed. Pour the poaching milk over the egg mixture and strain into a smaller saucepan. Bring the custard to a boil, stirring, then simmer briefly to thicken. Pour the custard into an attractive glass bowl, arrange the soft meringues over the top and chill.

RHUBARB AND CUSTARD TART

ingredients . . . .

Pastry
1½cups flour
¼cup sugar
1 stick cool butter
1 egg

Filling
1lb rhubarb, peeled and cut into
1½inch strips
¾cup milk
2 eggs
2tbsp sugar
½tsp ground ginger

To make the pastry: sift the flour together with the sugar into a mixing bowl or food processor. Add the butter and cut into the flour or process to form a large crumb consistency. Add the egg and mix to a pliable dough. If it seems a little moist, sprinkle with flour.

Preheat the oven to 400°F. Lightly grease an 8inch tart pan. Roll out the pastry on a floured work surface and use to line the pan. Arrange the pieces of rhubarb in the pastry case so that they overlap facing in one direction. Bake the tart in the oven for 25 minutes. Meanwhile, combine the milk, eggs, sugar and ginger in a bowl to make a simple egg custard. When the tart has had its 25 minutes baking, pour in the custard, return to the oven and bake for a further 25 minutes until the custard has set firmly in the middle.

OLD ENGLISH SYLLABUBS IN PRETTY STEM GLASSES

he syllabub has been a popular dessert in England for over 300 years. The earliest method of making this creamy confection was to take the frothy curds from the dairy milk and to blend them with ale or cider. The result had a tendency to settle out into a clear liquid with a foamy top and was enjoyed as a refreshing drink rather like an alcoholic milk shake. The recipe given here is for an "ever-lasting" syllabub which will hold together for up to 8 hours before serving.

ingredients ....

⅓cup fruity white wine
2tbsp brandy or sherry
finely grated zest of 1 orange
finely grated zest and juice of 1
 lemon
½cup packed pot cheese

1¼cups heavy cream
¼cup sugar
1-2tbsp chopped preserved
 stem ginger (optional)
4 twists of lemon peel, to
 decorate

Pour the wine and brandy or sherry into a bowl, add the orange and lemon zests followed by the lemon juice and leave for 30 minutes to allow the flavors to mingle.

Add the pot cheese and blend evenly. Whip the heavy cream with the sugar to a thick but soft consistency, then fold into the mixture.

Add the stem ginger if used, turn into 4 stem glasses and decorate each with a twist of lemon peel. Syllabub is at its best served at room temperature with ladyfingers.

A CHOCOLATE- AND ORANGE-SCENTED FLUMMERY

hoever invented the word flummery must have been as much a poet as a gourmet, since it describes this rather wobbly dessert perfectly. Originally the flummery was a somewhat solid affair of milk thickened with pounded wheat or oatmeal which set as it cooled. I have used a lighter mixture of farina, gelatin and whipped cream richly flavored with dark chocolate and orange.

ingredients ....

2½cups milk
finely grated zest of 1 orange
⅓cup farina
2tsp unflavored gelatine
6oz semisweet chocolate,
 chopped

¼cups whipping cream
¼cup sugar
orange segments, to decorate

Bring the milk to a boil with the orange zest, sprinkle over the farina and simmer to thicken for 15 minutes, stirring occasionally. Soften the gelatin in 2tbsp cold water and stir into the hot farina. Stir until the gelatin has dissolved completely, then stir in the chocolate and leave to melt and cool.

Whip the cream softly with the sugar. When the farina has cooled, fold in the cream evenly. Turn the flummery into a dampened decorative 5-cup mold and chill in the refrigerator for 1½-2 hours, until set.

To unmold the flummery, immerse the base in warm water for the count of 10, invert onto a serving dish and shake both the dish and the mold from side to side to release. Decorate with orange segments.

Mother's Day Lunch

The origin of Mother's Day, or Mothering Sunday as it was known during the last century, came about when young apprentices and girls in household service were given special leave to visit their mothers. Mothering Sunday thus became an ideal opportunity for visiting sons and daughters to prove their new-found skills by relieving mother of her usual household duties. To this day Mothering Sunday remains an important family gathering.

Cream of Leek and Potato Soup
•
Boiled Ham with Parsley Dumplings
•
Simmered Greens with Toasted Cashew Nuts
•
Butter-glazed Carrots
•
Scalloped Potatoes with Garlic and Herbs
•
Apple and Apricot Crumble with an Almond Topping
•
Banana Custard Creams

CREAM OF LEEK AND POTATO SOUP

ingredients

4tbsp butter	½tsp dried thyme
1lb leeks, split, washed and shredded	¼lb button mushrooms, sliced
¾lb potatoes, diced	⅔cup heavy cream
3¾cups chicken bouillon	salt and pepper

Melt the butter in a large saucepan, add the leeks and potatoes, cover and soften over a gentle heat for 3-4 minutes, stirring occasionally. Add the bouillon and the thyme and simmer for 35-40 minutes or until the potatoes have fallen apart completely. Add the mushrooms and continue to simmer for a further 5 minutes. (If you are planning ahead, the soup can be prepared to this stage up to a day in advance.)

To finish the soup: bring to a boil, remove from the heat and stir in the cream. Season to taste and serve with hot crispy bread.

Serves 6

BOILED COUNTRY HAM WITH PARSLEY DUMPLINGS

ingredients

one 4lb ham, preferably a country ham	1⅔cups self-rising flour
1 onion	½cup shredded beef suet
1 bay leaf	1tbsp chopped parsley
1 clove	2tbsp cornstarch
3 parsley stems	

If using a country ham, place it in a large saucepan, cover with cold water and leave to soak for 2-3 hours or longer to remove saltiness. Discard the water and replace with fresh. Secure the bay leaf to the onion with the clove and add to the pan with the parsley stems. Bring to a boil, then simmer for 1½ hours, skimming as necessary.

To prepare the dumplings: sift the flour into mixing bowl. Add the suet, parsley and the seasoning. Stir in 4tbsp cold water and mix to an even dough. One of the secrets of successful dumplings is to keep the dough fairly moist to enable them to rise properly. Sprinkle the dough with flour and shape into a thin sausage. Cut into even-sized pieces no larger than a walnut. (If you are planning ahead, the dumplings can be refrigerated for up to 8 hours before cooking.)

When the ham is cooked, transfer it to a plate, cover and keep warm. To make a simple sauce: strain 2cups of the ham cooking liquid into a small saucepan, reserving the remainder. Mix the cornstarch with 2tbsp water. Bring the cooking liquid to a boil and stir in the cornstarch to thicken. Season to taste with a little pepper.

Twenty minutes before you are ready to serve (when you sit down for the first course), bring the remaining cooking liquid to a boil in a saucepan, drop in the dumplings, reduce to a simmer and cook for 15-20 minutes, until the dumplings have risen and floated to the surface.

Serves 6

SIMMERED GREENS WITH TOASTED CASHEW NUTS

ingredients . . . .

1lb greens (cabbage, collards, mustard greens, etc.), finely shredded	2tbsp butter ⅓cup unsalted cashew nuts, toasted

Bring a large saucepan of salted water to a boil and simmer the greens, uncovered, for 6-8 minutes. Drain well, stir in the butter and strew with toasted cashew nuts.

BUTTER-GLAZED CARROTS

ingredients . . . .

1lb carrots, peeled and cut into fingers 1tsp sugar	1 pinch salt 2tbsp butter

Cover the carrots with cold water and add the sugar and salt. Bring to a boil, then simmer for 10-15 minutes depending on their age. Drain well, add the butter and serve.

SCALLOPED POTATOES WITH GARLIC AND HERBS

ingredients . . . .

2½lb potatoes, sliced ½tsp dried oregano or marjoram	1 garlic clove, minced 2cups milk

If you are planning ahead, the sliced potatoes can be kept in a bowl of water for up to 8 hours without discoloring.

Preheat the oven to 400°F. Spread the herbs and the minced garlic over the bottom of a roasting pan. Arrange the potatoes so that they overlap in the pan, pour over the milk and season. Bake the potatoes in the oven, uncovered, for 45-50 minutes until the milk has been absorbed and the potatoes are tender.

APPLE AND APRICOT CRUMBLE WITH AN ALMOND TOPPING

ingredients . . . .

	Topping
Serves 6 2lb tart baking apples, peeled, cored and chopped 14oz can apricot halves 2tbsp sugar	9tbsp flour 1cup rolled oats 1cup ground almonds 6tbsp sugar 6tbsp cool butter, diced

Preheat the oven to 375°F. Place the apples and apricots in a 2-quart baking dish together with the apricot syrup and the sugar.

To prepare the topping: measure all the dry ingredients into a mixing bowl, add the butter and rub together with the fingertips until the mixture resembles bread crumbs. Spread the almond topping over the fruit and bake in the oven for 50 minutes.

Serve hot with pouring cream.

BANANA CUSTARD CREAMS

❦

ingredients . . . .

1¼cups milk
⅔cup light cream
2 drops vanilla extract
3 eggs

3tbsp sugar
2 ripe bananas, sliced
3tbsp apricot jam

Preheat the oven to 375°F. Arrange four 3-inch ramekin dishes in a roasting pan and put to one side. To prepare the custard, bring the milk and the cream to a boil with the vanilla extract. Beat the eggs together with the sugar in a bowl. Pour the boiling milk over the eggs and strain the mixture into the ramekin dishes. Half fill the roasting pan with boiling water, place a baking sheet over the dishes and bake in the preheated oven for 25-30 minutes or until a skewer will come away cleanly from the center. Allow the custards to cool completely, then decorate with slices of banana. To glaze, stir the jam into 2tbsp of water in a small saucepan, bring to a boil, then brush evenly over the bananas. Chill well before serving.

April

*E*aster usually arrives at some time during April, with its mixture of showers and sunshine heralding the arrival of spring. This is an ideal time to gather family and friends around the table for a special celebration meal. New English lamb is always a popular feature on the menu, providing farmers have been successful with their lambing earlier in the year. Prices are usually high, but there is never a shortage of people prepared to pay for a taste of this sweet and tender meat.

April is often an unsteady month for the vegetable farmer, since the combination of rain and sunshine is rarely in his favor. Young vegetables like snow peas, zucchini, broad beans, carrots and turnips seem to do well under glass and are deliciously tender to eat, but prices are often high. New garlic with its familiar long stem is worth looking out for at the moment as a change from the usual dried garlic bulbs. The individual cloves are fatter and have a subtle sweetness in their flavor. English onions are still in good condition and offer better flavor than imported varieties. English leeks continue to be available, although at this time of the year they usually have a solid core up the center: they are perfectly edible, but may require extra cooking. English potatoes are still doing well and offer the best value for money, but you may well be tempted to try a pound or two of new potatoes boiled in their paper-thin skins with a sprig of mint to accompany the Easter roast. Cabbages continue to be available, although their flavor does seem to fade with the warmer weather. New arrivals include an increased variety of salad ingredients – butterhead lettuces, cucumbers, radishes, fennel, chicory, mustard and cress, tender shoots of spinach and imported tomatoes – all healthy and delicious. Fresh herbs, especially basil, tarragon, parsley, chives, dill and mint, come to life after their winter break and provide plenty of inspiration for salad dressings, sauces and garnishes.

On the fruit stalls, outdoor varieties of English rhubarb continue to be good value for money and combined with English Bramley apples give a really different flavor to a pie or crumble. Citrus fruits continue to be full of tang, especially thin-skinned oranges from Spain, Morocco and Cyprus. Juicy lemons and limes lend themselves well to a variety of puddings and desserts. Sweet and juicy pineapples from Kenya and the Ivory Coast are also worth looking out for.

Since the weather has taken a change for the better, fishmongers are able to offer an attractive display of wet fish, many of which have developed an improved flavor as the result of a slight rise in the temperature of the sea, which has brought to life hundreds and thousands of living organisms with which fish are able to fortify themselves after their winter spawning. Lemon and Dover soles, flounder, brill and halibut are among the first to show signs of improvement along with herring and mackerel which may continue to show a fall in price. April is a good time to try fillets of gray mullet, huss and monkfish, all of which are appreciated for their firm white flesh. Fresh-flavored cod, haddock and whiting combine well with the subtlety of spring vegetables. Wings of skate are still reasonably priced for the weekday menu, and supplies of fresh salmon for special occasions become more plentiful during the Easter period, with its price usually an indication of its quality. Cromer crabs appear on the stalls toward the end of the month with the start of their summer season. April is our last chance until September to enjoy oysters and mussels, but pink and brown shrimp, cockles, clams and winkles remain plentiful throughout the spring and summer months.

APRIL INGREDIENTS IN SEASON

FRUIT & NUTS

British at their best:
Apples
Cooking Apples
Pears
Rhubarb, outdoor

Also available:
Grapes
Hazelnuts (Filberts)
Walnuts

Imported in season:
Almonds, Apricots
Bananas
Brazil Nuts
Grapefruit
Kiwi Fruit
Kumquats
Lemons
Limes
Mangoes
Melons
Oranges
Papaya
Passion Fruit
Peanuts, Pecans
Pineapples
Pistachio Nuts
Plums
Pomegranates
Strawberries
Walnuts

VEGETABLES & HERBS

British at their best:
Carrots
Jerusalem Artichokes
Onions
Parsley
Potatoes
Rosemary
Sage, Salsify
Savory
Spinach
Spring Onions (Scallions)
Thyme, Turnips
Watercress

Also available:
Beets
Broad (Fava) Beans
Broccoli
Cabbages
Cauliflowers
Celeriac, Celery
Cherry Tomatoes
Chives
Courgettes (Zucchini)
Cucumbers
Dill, Fennel
Garlic
Globe Artichokes
Leeks, Lettuce
Marjoram, Mint
Mustard and Cress
Parsnips, Peas
Shallots
Spring Greens
Swedes (Rutabaga)
Tarragon

Imported in season:
Aubergines (Eggplant)
Avocados
Chicory (Belgian Endive)
Courgettes (Zucchini)
French (Green) Beans
Mange tout (Snow Peas)
Radishes
Sweet Peppers
Tomatoes

FISH & SHELLFISH

British at their best:
Brill
Dabs
Dover Sole
Gray Mullet
Haddock
Halibut
Herring
John Dory
Lemon Sole
Mussels
Oysters
Plaice
Prawns
Sea Trout
Shrimp
Skate
Squid
Trout
Turbot

Also available:
Cockles
Cod
Coley (Pollock)
Conger Eel
Crab
Freshwater Crayfish
Hake
Huss
Lobsters
Mackerel
Monkfish
Salmon
Sea Bass
Scallops
Scampi (Langoustines)
Torbay Sole
Whiting
Winkles

Imported in season:
John Dory
Red Mullet
Sardines
Squid

POULTRY & GAME

British at their best:
Goose
Turkey

Also available:
Chicken
Duck
Guinea Fowl
Pigeon
Quail
Rabbit
Venison

MEAT

Beef
Lamb
Offal
Pork
Veal

Starters

LITTLE ONION TARTLETS WITH NEW GARLIC AND FRESH HERBS

*A*pril sees the beginning of the season of new garlic when thick stems protrude from the familiar white heads. New garlic has a milder, sweeter character than older varieties, many of which have been in store since last year. The delicate flavor of new garlic is best appreciated combined in creamy onion tartlets with one or two fresh herbs and served as a light starter.

ingredients . . . .

3tbsp butter
basic pie pastry, made with 1½ cups flour
2 onions, sliced
2 new garlic cloves, minced
1tsp chopped fresh thyme or ½tsp dried

1tbsp chopped parsley
⅔cup light cream
2 eggs
salt and pepper

Lightly grease four 4-inch tartlet pans with about 1tbsp of the butter. Roll out the pastry as thinly as you can on a floured work surface, cut out four 6-inch circles and line the pans without stretching the pastry. Allow the tartlets to rest for 30 minutes to prevent them from shrinking. Preheat the oven to 375°F.

Place a square of foil in each tartlet case and bake unfilled in the oven for 20-25 minutes. Meanwhile, melt the remaining butter in a shallow saucepan, add the onions, cover and soften over a gentle heat for 8-10 minutes. Add the garlic and herbs and stir briefly. (Garlic has a tendency to stick and burn if softened with the onions.)

Divide the mixture among the baked tartlet cases. Combine the cream, eggs and seasoning in a measuring cup and pour carefully over the onions. Bake near the top of the oven for 20-25 minutes or until the egg mixture is just beginning to set.

If you are planning ahead, the tartlet cases and the filling can be prepared well in advance and baked nearer the time of serving.

TUNA FISH AND FLAGEOLET BEAN SALAD

*T*he subtle green color of flageolet beans is most attractive when combined with pink tuna fish and bound in a tomato mayonnaise. This conveniently quick and easy salad can be put together at any time of year but goes well with a new potato salad.

ingredients . . . .

two 7oz cans tuna fish in brine
14oz can flageolet, lima or cannellini beans
7oz can whole kernel corn
4 scallions, chopped

⅓cup mayonnaise
2tbsp chopped capers
2 shakes hot pepper sauce
salt and pepper
1 head lettuce, washed and separated into leaves

Drain the tuna, beans and corn. Flake the tuna fish into a bowl, add the remainder of the ingredients and stir to mix together. Chill well before serving on a bed of crisp lettuce leaves.

Serves 6

A SPINACH SALAD WITH CRISPY BACON AND HARD-COOKED EGGS

*O*ne of my favorites among the new salad ingredients are the first leaves of spinach, so sweet and tender that it would be a shame to cook them. To bring out their full flavor in this salad I have tossed the leaves together with lettuce, crispy bacon and hard-cooked egg. I have based the dressing on dry sherry, olive oil and mustard to accentuate the peppery nature of the spinach.

ingredients . . . .

½lb fresh bulk spinach
6oz slab bacon, cut into strips
1 small head lettuce
3 hard-cooked eggs
   (12 minutes), quartered

Dressing
3tbsp dry sherry
4tbsp olive oil
2tsp grainy mustard
1tbsp wine vinegar

Remove the stems from the spinach leaves and put them with the lettuce leaves into a sink of cold water. (As well as removing any unwanted slugs and bugs, the leaves will freshen up in the water.) Put the bacon in a skillet and fry until crisp. Drain on paper towels.

To prepare the dressing: measure all the ingredients into a screwtop jar and shake together. When ready to serve, dry the spinach and lettuce leaves thoroughly, combine with the hard-cooked egg wedges and crumbled crispy bacon and toss in the dressing.

WHISKEY-CURED SEA TROUT WITH FRESH SAGE AND LEMON

*T*he people of Scandinavia have been curing their salmon for as long as the Scots have been smoking theirs. Both preparations are equally delicious thinly sliced and served with brown bread and butter. Sea trout, like the salmon it resembles, is very special when cured in whiskey, sage and lemon.

ingredients . . . .

1½lb sea trout, filleted
1tbsp finely chopped fresh
   sage
finely grated zest and juice of ½
   lemon

1½tsp salt
1tsp sugar
freshly ground white pepper
⅓cup malt whiskey

Wash the sea trout fillets under cold running water. Using a pair of tweezers, remove the line of small bones that start at the head end and continue halfway along the fish. Lay the fillets in a shallow glass or porcelain dish, skin side down.

Mix the sage with the lemon zest, salt and sugar and spread evenly over the fish fillets. Season generously with pepper and pour over the whiskey. Turn the fillets over so that the skin is facing uppermost, cover with foil and leave in the refrigerator for 24 hours. During this time the salt and the alcohol will in effect cook the fish by slow tenderization. The flesh will be slightly firmer although it will appear to be quite raw. It is perfectly safe and delicious to eat and will keep in the refrigerator for up to 7 days.

To serve: slice the fillets as thinly as possible with a sharp knife and serve with slices of buttered brown bread. A few lettuce leaves make an attractive garnish.

Main Courses

A SMOKED HADDOCK AND AVOCADO CRUMBLE

*S*ome of the most practical ideas for midweek suppers seem to come during a frantic rush around the shops just as they are about to close. The fishmonger is often a good place to make for at such a time since he is usually able to help out with one or two pieces of smoked haddock. A flying visit to the greengrocer for an avocado, plus half a dozen eggs, and you have the makings of a delicious savory crumble.

ingredients ....

1½lb smoked haddock (finnan
  haddie)
1¼cups milk
2tbsp butter
1 onion, chopped
2tbsp flour
4 hard-cooked eggs (12
  minutes), quartered
1 large avocado, peeled and
  roughly chopped
salt and pepper

Crumble topping
9tbsp flour
1cup rolled oats
¾cup grated Cheddar cheese
6tbsp cool butter

Place the smoked haddock in a shallow saucepan, cover with the milk and simmer for 8-10 minutes. Transfer the fish to a plate, reserving the milk, and leave to cool.

Measure the butter into another saucepan, add the onion and soften over a gentle heat without letting it color. Stir in the flour and draw away from the heat. Add the smoked haddock cooking milk a little at a time and stir until completely absorbed. Return the sauce to the heat and simmer to thicken.

Flake the smoked haddock between the fingers, discarding the skin and any spare bones. Add the hard-cooked eggs and the avocado and season to taste with salt and pepper. Turn the mixture into a shallow gratin dish and set aside. Preheat the oven to 400°F.

To prepare the crumble topping, measure all the ingredients into a mixing bowl and rub together with the fingertips until the butter has dispersed into bread crumb-sized pieces. Spread the topping over the fish mixture and bake in the oven for 35-40 minutes or until golden-brown on top. Serve with buttered carrots and zucchini.

A RAGOÛT OF CRAB WITH EGG NOODLES

*T*he inspiration for this recipe came one evening while I was dining in my local Chinese restaurant. So delicious was the dish that I ordered, that I have since attempted to re-create it using English ingredients.

ingredients ....

2tbsp butter
1 bunch scallions, sliced
1 celery stalk, sliced
1 small carrot, sliced
½tsp tomato paste
¾cups light fish or chicken
  bouillon
10oz (about 2½cups) freshly
  cooked crabmeat

3tbsp dry sherry
salt and pepper
5oz thin egg noodles,
  cooked
2tbsp chopped scallion
  tops, for garnish

Melt the butter in a large saucepan, add the scallions, celery and carrot, cover and soften over a gentle heat without letting the vegetables color. Stir in the tomato paste, add the bouillon and simmer for 10-15 minutes.

Remove from the heat and add the crabmeat, sherry and seasoning. (It is best not to boil the soup for longer than is necessary to warm the crabmeat since the meat is inclined to toughen.) To serve: divide the egg noodles among 4 soup plates, ladle the soup over the top and sprinkle with chopped scallion tops.

TURBANS OF SOLE WITH A MUSHROOM FILLING

*N*umerous campaigns have been launched over the years to get the Englishman to eat more fish. Sounds like a good idea to most of us, but what do we do with the fish once we get it home? While standing in the queue at my fishmonger, I often overhear customers enquiring how certain fish should be cooked. The most common reply is, "Oh, you can boil it or you can fry it madam." My willingness to step in at this point with a suggestion often results in my giving a cookery class to the entire queue. One idea is to line ramekin dishes with fillets of sole and to stuff them with mushrooms cooked in wine. They are then baked in the oven, unmolded and served with a simple cream sauce. Ask your fishmonger to give you the bones after filleting the fish, to use in the bouillon.

lengthwise and use to line the dishes. Divide the mushroom filling among the dishes. (If you are planning ahead, the fish can be prepared to this stage and kept in the refrigerator for up to 8 hours.)

Preheat the oven to 400°F.

Twenty minutes before you are ready to serve the fish, stand the ramekin dishes in a roasting pan, pour in boiling water to come halfway up the sides of the dishes, cover with foil and bake in the oven for 15 minutes.

To prepare the cream sauce: measure approximately 1cup of the fish bouillon into a saucepan and bring to a boil. Combine the soft butter and the flour to make a smooth paste, remove the bouillon from the heat and gradually whisk in the paste to thicken. Add the heavy cream, simmer briefly and season to taste with salt and pepper.

Unmold the sole turbans onto a serving dish, pour the sauce around the edge and decorate with parsley sprigs. Serve with rice and a mixture of young vegetables.

ingredients................

4 fillets gray sole or flounder,
   skinned
2tbsp butter, for greasing

Simple fish bouillon
bones from 2 sole or flounder
1 small onion, sliced
1 small carrot, sliced
2 parsley stems

Filling
⅓cup dry white wine
2 shallots or 1 small onion,
   chopped

¼llb button mushrooms,
   chopped
1tsp chopped fresh thyme or
   ½tsp dried
¼cup heavy cream
salt and pepper

Sauce
2tbsp butter, softened
2tbsp flour
6tbsp heavy cream
parsley sprigs, for garnish

To make the bouillon: place the fish bones in a large saucepan, cover with cold water and add the vegetables. Bring to a boil, then simmer gently for 20 minutes and strain.

To prepare the filling: put the wine and shallots or onion into a small saucepan and simmer until the wine has evaporated completely and the shallots or onion are soft. Add the mushrooms and thyme and soften, uncovered, until their moisture is driven off. Stir in the cream and season to taste with salt and pepper.

Lightly butter eight 3-inch ramekin dishes. Cut the sole fillets in half

STUFFED LOIN OF PORK WITH ORANGE, LEMON AND THYME

*O*f all the meats that appear on display in the butcher's window, loin of pork is considered to be one of the best buys for roasting. Pork is sometimes thought of as a rather bland meat, but it takes well to additional flavors, particularly those of fresh fruit and herbs. For this recipe I have blended the flavors of citrus fruits with thyme to provide the basis for a delicious stuffing.

ingredients................

one 3lb loin roast of pork,
   boned

Stuffing
2tbsp butter
1 small onion, chopped
finely grated zest and juice of 1
   orange
finely grated zest and juice of 1
   lemon

1tsp chopped fresh thyme or
   ½tsp dried
1cup fresh bread crumbs
salt and pepper

Gravy
½cup dry white wine or hard
   cider
⅞cup chicken bouillon
1tbsp cornstarch

To prepare the pork for stuffing: open the meat out on a chopping board and make an incision down the eye of the meat to form a shallow pocket.

To prepare the stuffing: melt the butter in a small saucepan, add the onion, cover and soften over a gentle heat for 3-4 minutes. Remove from the heat and add the orange and lemon juices and zests, thyme, bread crumbs and seasoning and stir together.

Spoon the stuffing into the incision in the pork, fold the meat around the stuffing to make a neat, compact shape and secure in several places with fine string. (If you are planning ahead, the pork can be kept in the refrigerator for up to 24 hours before roasting.)

To roast the pork: preheat the oven to 400°F.

Place the pork in a roasting pan without any additional fat and roast in the center of the oven for 30 minutes.

Reduce the temperature of the oven to 350°F and continue to roast the pork for a further 1 hour. (Reducing the temperature of the oven at this stage will enable the fibers in the meat to relax and thus become tender.)

To prepare the gravy: transfer the pork to a plate, cover and keep warm. Tilt the roasting pan to one side and spoon off any visible fat, leaving only the sediment in the bottom. Heat the sediment on top of the stove until it bubbles, add the wine and reduce by half. Add the chicken bouillon, then thicken with the cornstarch mixed with 2tbsp water and season to taste.

Carve the pork in good thick slices to retain the stuffing and serve with roast potatoes, young carrots and broccoli.

A WHITE LAMB STEW WITH A COLLAGE OF SPRING VEGETABLES

———————————— ❦ ————————————

F or this recipe I have chosen to celebrate the arrival of spring by combining the subtlety of new season lamb with a variety of colorful spring vegetables in a creamy white stew.

ingredients . . . .

1½lb boneless shoulder of lamb, diced	2 baby turnips, cut into large dice
1 small onion	¼lb snow peas or fine green beans, trimmed
½ bay leaf	¼lb button mushrooms
1 clove	1 bunch large scallions
1 small carrot	
1 thyme sprig	
2 parsley stems	To finish
salt and pepper	4tbsp butter
	3tbsp flour
Vegetable garnish	⅓cup heavy cream
2 young carrots, cut into fingers	2tbsp chopped parsley

Place the diced lamb in a saucepan and cover with cold water. Bring to a boil, then simmer for 1 minute. (In this time a scum will appear on the surface.) Drain the lamb in a colander, discarding the water. Return the lamb to the saucepan with 3¾cups fresh water, the onion and the bay leaf secured with a clove, the carrot and the herbs. Add a large pinch of salt, cover and simmer for 45 minutes.

Meanwhile, prepare the vegetable garnish: bring the carrots and turnips to a boil in a pan of water and cook for 4-5 minutes. Place the remaining vegetables in a saucepan of boiling water and cook for just 2-3 minutes, to retain their crispness. When the vegetables are cooked, immerse them in cold water to prevent overcooking.

When the lamb is cooked, lift it out of its bouillon with a slotted spoon, discarding the onion, carrot and herbs. Strain the bouillon into a measuring cup, to give just over 2½ cups. In the same saucepan as the lamb was cooked in, melt the butter and stir in the flour to make a basic roux. Remove from the heat and gradually stir in the bouillon until smooth. Return to the heat and simmer for 6-8 minutes, to thicken. Add the lamb, stir in the cream and season to taste with salt and pepper. Just before serving add the cooked vegetables and heat them through briefly. Sprinkle with chopped parsley and serve.

PAN-FRIED LAMB CHOPS WITH GARLIC AND ROSEMARY

*L*amb chops are an attractive idea for the midweek menu, prepared with garlic and rosemary. Serve with sautéed new potatoes sprinkled with parsley and a colorful mixed salad.

ingredients........................

4   double or 8 single lamb chops
salt and pepper
2tbsp   olive oil
2   rosemary sprigs

2   garlic cloves, peeled and cut in
   half
1½lb   cooked new potatoes,
   sliced
chopped parsley, for garnish

Season the lamb on both sides with pepper (not salt) and set aside. (Salting meat before cooking tends to draw out the delicate juices, leaving the meat dry, although this does not apply to roasting cuts of meat covered with a thin layer of fat.)

Heat the oil in a heavy skillet and add the rosemary and garlic. Add the chops and cook for 6 minutes on each side for lightly pink lamb, 10-12 minutes for medium to well-done lamb.

Transfer the chops to a warm plate until ready to serve. Remove the rosemary sprigs and garlic from the pan and add a little more oil to the cooking juices. Fry the potatoes until golden. Sprinkle with parsley and serve with the chops seasoned with a little salt.

POT-ROASTED CHICKEN WITH FENNEL, GARLIC AND MUSTARD

*T*o get the best flavor out of a chicken, most of us would agree that it should either be roasted or casseroled. But the less common method of pot-roasting combines both, browning as well as casseroling the meat. In this recipe, white wine, aromatic vegetables, garlic and mustard are added to create a delicately balanced dish.

ingredients........................

4tbsp   butter, softened
½lb   bulb fennel, roughly
   chopped
1   small carrot, roughly chopped
1   onion, roughly chopped
4   chicken pieces
⅔cup   dry white wine

2tsp   spicy brown mustard
1   garlic clove, minced
2tsp   chopped fresh thyme or
   1tsp dried
2½cups   chicken bouillon, boiling
2tbsp   flour
salt and pepper

Preheat the oven to 425°F.

Melt half the butter in a flameproof casserole on top of the stove, add the roughly chopped vegetables and brown evenly. Place the chicken pieces over the browned vegetables, season and cook, uncovered, near the top of the oven for 35 minutes.

Add the wine, mustard, garlic, thyme and chicken bouillon to the casserole. Cover and return to the oven reduced to 350°F for a further 45 minutes. To thicken the sauce, combine the remaining butter and the flour to make a paste and beat into the casserole. Return to a simmer on top of the stove and season to taste. Serve with plain boiled rice, fried tomatoes and zucchini.

CHICKEN, LEEK AND MUSHROOM COBBLER

It is a healthy sign for anyone to long for the qualities of good home cooking. As a child, and even now, I spend a considerable amount of time dreaming about my favorite dishes. One such dish that I cannot live without is this mixture of chicken, leeks and mushrooms, crowned with a layer of cheesy scones that soften so invitingly in their own gravy.

ingredients . . . .

4 chicken pieces
1 celery stalk, roughly chopped
1 small onion, roughly chopped
1 small carrot, roughly chopped
1 thyme sprig

Cobbler topping
1¼cups self-rising flour
salt and pepper
4tbsp cool butter

½cup grated Cheddar cheese
milk or beaten egg, to glaze

Sauce
4tbsp butter
¾lb leeks, split, washed and
  shredded
3tbsp flour
¼lb button mushrooms,
  quartered

Place the chicken portions in a large saucepan with the celery, onion, carrot and thyme. Cover with 2½cups cold water and bring to a boil, then simmer for 45 minutes.

Meanwhlle, prepare the cobbler topping: sift the flour and seasoning into a mixing bowl, add the butter and cheese and rub together between the fingertips to form the consistency of large bread crumbs. Add 4tbsp cold water all at once and mix to an even dough without overworking. Cover with plastic wrap and leave to rest in the refrigerator until ready to use.

When the chicken is cooked, lift it out of the bouillon and cool on a plate. Strain the stock and set aside. Preheat the oven to 400°F.

To finish the sauce: melt the butter in a saucepan, add the leeks, cover and soften over a gentle heat for 3-4 minutes. Stir in the flour until absorbed. Remove the pan from the heat and gradually add the bouillon, stirring well. Return to the heat and simmer to thicken.

Remove the meat from the chicken pieces, add to the sauce with the mushrooms and season to taste with salt and pepper. Turn the mixture into a 5-cup baking dish.

Roll out the cobbler dough on a floured work surface, to a thickness of ¾inch and cut out as many 2inch circles as you can, using a plain or fluted cookie cutter. Arrange the circles overlapping around the edge of the dish and brush with milk or beaten egg to glaze. Bake the cobbler in the preheated oven for 25-30 minutes or until the topping is well-risen and golden.

Puddings

OLD ENGLISH LEMON POSSETS

The Englishman's taste for creamy confections dates back as far as the twelfth century when early literature records the taking of caudles and possets as a tonic to ward off minor illness. Gradually the posset has developed into a deliciously rich, creamy dessert to be served in little stem glasses with almond macaroons. It is worth mentioning that heavy cream will boil as readily as milk without curdling. It is essential, however, that it is as fresh as possible.

ingredients . . . .

1¼cups heavy cream	6tbsp sugar
juice of 1 lemon	12 almond macaroons

Rinse the bottom of a heavy saucepan with water, add the cream and bring to a boil. (Rinsing the saucepan with water is an old trick that will prevent the cream from burning. It also works with milk.)

Squeeze the lemon juice into a bowl and add the sugar. Pour the boiling cream over the lemon juice and sugar and stir well. Divide the lemon cream among 4 attractive stem glasses and leave in the refrigerator to set. The setting action occurs as the lemon begins to sour the cream. This usually takes between 1-1½ hours. Serve the lemon possets with almond macaroons.

TREACLE TART WITH LEMON AND BITTER ALMONDS

The treacle tart has been popular on the English table since we began importing sugar cane from the West Indies in the seventeenth century. Originally treacle tart was made from the sticky black residue that is left over from the refining of sugar cane, known today as molasses or black treacle. In the late 1800s, Tate and Lyle further refined this residue by a secret recipe into golden syrup, from which treacle tarts are still made today. For this recipe, I have included a squeeze of lemon and a few bitter almonds to counteract the sweetness of the tart. Serve it warm or cold, with custard sauce or cream.

ingredients . . . .

Pastry	finely grated zest and juice of 1
1⅔cups flour	lemon
1 pinch salt	1½cups fresh white bread
1 stick cool butter	crumbs
	½tsp ground ginger
Filling	⅔cups ground bitter almonds
½cup imported golden syrup or	
light corn syrup	

To make the pastry: sift the flour together with the salt into a mixing bowl and add the diced butter. Cut together until the mixture resembles large breadcrumbs. Alternatively use a food processor for the same result. Add 4-5tbsp cold water and mix to a dough. Dust with flour, wrap in plastic wrap and refrigerate for 30 minutes before using.

Preheat the oven to 375°F. Lightly grease an 8-inch pie pan, roll out the pastry on a floured work surface and line the pan. Save the trimmings for decoration. Put the golden syrup into a saucepan and warm over a gentle heat. Add the lemon zest and juice, the breadcrumbs, ginger and almonds. Spread the mixture into the pie pan and decorate the top with strips of leftover pastry. Bake the tart in the center of the oven for 25-30 minutes or until the pastry is golden.

A DARK CHOCOLATE MOUSSE

I t has been said that the finest chocolate mousses are made by people for whom chocolate is their first love. If you are such a person, it should go without saying that you cannot make a good chocolate mousse out of anything but the finest chocolate. For this recipe I have chosen a dark, slightly bitter chocolate that will blend smoothly with the remaining ingredients.

ingredients

7oz best-quality bitter sweet chocolate
3 eggs, separated
¼cup sugar
1¼cups heavy cream, softly whipped

Decoration
⅔cup whipping cream
3oz semisweet chocolate, flaked

Break the chocolate into a bowl and melt by standing over a saucepan of simmering water. It is important not to allow any moisture or steam into the chocolate or it may have a tendency to thicken.

Place the egg whites in a large mixing bowl. Remove the melted chocolate from the heat and stir in the yolks. Beat the egg whites with the sugar until soft peaks are formed. Pour the chocolate mixture into the beaten egg whites and fold in with a rubber spatula, retaining as much air as possible. Add the whipped cream and fold in evenly.

Turn the mousse into 4 pretty glasses or one large bowl and decorate with whipped cream and flaked chocolate.

ingredients

1 stick butter, softened
⅔cup light brown sugar
½tsp apple pie spice
2 eggs, beaten
1 cup self-rising flour
1 cup currants
⅔cup golden raisins
⅓cup raisins

finely grated zest of ½ orange
finely grated zest of ½ lemon
½lb yellow marzipan

To glaze
2tbsp apricot jam
1 egg yolk

Preheat the oven to 400°F. Lightly grease a 7-inch cake pan and line with a double layer of parchment paper. Place the butter, sugar and spice in a mixing bowl and beat together until pale and fluffy. It is important at this stage that the butter is of a similar consistency as the beaten egg to enable the two to be blended together evenly. Add the egg a little at a time and beat until smooth. If the egg begins to separate, add a little of the flour and continue to beat.

Place the remaining flour with the fruit and the citrus zest in a bowl and toss together. (Coating the fruit with flour will prevent the fruit from sinking during baking.) Stir the flour and the fruit into the creamed mixture and spread roughly half into the bottom of the prepared cake pan. Divide the marzipan in half, dust with a little flour and roll out one half into a circle that will fit into the pan. Spread the remaining batter in the pan and bake in the center of the oven for 30 minutes, then reduce the oven to 325°F and bake for 1 further hour, or until a skewer inserted into the center of the cake comes out clean.

Allow the cake to cool in the pan, then unmold it and trim the top level. Spread with warm apricot jam. Roll out two-thirds of the remaining marzipan to cover the top. Brush the surface of the marzipan with beaten egg yolk. Fashion 11 little balls from the leftover marzipan and position around the edge. Brush once again with egg yolk and brown under the broiler. The cake can be tied with a yellow ribbon and the top further decorated with sugar flowers if liked.

SIMNEL CAKE

S imnel cakes were traditionally baked and given on Mothering Sunday so that they could be kept for the remainder of Lent and enjoyed at Easter. To this day richly fruited simnel cake with its hidden layer of marzipan still marks the arrival of Easter and is decorated with 11 balls of leftover marzipan to symbolize Christ's faithful disciples.

Easter Dinner

Easter is the most important event in the Christian calendar, and whether or not we choose to follow the story of Easter, the Easter vacations have long been a time when family and friends have gathered at the table to enjoy a special dinner to mark the end of winter and the beginning of spring, with its variety of new produce to open the season. Spring lamb is usually ready for Easter and it could not taste better than when roasted in a simple way with new garlic and rosemary.

A Pâté of Cream Cheese, Pink Shrimp and Bacon
•
Roast Leg of Spring Lamb with Garlic and Rosemary
•
Zucchini, Tomato and Onion Layer
•
Boiled New Potatoes
•
Toasted Bread and Butter Pudding

A PÂTÉ OF CREAM CHEESE, PINK SHRIMP AND BACON

This delicious pâté can be served as individual portions or spooned from a larger dish to be accompanied by fingers of hot toast and a green salad.

ingredients

4 slices Canadian bacon, cut into strips
1½cups packed pot cheese
2tbsp chopped parsley
1tbsp lemon juice
1 pinch cayenne
½lb cooked shrimp, peeled and roughly chopped

4 scallions, chopped

Garnish
6 cooked shrimp in shell
6 parsley sprigs
6 lemon wedges

Fry the bacon until crisp and drain on paper towels. Blend together the pot cheese, parsley, lemon juice and cayenne in a food processor or using an electric food mixer.

Stir in the crispy bacon, shrimp and scallions and pack the mixture into 6 individual serving dishes or one large dish. Allow the pâté to chill for an hour or so before garnishing and serving with fingers of hot toast and a simple green salad. The pâté will keep in the refrigerator for up to 4 days providing it is well covered.

ROAST LEG OF SPRING LAMB WITH GARLIC AND ROSEMARY

English spring lamb is considered to have the finest flavor when the animal has fed on its mother's milk and been raised on salt marsh pastures, by the sea.

ingredients

one 2½-3lb new English leg of lamb
2 new garlic cloves, cut into slivers
1 bunch rosemary
2tbsp drippings or lard

Gravy
⅓cup red wine
⅞cup chicken bouillon
1tbsp cornstarch
1tsp raspberry or red wine vinegar

Preheat the oven to 425°F. Rub the skin of the lamb with plenty of salt to help it crisp in the oven. Pierce the skin with a small knife to make long pockets and place garlic slivers and sprigs of rosemary under the skin. Melt the drippings or lard in a roasting pan on top of the stove and brown the lamb evenly to seal in the flavor.

Roast the lamb in the oven, allowing 15 minutes per pound. When the lamb is cooked, transfer it to a plate and leave to rest in a warm oven while making the gravy. To make the gravy, tilt the roasting pan to one side and allow the meat juices to settle. Spoon off the layer of fat and bring the juices to a boil on top of the stove. Pour in the wine, stir to loosen the sediment and add the chicken bouillon. To thicken, mix the cornstarch with 2tbsp cold water and stir into the gravy. Season to taste and sharpen with a hint of vinegar.

Ragoût of Crab with Egg Noodles; Roast Leg of Spring Lamb with Garlic and Rosemary; Toasted Bread and Butter Pudding.

ZUCCHINI, TOMATO AND ONION LAYER

When entertaining a large number of people it is always useful to have the vegetables ready prepared and out of the way to allow more time when serving. This vegetable dish can be prepared well in advance, baked and brought to the table with very little fuss.

ingredients . . . .

1 garlic clove, halved	1lb firm tomatoes, sliced
1½lb zucchini, sliced at an angle	4tbsp butter
4 small onions, halved and sliced	salt and pepper

Preheat the oven to 400°F. Rub the bottom and sides of a 10inch gratin dish with the cut side of the garlic. This will give the finished dish a subtle flavor of garlic. Layer the sliced zucchini, onions and tomatoes into the dish. Strew with pieces of butter, season well and cover with foil.

Bake in the oven for 25-30 minutes or until the onions have softened and the zucchini nicely cooked. Remove the foil covering, season once more with freshly ground black pepper and bring to the table.

TOASTED BREAD AND BUTTER PUDDING

There is a certain magic about bread and butter pudding that recalls even the most hardened adults to their childhood. Some are attracted by the maternal softness of the milky egg custard. Others are lured by the delicate layers of buttered bread that point so invitingly in the brown crusty topping. Whichever aspect you look forward to, bread and butter pudding will always appeal to the young at heart.

ingredients . . . .

⅓cup golden raisins	½tsp vanilla extract
1 small loaf raisin bread, sliced,	6 eggs
or 8 slices of white bread	6tbsp sugar
4tbsp butter	confectioners' sugar for dusting
3¾cups milk	

Preheat the oven to 375°F. Scatter the raisins into a 5-cup baking dish. Remove the crusts from the bread. Butter the squares of bread generously with butter and arrange them overlapping neatly in the dish.

Bring the milk to a boil with the vanilla extract. Beat the eggs and sugar in a bowl, pour in the boiling milk and stir well. Strain the custard over the bread.

Stand the dish in a roasting pan, pour in boiling water to come halfway up the sides of the dish and bake in the oven for 35-40 minutes or until a small knife will come away cleanly when inserted into the center of the pudding. To finish, dust the pudding with confectioners' sugar and brown evenly under the broiler. Serve warm.

Teatime Favorites

*E*ntertaining is never easy during the Easter vacations, especially when unexpected guests turn up for tea and expect home-made cakes. At times like these we find ourselves searching for quick, easy recipes that can be made at a moment's notice. Sticky banana cake has been a favorite of mine ever since I was a lad.

STICKY BANANA CAKE

ingredients........................

6tbsp   soft butter
⅔cup   brown sugar
1   egg, beaten
2   large ripe bananas, mashed

1⅔cups   self-rising flour
½tsp   ground allspice
1   pinch salt

Preheat the oven to 375°F. Lightly grease an 8-inch loaf pan with oil or soft butter and line with parchment paper.

To make the cake, cream the soft butter and sugar together until pale and fluffy. Add the egg a little at a time and beat until smooth. Stir in the mashed banana. Sift the flour, allspice and salt together over the mixture and stir until even. Turn the mixture into the prepared pan and bake in the center of the oven for 35–40 minutes. The cake is cooked when a skewer will come away cleanly from the center. Allow the cake to cool in the pan. If you have time, the cake will improve if kept for a day or so before serving.

As a variation on the recipe you may like to add ½cup of chopped walnuts or mixed dried fruit to the mixture before baking. If you are expecting guests over the Easter vacations it is a good idea to make twice the recipe and keep the second cake in the freezer until needed. It will keep for up to 8 weeks.

Serves 8

ENGLISH FLAPJACKS

*Q*uick, easy and delicious: these are just three reasons why the English flapjack has remained such a popular item at tea time. Recipes for flapjacks are usually passed on from one generation to another through the family and remain a closely guarded secret.

ingredients........................

1½   sticks butter
½cup   brown sugar
2tbsp   imported golden syrup
3cups   rolled oats

1tbsp   sunflower seeds
1tbsp   pumpkin seeds
2tbsp   sesame seeds
3tbsp   sliced almonds

Preheat the oven to 350°F. Lightly grease a 9-inch square pan with butter or oil. Measure the butter, sugar and golden syrup into a heavy saucepan and melt over a gentle heat, taking care not to boil the mixture. Remove from the heat and stir in the remainder of the ingredients until even. Turn the mixture into the prepared pan, press lightly with the back of a wooden spoon and bake in the center of the preheated oven for 20 minutes. Allow to cool for 5 minutes, then cut into 12 fingers. Allow to cool completely. Transfer to an airtight container and store until required.

Makes 12

May is a month that is full of the promise and excitement of summer, while still very much part of spring.

Vegetable farmers can find little to complain about, with many of their crops benefiting from the warmer weather. New carrots are a common sight in vegetable markets and are particularly delicious when their feathery tops are attached. Other vegetables worth looking out for include new peas in their pods, which are delicious eaten raw in salads, green beans, broad beans and turnips. Many young vegetables appear more expensive at this time of the year, but providing they are cooked properly, their flavor will more than make up for their price. Most flavorsome of all are the neatly tied bunches of English asparagus that adorn vegetable stalls all over the country. Due to the intensive labor that is required to maintain and grow asparagus, graded bunches do tend to be expensive. Less expensive but equally delicious are the straggly lengths of asparagus known as sprue grass and often sold loose. Broccoli continues to be available throughout the month although short supplies can often cause the prices to rise. Cauliflowers, leeks, rutabaga and parsnips are now past their best.

The English potato season is at a bit of a loose end at the moment, as the first of our early varieties do not arrive until June. However, imported potatoes from Egypt, Cyprus and Israel are available and are considerably improved when boiled with a sprig of fresh mint. New potatoes no larger than Brussels sprouts are also worth having provided you don't object to the price. English cabbages are less plentiful now. Zucchini, eggplants and sweet peppers continue to be imported from Spain and France.

Along with the warmer weather comes a further variety of English salad ingredients; butterhead and curly lettuce, cucumbers, radishes, fennel, chicory, watercress, celery and scallions. English tomatoes are grown under glass at this time of the year and are worth having for their clean fresh flavor. Avocados are good and combine well in a variety of salad dishes. Fresh herbs are doing well and find their way into many seasonal dishes. Look out for cloves of new garlic, flat and curly parsley, chives, basil, tarragon, sage, dill and mint.

The fruit market is showing signs of improvement during May with the arrival of the first English strawberries. Prices are often high to start the season, although few can resist the first taste. Fresh apricots from Spain make a special appearance during May and are delicious eaten raw, made into creamy puddings or baked in a tart. Varieties of outdoor rhubarb continue to do well throughout the month and often show a fall in price. Oranges are full of flavor and are in good supply. Look out for Valencias, Navels and Jaffas. Melons are worth buying as the weather improves: Cantaloup, Charentais, Ogen and Galia offer the best flavor and are delicious chilled and served as a refreshing starter or dessert, or to take on a spring picnic.

The fishmonger is able to offer an attractive display during May with plentiful supplies of wild salmon, now at more reasonable prices. Farmed salmon is also available but doesn't have the same flavor and texture. Also on offer are a variety of crabs, both large and small, from Cromer and the West Country. Lobsters are appearing back on the stalls after their winter break and make fine eating with a crisp green salad. Fresh trout, available all year round, show signs of an improved flavor now. Herring and mackerel are a good buy during May and may even show a fall in price. Among the flat fish Dover, Torbay and lemon sole, brill, halibut, flounder and turbot are all in good condition and will remain so throughout the summer months. Fresh cod, haddock and whiting remain in good supply, although because cod is fished less extensively during the summer, many fish are kept frozen to maintain regular supplies. There are still plentiful supplies of pink and brown shrimp, cockles, clams, scallops and winkles to be had. With the warmer weather, samphire or poor man's asparagus, with its brilliant emerald color and sea-fresh taste, has started growing again on coastal marshes. Cook it in plenty of boiling water for 6-8 minutes and serve with melted butter and lemon juice to accompany fish.

$\mathcal{M}$AY INGREDIENTS IN SEASON

FRUIT & NUTS

British at their best:
Cooking Apples
Gooseberries
Pears
Rhubarb
Strawberries

Also available:
Apples
Grapes
Hazelnuts (Filberts)
Walnuts

Imported in season:
Almonds
Apricots
Bananas
Brazil Nuts
Cherries
Grapefruit
Kiwi Fruit
Kumquats
Lemons
Limes
Mangoes
Melons
Nectarines
Oranges
Papaya
Passion Fruit
Peanuts
Pecans
Peaches
Pineapples
Pistachio Nuts
Plums
Pomegranates
Watermelons

VEGETABLES & HERBS

British at their best:
Asparagus
Carrots
Cherry Tomatoes
Chives
Courgettes (Zucchini)
Cucumbers
Jerusalem Artichokes
Mange tout (Snow Peas)
Mint
Mustard and Cress
Onions
Parsley
Peas
Potatoes
Radishes
Rosemary
Sage
Savory
Spring Onions (Scallions)
Spinach
Tarragon
Thyme
Tomatoes
Turnips
Watercress

Also available:
Basil
Beets
Broad (Fava) Beans
Broccoli
Cabbages
Cauliflowers
Celeriac
Celery
Chervil
Dill
Fennel
Globe Artichokes
Lavender
Leeks
Lettuce
Marjoram
Shallots

Imported in season:
Aubergines (Eggplants)
Avocados
Chicory (Belgian Endive)
Courgettes (Zucchini)
French (Green) Beans
Garlic
Sweet Peppers

FISH & SHELLFISH

British at their best:
Brill
Conger Eel
Crab
Dabs
Dover Sole
Haddock
Halibut
Herring
John Dory
Lemon Sole
Lobsters
Mackerel
Plaice
Prawns
Red Mullet
Salmon
Sea Trout
Scampi (Langoustine)
Shrimp
Squid
Torbay Sole
Trout
Turbot
Whitebait

Also available:
Cockles
Cod
Coley (Pollock)
Freshwater Crayfish
Gray Mullet
Hake
Huss
Monkfish
Scallops
Sea Bass
Skate
Whiting
Winkles

Imported in season:
John Dory
Red Mullet
Sardines
Squid

POULTRY & GAME

British at their best:
Pigeon

Also available:
Chicken
Duck
Goose
Guinea Fowl
Quail
Rabbit
Turkey
Venison

MEAT
Beef
Lamb
Offal
Pork
Veal

Starters

A SOUP OF BABY CARROTS WITH THEIR TENDER TOPS

There is something very satisfying about a bunch of new carrots, especially if you have been able to grow them yourself. To make the most of their sweet and delicate flavor, I like to blend the carrots together with their feathery tops into a delicious soup that both captures and underlines their true character.

ingredients

¾lb baby carrots with their tops
1 small onion, chopped
1tsp chopped fresh thyme or
  ½tsp dried

2tbsp butter
3tbsp long-grain rice
2½cups light chicken bouillon
⅓cup light cream
salt and pepper

Trim the carrots of their tops and scrub clean. Cut half the carrots into short matchsticks and finely grate the remainder. Chop half the carrot tops, reserving 4 sprigs for the garnish. Place the grated carrot in a saucepan with the onion, chopped carrot tops, thyme and butter, cover and allow to soften over a gentle heat for 2-3 minutes. Add the rice and chicken stock and simmer for 20 minutes.

Blend the soup in a liquidizer until smooth. Return the soup to a clean saucepan with the carrot matchsticks and simmer for 4-5 minutes. When ready to serve, stir in the cream and season to taste. Decorate each serving with a sprig of carrot top.

A SPINACH AND MUSHROOM SOUFFLÉ SCENTED WITH NEW GARLIC

Milky white heads of new garlic quite literally bulge with flavor and lend a wonderfully sweet aroma and subtle taste to this soufflé of spinach and mushrooms.

ingredients

6tbsp butter
¼lb button mushrooms,
  chopped
1tsp chopped fresh thyme or
  ½tsp dried
2 new garlic cloves, minced
¼cup flour

1¼cups milk
5 eggs, separated
1lb fresh bulk spinach, cooked
  and finely chopped, or 6oz
  frozen chopped spinach,
  thawed
salt and pepper

Grease a 7-inch straight-sided soufflé dish with about 1tbsp of the butter.

Place the mushrooms in a saucepan with 1tbsp of the butter and thyme and soften, uncovered, until the moisture has been driven off. Add the garlic and set aside.

Melt the remaining butter in a saucepan and stir in the flour, then remove from the heat and stir in the milk a little at a time. Return to the boil and simmer briefly to thicken. Stir in the egg yolks, the well-drained chopped spinach and the mushrooms. Season to taste with salt and pepper. (If you are planning ahead, the mixture can be reheated up to 2 hours later.)

Thirty minutes before you intend to serve the soufflé, preheat the oven to 400°F. Beat the egg whites until they are smooth and hold their weight on the beater. (If the whites become grainy, give them a final beating by hand before folding in.) Stir a large spoonful of beaten egg white into the spinach and mushroom mixture until evenly distributed, then fold in the remainder, retaining as much air as possible. Turn the mixture into the prepared soufflé dish and spread the top level. Bake in the center of the oven for 20-25 minutes, until the soufflé is risen and set, but still creamy in the center. (Test with a skewer as you would a fruit cake.) Serve immediately.

AVOCADO-STUFFED TOMATOES IN A SIMPLE GREEN SALAD

*A*s the weather changes favorably with the approach of summer, those wonderful salad days return when one can exist quite happily on a colorful variety of seasonal produce. For this salad I have made use of the first English tomatoes of the season and have stuffed them with a smooth avocado mayonnaise blended with fresh herbs. The stuffed tomatoes are then hidden in the midst of a green salad and served as a starter or light main course.

Wash the lettuce and watercress in plenty of cold water and leave them in the water to freshen up. Score the tomatoes with a sharp knife, place them in a bowl and cover with boiling water to loosen their skins. Cool under cold running water, then peel. Slice off the tops and scoop out the insides with a teaspoon.

To prepare the filling, place all the filling ingredients in a blender or food processor and combine until smooth. Fill each tomato and set aside. Combine all the dressing ingredients.

When ready to serve, dry the salad leaves thoroughly and toss together with the dressing. Distribute the salad among 4 plates and arrange three stuffed tomatoes in the center of each plate.

ingredients

1 head crisp lettuce
1 bunch of watercress
12 ripe tomatoes

Filling
2 ripe avocados, peeled and
  seeded
¼cup mayonnaise
1 garlic clove, minced
2tbsp chopped chives

2tbsp chopped parsley
1tbsp lemon juice
3 shakes of hot pepper sauce

Dressing
⅓cup olive oil
2tbsp lemon juice
1tsp Dijon-style mustard
1 pinch sugar
salt and pepper

RAW TOMATO, CUCUMBER AND GARLIC SOUP

ingredients

3 slices stale white bread, crusts
  removed
⅔cup olive oil
3tbsp red wine vinegar
1 small onion, roughly chopped
2 cloves garlic, minced

1 small hothouse cucumber,
  roughly chopped
2lb tomatoes, skins removed
1tbsp Worcestershire sauce
salt and pepper

Place the stale bread in a shallow dish with the oil and vinegar to soften for 3-4 minutes. In the meantime process the onion, garlic and cucumber until smooth. Add the tomatoes, Worcestershire sauce and the softened bread and blend. Measure in 1¼cups of water and season to taste with salt and pepper. Chill before serving.

Main Courses

A WHITE FISH GRATIN WITH YOUNG VEGETABLES

One of the greatest incentives that should stimulate every cook is the desire to bring the natural freshness of ingredients to the table. At this time of the year I like to take full advantage of the variety of young vegetables on the market. Some are best eaten raw, but most will improve with a brief cooking. To extend their flavor still further, I like to combine these vegetables into a creamy gratin of white fish finished with a golden layer of cheese. Brill, halibut, haddock or a combination of the three could be used.

ingredients . . . .

¼lb baby carrots, scrubbed and sliced
¼lb asparagus spears, scraped and cut into short lengths
2oz snow peas, trimmed and halved
¼lb young turnips, peeled and cut into fingers
2oz fine green beans, trimmed and halved

1½lb white fish, filleted and skinned
2cups milk
4tbsp butter
¼cup flour
salt and pepper
½cup grated Cheddar cheese
1cup fresh white bread crumbs

Preheat the oven to 400°F.

Bring a saucepan of water to a boil with a large pinch of salt and simmer the carrots and asparagus for 6 minutes. Add the snow peas, turnips and beans to the same pan and continue to cook for 4 minutes. Drain the vegetables and cool under running water.

Season the fish with salt and pepper, place it in a shallow saucepan, cover with milk and simmer for 8 minutes. Lift the fish out of the milk and arrange it in a 9-inch gratin dish.

To make the sauce, melt the butter in a saucepan and stir in the flour. Remove from the heat and gradually stir in the milk used to cook the fish. Return to the heat and simmer to thicken. Season the sauce to taste. Spread the cooked vegetables over the fish and pour the sauce over the top. Combine the grated cheese with the bread crumbs and sprinkle evenly over the gratin. Finish the gratin under the broiler until crisp and golden, and serve with new potatoes.

FILLETS OF FLAT FISH WITH A SPICY SHRIMP STUFFING

In this recipe I have given a new look to fillets of flat fish, stuffing them with a spicy shrimp butter and serving with a delicate cream sauce.

ingredients . . . .

4 fillets of flat fish such as flounder, skinned
1tbsp flour
1cup milk
3tbsp heavy cream
salt and pepper

Stuffing
½lb peeled cooked small shrimp
2 scallions
2 pinches paprika
1 pinch turmeric
1 pinch ground mace
1 pinch cayenne
6tbsp soft unsalted butter

Preheat the oven to 375°F.

Place half the shrimp in a food processor with the scallions, spices and butter and blend until smooth. Spread the mixture onto the fish fillets, roll up neatly and secure with a wooden toothpick. Place the fish in a flameproof casserole, cover loosely with foil and bake in the preheated oven for 20 minutes. Transfer the fish to a plate and keep warm.

Stir the flour into the buttery juices in the casserole, add the milk a little at a time and stir until smooth. Add the remaining shrimp and the cream and simmer briefly to thicken. Taste for seasoning and spoon the sauce over the fillets. Serve at once with Basmati rice, and buttered carrots and zucchini.

FILLETS OF PINK TROUT WITH A TARRAGON CREAM SAUCE

ingredients . . . .

2tbsp butter
1tbsp peanut oil
four ¾lb pink trout, filleted by
  your fishmonger
salt and pepper
1tsp cornstarch

⅞cup light cream
2tbsp chopped tarragon
3 firm tomatoes, skinned,
  seeded and diced
1tsp white wine vinegar

Heat the butter and oil in a large non-stick skillet. Season the trout fillets with salt and pepper and cook for 3 minutes on each side. Transfer to a plate, cover and keep warm. Mix the cornstarch with 2tbsp cold water and stir into the cream, to prevent it from separating when heated.

Stir the cream and tarragon into the skillet and simmer to thicken. Add the diced tomato, sharpen to taste with the white wine vinegar and season.

Arrange the trout fillets on a serving dish and cover with the sauce. Serve with buttered new potatoes, snow peas and zucchini.

LOIN OF LAMB IN THE STYLE OF WELLINGTON

 In his day, the Duke of Wellington inspired the name of one of our most celebrated beef dishes, Fillet of Beef Wellington, covered with liver pâté, mushrooms and a layer of golden pastry. Contrary to popular belief, the Duke was not a great gourmet and it is thought that the dish was so named because of its resemblance to one of Wellington's riding boots! Since fillet (tenderloin) of beef has almost priced itself out of the market, I have taken to making the dish with a tender loin of lamb: still expensive, but for my money twice as delicious.

ingredients . . . .

2tbsp drippings or butter
one 2½lb boned loin of lamb,
  trimmed of all fat and tied
salt and pepper
1 onion, finely chopped
1tsp chopped fresh thyme or
  ½tsp dried
6oz button mushrooms, finely
  chopped
½lb puff pastry

3oz smooth liver pâté
a little milk (optional)
1 egg, beaten with a pinch of
  salt
1 bunch parsley, for garnish

Sauce
⅓cup red wine
1¼cups light beef bouillon
1tbsp cornstarch

Preheat the oven to 425°F. Heat the drippings or butter in a roasting pan on top of the stove. Season the lamb and seal by turning in the fat. Transfer to the oven and roast for 15 minutes, then remove from pan and allow to cool. Pour the cooking fat into a small saucepan. Keep the roasting pan for making the sauce. Add the onion and soften over a gentle heat. Add the thyme and mushrooms and continue to soften. Reserve 2tbsp of this mixture for the sauce and cool the remainder on a plate.

Roll out the puff pastry into a rectangle on a floured work surface. Soften the pâté if necessary with a little milk and spread over the lamb. Spread the mushroom mixture over the pastry, position the lamb in the center, cut off the corners of the pastry and cover the lamb with pastry, sealing the edges firmly. Brush with beaten egg and decorate with pastry trimmings. (If you are planning ahead, the Lamb Wellington can be kept in a cool place – not the refrigerator – for up to 4 hours.)

To cook, preheat the oven to 400°F. Brush the pastry once more with egg glaze if the dish has been kept waiting. Bake for 20-25 minutes or until the pastry is brown; the lamb will be slightly pink in the middle.

To prepare the sauce: pour the wine into the roasting pan that was used to brown the meat. Bring to a boil on top of the stove and stir to loosen the sediment. Add the reserved mushroom mixture and bouillon and simmer. To thicken, mix the cornstarch with 2tbsp cold water and stir into the sauce. Season to taste with salt and pepper. Bring the lamb to the table, garnished with parsley, and serve, with a selection of spring vegetables and new potatoes.

SPARERIBS OF PORK WITH A SPICED APRICOT SAUCE

———————— ❦ ————————

aintaining a young family's interest in their meals throughout the week is becoming an increasingly difficult task, especially when all children seem to want these days is an endless succession of junk food. Can you blame them when they are lured by so much television advertising? One way to tempt them back to home cooking is to offer them a supper of spareribs in a spicy apricot sauce. As soon as they realize that the ribs are best eaten with the fingers, it won't be long before junk food becomes second best.

ingredients . . . .

2lb pork spareribs	2tbsp olive oil
salt	1tbsp Worcestershire sauce
6oz fresh apricots, pitted and roughly chopped	2 shakes hot pepper sauce
1 small onion, finely chopped	1tbsp wine vinegar
1 garlic clove, minced	3tbsp apricot jam

Season the pork with plenty of salt and set aside. (Salting will help the ribs crisp evenly.) To prepare the sauce: place the apricots, onion, garlic and oil in a saucepan, cover and soften over a gentle heat for 6-8 minutes. Add the Worcestershire sauce, hot pepper sauce, vinegar and jam and stir until well blended.

Pour the sauce over the ribs and leave to marinate for a minimum of 30 minutes – longer if you have time. Broil the ribs under a moderate heat for 10-12 minutes on each side, basting occasionally. Serve with parsley potatoes, zucchini and carrots.

ROAST DUCK WITH KUMQUATS AND LIME

———————— ❦ ————————

ne of the secrets I have learned is that there are very few entirely new recipe ideas: most stem from age-old traditions. There is nothing new, for instance, about combining the acidity of fresh oranges with the richness of roast duck; in fact, this combination is a classic. In this recipe I have used the tangy flavor of kumquats together with the sharpness of lime to create an equally delicious contrast: a simple variation on a common theme.

ingredients . . . .

one 5lb duck	¼cup dry sherry
salt and pepper	finely grated zest and juice of 2 limes
¼lb kumquats, sliced	
3tbsp sugar	2tsp wine vinegar
1¼cups chicken bouillon	2tbsp cornstarch

Preheat the oven to 425°F.

Pierce the duck skin several times with a fork to enable the juices to flow while cooking. Rub the skin with fine salt to ensure crispness, and season the inside with salt and pepper. Place the duck breast side down on a trivet in a roasting pan. Roast in the center of the oven for 30 minutes, then reduce the oven temperature to 375°F, turn the duck breast side up and continue to roast for a further 45 minutes.

Meanwhile, to prepare the sauce: place the sliced kumquats in a small saucepan, cover with water and simmer for 6-8 minutes until tender. Place the sugar in a heavy saucepan and stir over a moderate heat until it has caramelized. Remove from the heat, stand well back and add the chicken bouillon. Bring to a boil and simmer until the caramel has dissolved.

When the duck is cooked, transfer it to a plate, cover and keep warm. Allow the sediment to settle in the roasting pan and spoon off the layer of fat, saving it for another occasion (potatoes are delicious roasted in duck fat). Heat the sediment on top of the stove, add the sherry and stir with a wooden spoon. Pour the contents of the roasting pan into the caramel. Add the kumquats and adjust the acidity with lime zest and juice and wine vinegar. To thicken, mix the cornstarch with 2 tbsp cold water, stir into the sauce and simmer to thicken. Carve the duck and serve with roast potatoes and a variety of spring vegetables, with the sauce handed separately in a sauce-boat.

English Asparagus Season

Few vegetables evoke such happy memories as the slender green shoots of English asparagus that appear on the market during May and June. Imported asparagus often appears a few weeks earlier and can look most appealing, but rarely does it match the true flavor of home-grown varieties. The finest spears are graded according to their size and are bound with lengths of colored ribbon: blue indicates thicker varieties, while red is used to gather more slender shoots. Straggly sprue grass is often sold cheaply and despite its appearance, is full of flavor.

Due to the intensive labor required to establish and maintain a good bed, asparagus is an expensive luxury. To ensure the best flavor, spears must be of an even size and the cut ends should show little signs of drying out. Fine-flavored fresh asparagus makes a really special starter, particularly when accompanied by a very rich and creamy egg- and butter-based sauce. Since an entire summer of healthy salads lies ahead of us, I can think of few reasons why one should abstain from the pleasures of eating asparagus in this way during its short season.

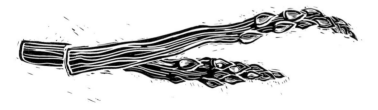

How to cook asparagus

If you are serving asparagus as a first course, a 2lb bunch will provide 4 generous portions. Whether you have chosen thick or thin spears, a little under one-third of the woody stem must be trimmed away. (These trimmings, if you have enough of them, can be turned into an excellent soup.)

Then hold each spear flat against a chopping board and stroke it with a fine vegetable peeler or sharp knife, turning as you go, to remove the tough outer covering.

There are several methods of cooking asparagus, many of which rely on expensive steamers that rarely earn their keep in a small kitchen. The principle of the steamer is to hold the asparagus upright in boiling water so that the tips, which take less cooking, can steam above the water level. The method that I use year after year involves a skillet and a chopstick. Three-quarters fill a large skillet with salted water and bring to a boil. Rest the chopstick against the side of the pan and prop the spears up so that the tips are out of the water. Cover and simmer for 10-12 minutes, depending on the thickness of the spears.

If you are serving the asparagus cold, immerse in cold water to prevent over-cooking. If serving warm, drain thoroughly and allow the steam to dry briefly. There are several sauces that are worth trying, the simplest of which is melted butter and lemon juice. Others include hollandaise flavored with orange or tarragon, or a mild horseradish sauce enriched with softly whipped cream. Asparagus is also delicious cold with a vinaigrette sauce to which a little mustard has been added.

HOMEMADE CHICKEN AND ASPARAGUS SOUP

ingredients...................

¾lb asparagus trimmings, chopped (2½-3 cups)
1 small onion, roughly chopped
1 chicken leg
½lb new potatoes, chopped
1 thyme sprig
salt and pepper

1 pinch sugar (optional)
⅔cup heavy cream

To finish:
2 slices of bread, diced
4tbsp unsalted butter

Place the asparagus trimmings, onion, chicken, potatoes and thyme in a large saucepan and cover with 2½cups water. Bring to a boil, then simmer for 45-50 minutes.

Fish out the chicken leg and the thyme. Remove the chicken meat from the bone, return to the soup and liquidize until smooth. Season to taste with salt and pepper. A pinch of sugar may also help to lift the flavor. Stir in the cream and return to the heat. (The cream is unlikely to separate due to the amount of starch in the soup.)

As an added touch you may like to serve a handful of croûtons with the soup. These are made by frying the cubes of bread in butter until crisp and golden.

Pink Salmon and Asparagus Pillow Case; Roast Duck with Kumquats and Lime;
Chocolate and Rum Truffle with a Coffee Custard Topping.

ASPARAGUS WITH A BEAUTIFUL EGG SAUCE

ingredients.....................

1tbsp white wine vinegar
½tsp English mustard powder
2 egg yolks
1½ sticks unsalted butter, diced

salt and pepper
2lb asparagus
4 squares of toast

To prepare the sauce: place the vinegar, mustard and egg yolks in a heatproof bowl that will fit neatly into the top of a saucepan (or use a double boiler). Bring an inch or so of water to a simmer in the pan and beat the egg yolks into a thick froth. It is important that the base of the bowl does not touch the water and the sauce does not become too hot, otherwise the yolks will scramble.

Whisk in the butter one piece at a time until evenly blended. Gradually the sauce will begin to thicken to the consistency of thick cream. Season the sauce with salt and pepper, cover with a small plate and keep warm by standing the bowl over the saucepan away from the heat. Cook the asparagus, arrange the spears on squares of buttered toast and spoon the sauce over the top. Serve immediately.

PINK SALMON AND ASPARAGUS PILLOW CASES

ingredients.....................

¾lb puff pastry
1 egg
1 pinch salt
2tsp wine vinegar
½tsp English mustard powder
2 egg yolks
1½ sticks unsalted butter, diced

1tbsp chopped tarragon
salt and pepper
2tsp lemon juice
1lb asparagus
1tbsp olive oil
¾lb salmon tail, skinned and
  thinly sliced crosswise

Roll out the pastry in a dusting of flour to a thickness of ¼inch and cut out four 3×5inch rectangles. Beat the egg with the salt and use to glaze the pastry, then leave to rest for 30 minutes.

To prepare the sauce: measure the vinegar, mustard and egg yolks into a heatproof bowl that will fit snugly into a saucepan (or use a double boiler). Bring an inch or so of water to a simmer in the pan and beat the yolks for 8-10 minutes until firm and frothy. Whisk in the butter one piece at a time until the sauce begins to thicken to the consistency of thick cream. Add the tarragon and seasoning and sharpen to taste with lemon juice. To keep the sauce warm, cover with a small plate and leave the bowl over the saucepan away from the heat.

Preheat the oven to 400°F. Arrange the pastry rectangles on a baking sheet, brush once again with beaten egg and bake in the center of the oven for 30-35 minutes or until well-risen and golden. Split the pastry rectangles in half horizontally and set aside.

Cook the asparagus as directed and cut into short lengths. Fifteen minutes before you are ready to serve, season the salmon slices with salt and pepper, heat the olive oil in a heavy skillet and cook the salmon for 1 minute on each side. To assemble the pillow cases, place the middle lengths of asparagus on the lower halves of the pastry rectangles, arrange the salmon slices over the top and place on four plates. Cover the salmon with the sauce, decorate with asparagus tips and half cover with the pastry lid. Serve immediately.

ASPARAGUS AND MUSHROOM TARTLETS

ingredients.....................

basic pie pastry, made with 1½
  cups flour
1lb asparagus
2tbsp butter
¼lb button mushrooms,
  chopped

1 thyme sprig
2 eggs
⅔cup light cream
salt and pepper

Lightly grease four 4inch tartlet tins with butter. Roll out the pastry as thinly as you can on a floured work surface and line the pans without stretching the pastry. Allow the tartlets to rest for 30 minutes to prevent them from shrinking. Preheat the oven to 375°F. Place a square of foil in each tartlet case and bake unfilled in the oven for 20-25 minutes.

Meanwhile, cook the asparagus as directed and cut into short lengths. Melt the butter in a saucepan, add the mushrooms and thyme, cover and soften over a gentle heat for 3-4 minutes. Divide the mushrooms among the tartlet cases and arrange the asparagus over the top.

Twenty minutes before you are ready to serve, heat together the eggs, cream and seasoning. Pour into the tartlets and bake in the center of the oven for 20 minutes or until the filling is just beginning to set. Serve with a crisp green salad with a fresh herb dressing.

Picnic

*A*s soon as the weather cheers up, many of us are keen to pack our hampers and make off for a quiet spot in the country.

Cold soups are delicious for picnics and are best sealed in plastic containers with one or two cubes of ice to keep them fresh. Potato, rice and pasta salads can be made ahead of time and kept well-sealed in plastic containers. English cheeses lend themselves well to outdoor eating since their flavor is reminiscent of the country air. Fresh fruit is the most practical and tasty solution for dessert. An inexpensive bottle of white or rosé wine chilled in a near-by stream will enhance the flavor of the cheese and may even encourage a lengthy snooze in the afternoon, while more energetic members of the party amuse themselves with various games.

A NEW POTATO SALAD WITH CHIVES

ingredients

3lb new potatoes
1cup mayonnaise
1 small onion, finely chopped

1tbsp white wine vinegar
salt and pepper
3tbsp freshly chopped chives

Cover the potatoes with cold water, add a pinch of salt and simmer for 15-20 minutes. Refresh under cold water and drain. Dice the potatoes evenly. I like to leave the skins on for extra flavor, although you may

choose to remove them. Place the potatoes in a bowl and combine with the mayonnaise, onion, vinegar and seasoning. The salad is best served 3-4 hours after making to allow the onions to soften. Just before serving add the chives.

SAUSAGE, BACON AND MUSHROOM CRUST

*P*ies and crusts are ideal for picnics, since they travel well and are convenient to eat with the fingers. The crust, as it is known, is made from pie or flaky pastry and is fashioned into a simple parcel. Fillings are usually savory, in this case sausage meat, bacon, mushrooms and herbs shaped into a neat square.

ingredients

2tbsp butter
1 small onion, chopped
¼lb slab bacon, chopped
6oz button mushrooms
1tsp dried thyme
1lb bulk pork sausage meat

2tbsp chopped parsley
3 twists freshly ground pepper
basic pie pastry made with
   1⅔cups flour
beaten egg, to glaze

Melt the butter in a shallow saucepan, add the onion, bacon, mushrooms and thyme, cover and soften over a gentle heat for 3-4 minutes. Allow to cool slightly and combine with the sausage meat. Add the chopped parsley and seasoning. To prepare the pastry, remove ¼ of the dough and reserve for the lid. Roll out the remainder in a dusting of flour to form a 9inch square. Lay the pastry on a baking sheet. Shape the filling into a 6inch square and place it in the center of the pastry. Bring the edges of the pastry up the sides without stretching it. To make the lid, roll out the reserved pastry into a 6inch square. Brush the edges with beaten egg and place the lid on top. Brush the entire parcel with beaten egg to glaze and decorate with leftover pastry trimmings. Allow to rest in a cool place for 30 minutes. Bake in a preheated 375°F oven for 1 hour until the pastry is golden. Allow to cool before wrapping.

SPINACH AND TARAMASALATA ROULADE

The roulade has become very popular in recent years and every cook worth his or her salt is expected to be able to russle one up at a moment's notice. For this recipe I have chosen a green spinach base to contrast with a filling of taramasalata (Greek cod roe spread). Other filling ideas could include combinations of cream cheese, chopped ham, shrimp, mushrooms and fresh herbs.

ingredients . . . .

1lb fresh bulk spinach or 6oz
   frozen chopped spinach
1 pinch grated nutmeg

salt and pepper
4 eggs, separated
1cup taramasalata

Lightly grease a 9×12inch jelly roll pan and line with parchment paper. Preheat the oven to 400°F.

If using fresh spinach, break off the tough stems, rinse the leaves well in cold water and place in a large saucepan. Cover and steam over a gentle heat for 6-8 minutes. Cool the leaves under running water, squeeze dry thoroughly and chop finely. If using frozen spinach, simply squeeze it dry. Place the spinach in a large mixing bowl, add the nutmeg, seasoning and the egg yolks and stir until even. Beat the egg whites in another bowl until firm and fold evenly into the spinach mixture, retaining as much air as possible. Spread the mixture into the prepared pan and bake near the top of the oven for 20-25 minutes or until firm to the touch. Allow to cool and peel off the paper. Spread the taramasalata over the surface and roll from the short edge. The best way to wrap the roulade is to roll it in a piece of wax paper and secure each end. Cut with a serrated knife and serve with a mixed salad.

THREE ENGLISH CHEESES

There are several good cheeses available during the summer months, some of which owe their existence to enthusiastic dairy farmers who are beginning to realize the advantages of turning surplus milk into profitable cheeses. As a result, an increasing variety of regional cheeses are beginning to appear in our supermarkets and cheese shops. Many English cheeses have a brief season and are produced on a small scale. They are often prepared according to age old traditions and should be seized upon without a moment's hesitation. What better place to enjoy our finest English cheeses than on a lazy picnic in the English countryside with a bottle of wine and a loaf of crusty bread. Depending on what is available, I like to select three cheeses that will complement the lighthearted atmosphere of the picnic. I would avoid heavy cheeses such as Stilton, Shropshire blue and rich Cheddars that are associated with winter, and settle for lighter cheeses such as a farmhouse Cheshire, a Swaledale and a Ladywell goat's cheese. Alternatively, try an unpasteurized single Gloucester, a Cotherstone and a Colwick goat's cheese from Wokingham in Berkshire. Depending on where you live, a cheesemonger will be able to recommend local cheeses for you to try as and when they are available. For six people on a picnic, allow 1½lb of cheese, two bottles of wine and a large loaf of bread.

Puddings

STRAWBERRIES AND CREAM

*M*ay sees the beginning of the wonderful English strawberry sea-son, which lasts until the end of July, to be followed by a second crop in September/October. To my mind there is no better way to freshen the palate at the end of a meal or perfect picnic than a bowl of beautifully sweet English strawberries over which a spoonful of cream has been poured. Those who are health conscious may prefer plain whole-milk yogurt. For a party of six, allow 2½lb (about 4pints) of strawberries. A generous cup or more of heavy cream (or creamy yogurt) will keep most people happy.

STRAWBERRY SPECTACULAR

*A*s an indulgence, I have created this wonderful concoction based on the freshness of English strawberries, with crushed macaroons and an abundance of creamy yogurt. The result is as pink and creamy as an elephant on cloud nine. This recipe is also delicious made with raspberries, black currants or sweet gooseberries.

ingredients . . . .

½lb (about 1½ cups)   2 egg whites
  strawberries   ⅓cup sugar
finely grated zest of 1 orange   1-2 macaroons, broken
1½cups thick creamy yogurt   4 strawberries, to decorate

Hull the strawberries and mash them roughly with a fork. Recognizable pieces are preferable to a smooth paste. Add the orange zest and stir in the yogurt. Place the egg whites in a clean bowl with 2tbsp of the sugar and beat until the mixture will hold a firm peak. Add the remaining sugar a little at a time and beat until smooth.

Fold the beaten egg whites into the yogurt, add the macaroons and spoon into 4 stem glasses or an attractive serving bowl. Decorate with strawberries and chill before serving.

STRAWBERRIES FLOATING IN PORT WINE AND GRAND MARNIER

*H*ere is another sensational way to enjoy our most popular fruit, by floating them in port wine and Grand Marnier and to serve them with a delicious cream sauce. Not good for the waistline but quite a taste sensation!

ingredients . . . .

1½lb (about 2½pints) strawberries   ¼cup Grand Marnier
1cup orange juice   1tbsp sugar
½cup ruby port wine   1¼cups heavy cream

Place a heaping cup of the largest strawberries in a blender and purée until smooth. Place the remainder of the strawberries in a bowl and pour over the orange juice, port wine, Grand Marnier and sugar. Leave the strawberries to macerate for at least 2 hours in the refrigerator, the longer the better.

To prepare the sauce: softly whip the cream and stir in the strawberry purée. (You may like to add a little sugar to taste.)

To serve: lift the strawberries out of their macerating liquid and serve with the sauce poured over the top. The liquid can be re-used on another occasion when you are celebrating, as it makes a good base for a rather special punch.

CREAMY RICE, APRICOT AND ALMOND MOUSSE

※

*W*hen I was a lad I developed an uncontrollable desire for Mum's rice pudding; hot or cold, I simply couldn't get enough of it. Since leaving home and training as a cook, it has become a vested interest of mine to explore new and exciting ways with rice pudding. My latest discovery is to cook the rice with a piece of marzipan which dissolves deliciously into the milk. When the rice has cooled, it is combined with fresh apricots and turned into a creamy mousse. Rice pudding will never be the same again!

ingredients ....

2½cups milk
5tbsp short-grain rice
1oz white marzipan
½tsp almond extract
3 eggs, separated
½lb apricots, pitted and cut into
    thin wedges
1 envelope unflavored gelatin

¼cup sugar
⅔cup heavy cream, softly
    whipped

Topping
½lb apricots, halved and pitted
6tbsp sugar

Rinse a heavy saucepan out with water and bring the milk to a boil. (Rinsing the saucepan is an old trick that will prevent the milk from burning.) Place the rice and marzipan in the milk and simmer for 45-50 minutes until the rice is thick and creamy. Remove from the heat and stir in the extract, egg yolks and apricots. Soften the gelatin in 1tbsp cold water, stir into the hot rice mixture and leave until cold.

Beat the egg whites together with the sugar until firm, then fold evenly into the rice. Fold in the whipped cream and turn into individual serving dishes or one large bowl.

To prepare the topping: place the apricots in a small saucepan with the sugar and 1cup water and simmer for 10-12 minutes. Allow to cool, then drain and arrange over the top of the mousse. Chill well before serving.

A CHOCOLATE AND RUM TRIFLE WITH A COFFEE CUSTARD TOPPING

※

*T*here are three essentials in a true English trifle. Firstly, the cake base must be light and moistened to its full capacity with an alcohol-enriched syrup, and secondly, the cake must be covered with an inviting layer of smooth custard. Then, when the custard has set, the trifle is covered with a layer of whipped cream and decorated. Retaining these well-established contrasts of taste and texture, I have put together this delicious variation, making use of a rum-soaked chocolate cake and a coffee-scented custard concealed by the usual layer of cream.

ingredients ....

Chocolate sponge cake
butter for greasing
3 eggs
6tbsp sugar
9tbsp flour
2tbsp cocoa powder

Syrup
3tbsp marmalade
3tbsp sugar
⅓cup dark rum

Custard topping
2½cups milk
½tsp vanilla extract
3tbsp custard powder or
    cornstarch
2tbsp instant coffee granules
2tbsp sugar

To decorate
⅔cup heavy cream, softly
    whipped
3oz semisweet chocolate, flaked

To make the cake: preheat the oven to 400°F. Lightly grease an 8inch cake pan, line the bottom with parchment paper and dust with flour. Beat the eggs and sugar together in a mixing bowl for 10-12 minutes until the mixture will leave a thick trail across the surface. Sift the flour and cocoa powder into the mixture and fold in with a large metal spoon, retaining as much air as possible. Turn the mixture into the prepared pan and bake in the oven for 30-35 minutes or until springy to the touch. Unmold onto a wire rack to cool.

To prepare the syrup: place the marmalade, sugar and rum in a measuring cup and add boiling water to make 2cups. When the cake has cooled, slice it into large cubes, scatter into a 9inch serving bowl and moisten with the syrup.

To prepare the custard: measure 3tbsp of the milk into a bowl and bring the remainder to a boil with the vanilla extract. Place the custard powder, coffee and sugar in the bowl and stir until smoothly blended. Remove the milk from the heat, pour into the custard mixture and return to a boil to thicken. Pour the custard over the cake and leave to cool completely.

To decorate: spread the whipped cream over the surface of the trifle and sprinkle with flaked chocolate. Chill before serving.

June

Much of England's finest weather appears in June and gives rise to a hive of activity in the market place. As we feast our eyes on all that is fresh and full of life, we are inspired to put together new and exciting dishes, many of which lend themselves to the relaxed style of long summer evenings. Sporting events such as the Derby at Epsom and lawn tennis at Wimbledon coincide deliciously with beautifully dressed salmon, asparagus, salads and, of course, strawberries and cream. At no other time of the year can the English be seen exulting in the pleasures of their table with such a sigh of contentment.

There is plenty of freshness and variety in the vegetable market during June. Carrots, turnips and beets are fattening up and are still sweet and tender. Peas in their pod are becoming more plentiful and may even show a fall in price. Snow peas, spinach and zucchini continue to be as tender as they are delicious. English asparagus is still in good condition and will continue to be available until the end of the month. The beginning of June sees the arrival of the first English new potatoes. Prices often start high, but their flavor makes them well worth the extra. June is the month when salad leaves are at their most tender. Varieties too numerous to mention combine well with English cucumbers, tomatoes, watercress and scallions. Fresh herbs are doing well and beautifully enhance fish and salad dishes. Look out for flat and curly leaf parsley, new garlic, chives, chervil, basil, tarragon, marjoram and mint.

English strawberries are at their best during June. Quality and flavor can vary from week to week according to the weather, but nothing can beat the true character of these home-grown strawberries. Raspberries start to appear toward the end of the month but will not reach their peak until July. Red currants are plentiful at the moment and will become sweeter as the season progresses. Gooseberries can be a little sour in June, but will come alive if poached in a sugar syrup with a sprig of elderflower and the zest of an orange.

English cherries become a familiar sight on fruits stalls towards the end of the month. Sour cherries such as Morellos have a sharper flavor and are ideal for cooking. Imported peaches, nectarines and apricots are in good condition and their season will continue well into summer. The summer also sees the arrival of a variety of tropical fruits, many of which make delicious fruit salads. Look out for mangoes, papayas, guavas and passion fruits.

The fine weather has done much to improve the display of fish at the fishmongers. Flat fish, such as Torbay, Dover and lemon sole, flounder, brill, halibut and turbot are all plump and full of flavor, while herring and mackerel are also in good condition. The fry of mackerel known as whitebait are delicious dipped into milk, tossed in seasoned flour and deep fried for 2-3 minutes. Monkfish is a popular summer fish and is well suited to fish kabobs. A little more unusual for the barbecue are red mullet and John Dory or St Peter fish. Both should be lightly scored, seasoned and given 10-12 minutes on each side. Wild salmon is more expensive than farmed salmon, but the difference in flavor is well worth the extra. Less expensive are pink trout and river trout, both of which are delicious pan-fried and served with new potatoes and a green salad. Crabs and lobsters are at their best now and provide a wonderful feast if you are near the coast and can buy them really fresh. Cockles, winkles, prawns and shrimp are available all year round but have their best flavor during the summer months.

JUNE INGREDIENTS IN SEASON

FRUIT & NUTS

British at their best:
Black Currants
Blueberries
Cherries
Elderflowers
Gooseberries
Pears
Red Currants
Rhubarb
Strawberries

Also available:
Apples
Hazelnuts (Filberts)

Imported in season:
Apricots
Bananas
Brazil Nuts
Grapefruit
Grapes
Kiwi Fruit
Kumquats
Lemons
Limes
Mangoes
Melons
Oranges
Nectarines
Papaya
Passion Fruit
Peaches
Peanuts
Pecans

VEGETABLES & HERBS

British at their best:
Asparagus
Basil
Beets
Broad (Fava) Beans
Carrots
Cherry Tomatoes
Chervil
Chives
Courgettes (Zucchini)
Cucumbers
Dill
Fennel
French (Green) Beans
Garlic
Globe Artichokes
Jerusalem Artichokes
Lettuce
Onions
Mange tout (Snow Peas)
Marjoram
Mint
Mustard and Cress
Nasturtium Flowers
New Potatoes
Parsley
Peas
Radishes
Rosemary
Sage
Samphire
Savory
Spring Onions (Scallions)
Sorrel
Spinach
Tarragon
Thyme
Tomatoes
Turnips
Watercress

Also available:
Broccoli
Cabbages
Cauliflowers
Celeriac
Celery
Horseradish
Leeks
Marrows and other
  Large Summer Squashes
Pickling Cucumbers
Shallots

Imported in season:
Aubergines (Eggplant)
Avocados
Chicory (Belgian Endive)
Globe Artichokes
Sweet Peppers
Tomatoes

FISH & SHELLFISH

British at their best:
Brill
Cockles
Conger Eel
Crabs
Dover Sole
Freshwater Crayfish
Hake
Halibut
Herring
John Dory
Lemon Sole
Monkfish
Lobsters
Mackerel
Plaice
Prawns
Red Mullet
Salmon
Scampi (Langoustines)
Sea Trout
Shrimp
Squid
Torbay Sole
Trout, Turbot
Whitebait
Winkles

Also available:
Cod
Coley (Pollock)
Freshwater Crayfish
Gray Mullet
Haddock
Huss
Scallops
Sea Bass
Skate
Whiting

Imported in season:
John Dory
Red Mullet
Sardines
Squid

POULTRY & GAME

British at their best:
Guinea Fowl
Pigeon

Also available:
Chicken
Duck
Goose
Quail
Rabbit
Turkey
Venison

MEAT

Beef
Lamb
Offal
Pork
Veal

Starters

ICED BEET AND ORANGE SOUP

Many greengrocers cook their own beets for customer's convenience, and a quick and easy way to enjoy them is in this colorful soup. Instead of sour cream, you can squeeze 2tsp fresh lemon juice into ⅔cup of whipping cream and let it stand in a warm place for 3-4 hours. The acid will cause the cream to thicken slightly and become slightly tart.

ingredients . . . .

1 onion, chopped
1tbsp vegetable oil
2tsp chopped lemon thyme or savory
finely grated zest and juice of 1 orange
finely grated zest and juice of ½ lemon

½lb cooked beets, peeled and chopped
1¾cups carton of unsweetened orange juice

Garnish
⅔cup sour cream
4 thyme sprigs

Place the onion in a stainless steel saucepan, add the oil and soften over a low heat. Stir in the thyme or savory and add the orange and lemon zests and juices. Simmer for 3-4 minutes.

Add the beets and blend in a liquidizer for 1-2 minutes until quite smooth. Season with salt and pepper to taste, pour in the orange juice and chill for 1-1½ hours.

Serve the soup in individual bowls, topped with a swirl of sour cream and garnished with a thyme sprig.

COLD SALMON AND CUCUMBER SOUP

Cucumber soup has made quite a name for itself at dinner parties. Goodness knows why. Certainly versions I have tasted have not been very exciting. Reduce the amount of cucumber and introduce a little fresh salmon and your guests will mean what they say when they tell you it was delicious.

ingredients . . . .

2tbsp butter
1 onion, chopped
1 garlic clove, minced
½tsp chopped thyme
1tsp chopped tarragon
½ hothouse cucumber, chopped
10oz salmon tail

salt and pepper
1¼cups milk
⅔cup soured cream

Garnish
thyme sprigs
4 cucumber slices

Melt the butter in a saucepan, add the onion, garlic, herbs and cucumber, cover and cook over a gentle heat until softened.

Season the salmon, place in a shallow saucepan, add the milk and bring to a boil. Immediately remove the pan from the heat and leave the salmon to cook in the heat of the milk for 4-5 minutes.

Transfer the cucumber mixture to a liquidizer and blend until smooth. Add the milk in which the salmon was cooked, blend briefly and pour into a soup tureen. When cool, remove the skin and flake the fish from the bone into the soup.

When ready to serve, stir in the soured cream and decorate with thyme sprigs and cucumber slices.

CRAB AND POTTED SHRIMP SALAD

 his is an eighteenth-century recipe taken from a Suffolk manor recipe book. It is set into individual portions and served in a green salad. Serves 8 as a starter, 4 as a main course.

ingredients...................

6oz peeled cooked bay or other
  small shrimp
½-¾cup fresh crabmeat
3tbsp medium sherry
1 pinch ground mace
¼tsp ground ginger
1 pinch cayenne
1½ sticks salted butter

4cups green salad leaves
3tbsp olive oil
1tbsp lemon juice
ground white pepper

Garnish
1cup cherry tomatoes
4 parsley sprigs

Trim eight 1-cup yogurt cartons with a pair of kitchen scissors to half their height, stand them on a pan and set aside.

Finely chop half of the shrimp with the crabmeat and place in a bowl. Stir in the sherry, mace, ginger and cayenne. Heat the butter in a small heatproof bowl set over a saucepan of simmering water. Stir the butter until very soft but not completely melted. Pour the butter over the chopped shrimp mixture, add the whole shrimp and stir evenly. Distribute the mixture among the yogurt cartons and leave in the refrigerator for 1½-2 hours to set.

Wash the green leaves. Combine the olive oil, lemon juice and pepper and dress the salad. When ready to serve, place the salad on individual plates and unmold the potted shrimp into the center of each plate. Garnish with halved cherry tomatoes and parsley sprigs.

WARM DANDELION SALAD WITH BACON AND FRESH SPINACH

 oung dandelion leaves have been sought after by salad lovers in France for many years. Our dandelion leaves are just as tasty, if picked from the center of the plant.

ingredients...................

6oz (2-3cups) young dandelion
  leaves
5oz (2-3cups) young spinach
  leaves
3oz (1-2 cups) field lettuce

2tbsp salad oil
¼lb Canadian bacon, cut into
  strips
2tbsp wine vinegar
freshly ground black pepper

Wash the dandelion leaves, spinach and field lettuce under plenty of cold running water and shake the leaves dry in a dish towel.

Heat the salad oil in a non-stick skillet, add the bacon strips and cook until browned. Transfer the bacon to a small plate. Measure the vinegar into the skillet, increase the heat and allow the juice to reduce by half. Add the bacon to reheat.

Place the leaves in a large bowl. Pour over the warm dressing from the pan, toss well and season with plenty of black pepper.

CURRIED SHRIMP AND MELON COCKTAIL

ingredients...................

1 cantaloupe or similar-sized
  melon
½tsp ground ginger
juice of 2 limes or 1 lemon
½lb peeled cooked shrimp
¼cup mayonnaise
2tsp medium hot curry paste
1tbsp tomato catsup

1tbsp chopped coriander (cilantro)
1tbsp lemon juice
1 small head crisp lettuce

Garnish
4 lime twists
4 cooked shrimp in shell
4 coriander (cilantro) sprigs

Cut the melon in half and remove the seeds. Scoop out as many little balls as you can with a melon baller. Place the melon balls in a bowl with the ginger, add the lime or lemon juice and set aside. Place the shrimp in another bowl with the mayonnaise, curry paste and tomato catsup. Add the chopped coriander and stir in the lemon juice.

Shred the lettuce and distribute among 4 glasses. Spoon the combined melon balls and shrimp over the shredded lettuce. Decorate each glass with a lime twist, shrimp in shell and coriander sprig.

Main Courses

BROILED SALMON STEAKS WITH A TOMATO VINAIGRETTE

ingredients . . . .

6oz small new potatoes
four 5oz salmon steaks
4tbsp butter, melted
salt and pepper
¼lb baby carrots, scraped with
  their feathery green tops
  trimmed short
6oz baby turnips, peeled and
  diced
¼lb young zucchini, peeled in
  stripes and cut diagonally into
  thin slices
2oz snow or sugar peas,
  trimmed and de-stringed if
  needed

Tomato vinaigrette
¼cup olive oil
2tbsp wine vinegar
½ garlic clove, minced
4 ripe tomatoes
2tbsp chopped parsley
1tbsp chopped tarragon
1 pinch sugar
2 grindings black pepper

Wash the new potatoes, cover with plenty of water, add a pinch of salt and boil for 15-20 minutes until tender

To prepare the tomato vinaigrette: measure the oil into the top of a double boiler with the vinegar and garlic and keep warm over a low heat. Pierce the tomatoes with a small knife, place them in a bowl and pour boiling water over them to loosen their skins. Pour the hot water away and cool under running cold water. Remove the skins and chop the tomatoes into small dice. Add the tomatoes to the double boiler with the herbs, sugar and pepper, cover and keep warm.

Brush the salmon steaks with melted butter and season with salt and pepper. Arrange the salmon on a broiler rack and cook under the broiler for 6 minutes on each side.

Meanwhile, bring a large saucepan of water to a boil, add a little salt and lightly cook the carrots, turnips, zucchini and snow peas for 4-5 minutes, then drain. (Young vegetables are at their best when a little under-cooked.)

To serve the salmon, remove the central bone from each salmon steak and fill the cavity with the warm tomato vinaigrette. Serve with the potatoes and mixed vegetables.

POACHED RIVER TROUT WITH CUCUMBER AND FENNEL

*A*t one time fresh river trout were enjoyed only by country folk who knew the secrets of the rod, line and fly. Anglers who had mastered their technique became popular figures in village life, as they were often able to provide locals with a regular supply of trout. Nowadays, trout are fortunately available in abundance from trout farms, where one can "catch" one's own fish, and at fishmongers in towns. Trout is a deliciously tender fish, full of subtle flavor, particularly good with cucumber, fennel and new potatoes.

ingredients . . . .

4 trout, cleaned, heads left on if
  liked
salt and pepper
2tbsp butter, softened
1 small onion, sliced
½ garlic clove, peeled
1tsp fennel seeds

¼cup dry vermouth or dry white
  wine
1 small hothouse cucumber
1 fennel bulb
2tbsp butter, melted
1tbsp chopped dill

Preheat the oven to 350°F. Season the trout inside and out with salt and pepper and set aside. Line a large roasting pan with foil and brush with soft butter. Scatter the onion over the bottom. Bruise the garlic with the side of a large knife. This will release the flavor sufficiently but not overpower the fish. Add to the onion.

Lay the trout over the onion and sprinkle on the fennel seeds, the vermouth or wine and ⅓cup water. Cover with a sheet of foil and seal the edges. Bake in the center of the preheated oven for about 35 minutes.

Meanwhile, peel the cucumber and cut into 2inch batons. Cut the fennel into even-sized pieces and boil together with the cucumber for 6-8 minutes or until the cucumber has become translucent. Drain and toss in the melted butter. Lift the cooked trout out of the poaching liquid and drain on paper towels. Place in a serving dish. Serve accompanied by the fennel and cucumber sprinkled with the dill and a dish of new potatoes sprinkled with chives.

BAKED MACKEREL WITH GOOSEBERRY MAYONNAISE

ingredients . . . .

four ¾lb mackerel, filleted by the
  fishmonger
salt and pepper
1 small onion, chopped

½lb (1½cups) fresh gooseberries,
  trimmed
1 large orange
6tbsp mayonnaise

Preheat the oven to 350°F. Arrange the mackerel fillets in a 9inch square casserole and season with salt and pepper. Sprinkle the onion over the fish and add the gooseberries. Remove the outer zest from half the orange with a vegetable peeler and add to the casserole. Cut the orange in half and squeeze the juice over the fish. Cover the casserole and bake in the oven for 15 minutes.

Remove half the gooseberries from the casserole and save them for garnish. Return the casserole to the oven and cook for a further 15 minutes. By this time the remaining gooseberries will begin to burst in readiness for a delicious sauce.

To prepare the sauce: transfer the mackerel fillets to a warm serving dish and cover. Discard the pieces of orange zest, pour the cooking juices into a liquidizer and blend until smooth. Add the mayonnaise and blend for a further 30 seconds. Pour the sauce over the mackerel fillets and garnish with the reserved gooseberries. Serve the dish with young turnips, baby carrots and new potatoes.

ROAST LAMB STUFFED WITH PARSLEY, LEMON AND THYME

ack of lamb, with six or seven chops joined together, is available from many supermarkets. Once the small bones have been removed, the meat is ideal for stuffing and roasting.

ingredients . . . .

one 2lb rack of lamb, boned
salt and pepper
1tbsp drippings or vegetable oil

Stuffing
4tbsp butter
1 onion, chopped
1 garlic clove, minced
3tbsp chopped parsley

1tbsp chopped thyme
finely grated zest and juice of 1
  lemon
1cup fresh bread crumbs

Gravy
⅓cup red wine
1tbsp cornstarch
⅔cup vegetable bouillon

Preheat the oven to 425°F. Season the lamb inside and out with salt and pepper and set aside.

To prepare the stuffing: melt the butter in a saucepan, add the onion and garlic and soften over a gentle heat without allowing to color. Add the parsley, thyme, lemon zest and juice, then add the bread crumbs and season with salt and pepper. Open the lamb out on a chopping board, spoon in the stuffing, roll up tightly and secure in several places with fine string.

To cook the lamb, heat the drippings or oil in a roasting pan on top of the stove and seal both ends of the roast, to keep the juices inside during cooking. Turn the meat once in the hot fat, then roast in the oven for 15 minutes per pound weight before stuffing if you like slightly pink lamb (20 minutes per pound if you prefer your lamb medium to well-done).

When the lamb is cooked, take it out of the oven and leave to rest for at least 15 minutes before carving to allow the juices to settle. Meanwhile, make the gravy. Allow the sediment to settle in the roasting pan and pour off the layer of fat. Place the roasting pan on top of the stove, pour in the wine and stir with a wooden spoon to loosen the sediment. Increase the heat and let the sediment reduce by half. Mix the cornstarch with 2tbsp cold vegetable bouillon or water and stir into the remaining bouillon. Add the bouillon and cornstarch mixture to the roasting pan and bring back to a boil, stirring. Season to taste and serve with the lamb. Offer a selection of delicious young vegetables as accompaniments to this dish (see page 96).

POACHED BREAST OF CHICKEN WITH BROCCOLI CREAM SAUCE

 I must share with you one of my favorite sauces to go with chicken. It tastes even better than it sounds and is a perfect light dish for the hot summer months.

ingredients . . . .

1 small onion, sliced	salt and pepper
4tbsp butter	10oz broccoli
⅓cup dry white wine	6tbsp heavy cream
⅔cup chicken bouillon	
4 chicken breast halves, skinned and boned	

Place the onion and 2tbsp butter in a shallow stainless steel or enamel saucepan and soften over a gentle heat. Add the wine and simmer until nearly evaporated. Pour in the chicken bouillon and add the chicken breasts. Cover and simmer over a low heat for 15 minutes. (If the chicken is cooked too quickly it will lose its delicate texture.)

Meanwhile, bring a saucepan of salted water to a boil, divide the broccoli into small florets and cook for 6-8 minutes. (Save the stems as they can be served sliced with other vegetables.) Reserve half the cooked broccoli florets and then place the remainder in a blender with the cream.

Strain the chicken cooking liquid into a saucepan, bring to a boil and simmer briskly for 3-4 minutes until reduced by half. Pour the reduced liquid into the blender with the broccoli, add the remaining butter and blend until smooth. Pour the sauce into a small saucepan, add the reserved broccoli florets and reheat gently. Season to taste. Slice each chicken breast piece diagonally into long strips, arrange on a serving dish and spoon over the broccoli cream sauce. Serve with buttered new potatoes and baby carrots.

ROAST DUCKLING WITH CHERRIES AND GINGER WINE

ingredients . . . .

4½lb duckling, with neck and giblets	2tbsp sugar
½ small onion, sliced	finely grated zest and juice of 1 orange
½ small carrot, roughly chopped	2inch cinnamon stick or 1tsp ground cinnamon
1 celery stalk, roughly chopped	½cup imported British green ginger wine
1 pinch of chopped fresh or dried thyme	2tsp cornstarch
½ bay leaf	1 bunch of watercress
salt and pepper	
1½lb (6 cups) black cherries	

To prepare a simple duck bouillon for the sauce: place the duck neck and giblets in a small saucepan of cold water, discarding the liver as it would make the bouillon bitter. Add the onion, carrot, celery, thyme, bay leaf, salt and pepper. Bring to a boil, then simmer for 50 minutes.

Meanwhile, remove the pits from the cherries with a cherry pitter. Season the inside of the duck with plenty of salt and pepper. Place the cherries inside the duck with the sugar. Add the orange zest and juice, and the cinnamon.

Preheat the oven to 425°F. Truss the duck securely with string. Pierce the duck skin in several places with a fork and rub with salt. Place the duck on its side on a rack in a roasting pan and roast in oven for 20 minutes. Turn the duck over to its other side and roast for a further 20 minutes, then turn it onto its back to roast for a final 20 minutes. (This method of roasting will ensure that the bird is properly basted.) When the bird is cooked, keep it covered in a warm place while making the sauce.

Tip the roasting pan to one side and let the sediment settle to the bottom. Spoon off the visible fat. Add the ginger wine to the roasting pan and boil briskly on top of the stove until reduced by half, stirring all the time with a wooden spoon.

Strain the duck bouillon and add ⅔cup to the pan. Mix the cornstarch with 2tbsp cold water and stir into the sauce. Stir over a gentle heat to thicken and season to taste with salt and pepper.

To finish the dish, remove the cherries from inside the duck. Stir into the sauce. Arrange the duck on a serving dish, spoon some of the sauce around it, place a small bunch of watercress between the legs and serve with buttered turnips and garden peas, with the remaining sauce handed separately.

OMELETTE OF GOOSE EGGS WITH MUSHROOMS AND SORREL

With the warmer weather, geese are now laying eggs in increased numbers. Goose eggs have a subtly rich flavor: they are available at farm shops in many parts of England. If you cannot obtain sorrel, young spinach can be used instead.

ingredients . . . .

3 fresh goose eggs
salt and pepper
1tbsp goose fat or butter
2oz button mushrooms, sliced
   (²/₃cup)

1 pinch of chopped fresh thyme
1cup shredded fresh sorrel

Break the goose eggs into a bowl, season and beat lightly with a fork. Melt the goose fat or butter in a 9inch non-stick omelette pan, add the mushrooms and thyme and cook over a gentle heat until soft. Sprinkle in the sorrel, cover and allow to cook for 3-4 minutes.

When the sorrel has reduced in volume, increase the heat and pour the beaten eggs into the pan. Keep stirring the eggs with the back of a fork so that they cook evenly. When they are just beginning to look scrambled, stop stirring and leave the omelette to set enough to fold in half. If you enjoy your omelette soft tip it out quickly onto a warm serving dish and serve immediately. Firmer omelettes will need slightly longer in the pan, but it is worth mentioning that the best-tasting omelettes should take no longer than 60 seconds to cook.

Serve the omelette with a crisp green salad tossed in a vinaigrette dressing flavored with mustard and tarragon.

Serves 2.

SPICED BABY TURNIPS AND BEETS IN A CHEESE SAUCE

ingredients . . . .

2tbsp butter
1 onion, chopped
3tbsp flour
1tsp English mustard
   powder
¼tsp ground coriander
2cups milk

salt and pepper
¾cup grated Cheddar cheese
1cup fresh bread crumbs
1½lb baby turnips
¾lb cooked beets
butter for greasing

Melt the butter in a saucepan, add the onion and soften over a gentle heat without coloring. Stir in the flour, mustard and coriander, using a wooden spoon. Bring the milk to a boil and add to the onion mixture a little at a time, away from the heat, stirring until smooth. Continue to add the milk until completely absorbed. Return the sauce to a low heat, season with salt and pepper and simmer for 3-4 minutes. Add three-quarters of the grated cheese, cover and leave to cool. Preheat the oven to 350°F.

Mix the remaining cheese with the bread crumbs and set aside. To prepare the turnips: cut off their tops and bottoms with a small knife. Peel them and boil in enough salted water to cover for 6 minutes. Hold the turnips under cold running water to cool, then slice into¼inch disks. Peel the beets and slice into similar-sized pieces.

Lightly grease a 7inch baking dish with butter and arrange half the cooked turnips and beets overlapping in the bottom. Stir the cheese sauce and add half to the pan, followed by the remaining turnips and beets. Cover with the remaining sauce and top with the cheese and bread crumb mixture. Bake in the center of the oven for 40 minutes. To finish, place under the broiler until golden. Serve with buttered egg noodles dressed with poppyseeds.

*Warm Dandelion Salad with Bacon and Fresh Spinach;
Broiled Salmon Steak with a Tomato Vinaigrette; Strawberry Layer Cake.*

COMBINATION SUMMER VEGETABLES

*W*andering through the garden at this time of year you see a wonderful variety of young and tender vegetables. Scallions, baby carrots and turnips, which may need thinning, are worth preparing for their delicate flavor. Broad (fava) beans and snow peas are at their most delicious at the moment and can be eaten raw in simple salads. Listed below are some unusual combinations which you might like to try.

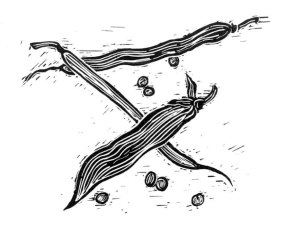

Baby Carrots with Thyme Flowers

•

Young Turnips with Honey and Coriander

•

Buttered Broad (Fava) Beans with Savory

•

Zucchini hollowed out and stuffed with Baby Carrots

•

Crisp New Peas with Garden Mint

•

Poached Cucumber stuffed with Tomato and Chives

•

Green Bean Parcels tied with Ribbons of Zucchini

•

Baby Carrots, Snow Peas and Scallions

•

Broccoli, Cherry Tomatoes and Bean Sprouts

STUFFED SQUASH FLOWERS

*F*or this recipe you will need zucchini from the vegetable garden with the flowers attached, sometimes obtainable from good greengrocers or in farm shops. The flowers are stuffed and cooked together with the vegetable.

ingredients ....

2tbsp olive oil
2 shallots, finely chopped
1 garlic clove, minced
¼tsp chopped lemon thyme
2tbsp porcini (dried ceps),
   soaked in warm water for 20
   minutes, then drained and finely
   chopped

¼lb button mushrooms,
   chopped
½cup chopped cooked ham
salt and pepper
4 baby zucchini with their
   flowers

Heat the oil in a small saucepan, add the shallots, garlic and thyme and soften over a gentle heat without allowing to color. Add the porcini and fresh mushrooms to the pan, cover and cook for 6-8 minutes. If necessary remove the lid to allow some of the moisture to evaporate. Add the ham and remove from the heat. Season to taste with salt and pepper.

Wash the zucchini carefully in a bowl of cold water. Trim the stalk end of each zucchini and spoon the filling into the flower end. Lay the zucchini in a steamer and cook for 8-10 minutes.

To finish, slice the zucchini lengthwise into strips and fan out on an attractive plate. Serve with a fresh tomato sauce.

Puddings

APRICOT AND GOOSEBERRY TART

*D*uring my apprenticeship years in Switzerland, my chef used to tell me that pastry is like a baby, needing time, patience and plenty of love. Once you have mastered the art of pastry-making, ideas for tarts, pies and quiches will become endless. And you will see that there is no comparison between frozen bought pastry and the home-made variety.

ingredients.................................

2½cups sweet gooseberries	Sweet pie pastry
2tbsp butter	1⅔cups flour
⅔cup ground almonds	3tbsp sugar
6tbsp sugar	1 stick cool salted butter, diced
1½lb fresh apricots	extra butter for greasing

To make the pastry: sift the flour with the sugar into a mixing bowl, add the butter and rub together with the fingertips until the mixture resembles large bread crumbs. If you have been blessed with hot fingers, try using a pastry blender. Better still, if you don't mind the dish washing, you can make the pastry in a food processor. Add 4tbsp cold water and mix into an even dough. Wrap the pastry in plastic wrap and leave it in the refrigerator to rest for at least 30 minutes.

Meanwhile, trim the gooseberries and place all but 10 of them in a stainless steel or enamel saucepan with the butter and ground almonds. Cover and simmer over a gentle heat for 5 minutes or until the gooseberries have fallen apart. Stir in the sugar and set aside.

Preheat the oven to 400°F. Lightly grease a 9inch tart pan with butter. Roll out the pastry on a floured work surface to a thickness of ⅛inch. Pick the pastry up on the rolling pin and position it over the pan. Lift the edges carefully into the sides of the pan without stretching the pastry. Trim neatly and pierce the bottom with a fork. Place a circle of parchment paper in the pastry case and fill with dried beans or rice. Place the pan on a baking sheet and bake the case unfilled in the oven for 20 minutes.

Remove the lining paper and beans and spread the cooked goose-berries into the pastry case. Halve the apricots and remove their pits. Arrange the apricot halves around the edge so that they stand up like the petals of a flower. Make another circle overlapping with the first. Place the reserved gooseberries in the center and return the tart to the top shelf of the oven to bake for 25-30 minutes until the fruit is tender. Serve the tart warm or cold.

POACHED GOOSEBERRIES WITH ELDERFLOWER AND ORANGE

*G*ooseberries, now in season, benefit like so many other fruits from simple cooking to bring out their very best flavor. Here the gentle muscat fragrance of elderflower combines with a hint of fresh orange to enhance this humble berry.

ingredients.................................

½cup sugar	1½lb (2½pints) gooseberries,
2cups water	trimmed
2 oranges	
2 heads of elderflower, tied in a	
cheesecloth bag	

Place the sugar and water in a stainless steel or enamel saucepan and bring to a boil. Thinly pare the zest from the oranges with a vegetable peeler and tie together with the elderflower in a piece of cheesecloth. Simmer gently in the syrup for 3-4 minutes.

Add the gooseberries, squeeze in the juice from the oranges, cover and cook for no longer than 2 minutes. Gooseberries need watching very carefully as they overcook and fall apart very easily. Remove from the heat and leave to cool.

Serve the gooseberries at room temperature with a spoonful of whipped cream or vanilla ice cream.

STRAWBERRY LAYER CAKE

For a very special party in the summer, there's nothing nicer than this fresh strawberry cake with its pretty chocolate decoration.

ingredients

Sponge cake
4 eggs, at room temperature
¾cup sugar
1cup whole wheat flour
1⅓cups ground almonds

Filling
1½lb (2½pints) strawberries
2tbsp confectioners' sugar
2cups whipping cream

2oz semisweet chocolate, to decorate

Preheat the oven to 375°F. Line two baking sheets with parchment paper. Mark out three 7inch circles with a pencil and set aside.

Separate the eggs into two large bowls. Add half of the sugar to the yolks and beat until a thick ribbon can be drawn across the surface. Add 2tbsp of the remaining sugar to the egg whites and beat with a clean beater until soft peaks are formed. Continue to beat in the remaining sugar, a little at a time. Fold the beaten egg whites into the yolks, using a large metal spoon. Sift the flour and ground almonds over the egg mixture and fold in as lightly as possible.

Distribute the cake batter among the marked circles and spread out evenly. Bake the cakes near the top of the oven for 25-30 minutes, until risen and springy to the touch. Cool on a wire rack.

To prepare the filling: reserve 8 of the best-looking strawberries. Place 1 heaping cup of the softest strawberries in a small bowl and crush them with the back of a spoon. Add the confectioners' sugar. Softly whip the cream and blend in the crushed strawberries.

When the cake layers are cold, put them together with layers of strawberry cream and the remaining strawberries, sliced if necessary, saving a little of the strawberry cream to spread over the top of the cake.

To decorate: place the chocolate in a small heatproof bowl. Pour 1inch water into a saucepan and bring to a boil. Set the bowl of chocolate over the water and stir until melted. Be careful not to overheat the chocolate.

Dip the reserved strawberries in the melted chocolate and set aside on a sheet of wax paper to harden. Dip a teaspoon in the remaining chocolate and spin over the top of the cake to make an attractive pattern. Lastly position the chocolate-dipped strawberries around the edge of the cake and chill until ready to serve.

KENTISH CHERRY PIE

By the middle of June in the south of England the cherry trees are laden with fruit, a great attraction for birds as well as children! The cherry season is short and it is worth making the most of it. A special cherry pitter is invaluable for use in recipes like this, where a large quantity of cherries is required.

ingredients

Filling
⅞cup full-bodied red wine
1tbsp cornstarch
6tbsp sugar
1½inch cinnamon stick
1 small bay leaf
3½pints sweet cherries, pitted

basic pie pastry, made with
1½cups flour

To glaze
1 egg, beaten with a large pinch
of salt

To prepare the cherry filling: bring the wine to a boil in a stainless steel or enamel saucepan. Mix the cornstarch with 2tbsp cold water and stir into the wine to thicken, along with the sugar, cinnamon and bay leaf. Add the cherries and simmer for 4-5 minutes. Turn the cherries into a deep 1-quart pie dish or baking dish and leave to cool. Preheat the oven to 400°F.

Roll out the pastry on a floured work surface to a thickness of ⅛inch. Brush the rim of the pie dish with beaten egg, cut a 1inch strip from one side of the pastry and place around the rim. Brush once more with egg and cover with the pastry. Press to seal to the strip. Trim the edges, use the trimmings to decorate the top of the pie, and brush with beaten egg. (Adding a large pinch of salt to the egg gives the glaze an attractive shine.)

Bake the cherry pie in the oven for 45-50 minutes, until the pastry is golden. Serve with lightly whipped cream.

Summer Drinks Party

What better way to entertain friends than at an *al fresco* drinks party one balmy June evening? Choose the evening of 21 June – the longest day of the year – and the party will go on and on! Serve a selection of exciting cocktails along with interesting nibbles. The following 4 cocktail recipes each serve one person.

PRINCE OF WALES

Three-quarters fill a tall glass with crushed ice and add 3 dashes of Angostura bitters and a wine glass of champagne or sparkling wine. Top up with soda water and decorate with a twist of lemon, a Maraschino cherry, a paper umbrella and a fancy straw.

SILVER FIZZ

Dip the rim of a julep glass into egg white, then into superfine sugar to give a frosted effect. Half fill a cocktail shaker with cracked ice, add the juice of ½ lemon, 1tbsp confectioners' sugar, an egg white, 1 measure of gin and 3 bruised juniper berries. Shake until frothy, pour into the julep glass and decorate with slices of lemon and lime.

TEQUILA SUNRISE

Half-fill a slender glass with crushed ice. Pour in one measure of tequila and half a measure of grenadine syrup. Top up with fresh orange juice and decorate with an orange slice, a chunk of fresh pineapple and a sprig of mint on a cocktail stick.

LEAVE IT TO ME

Half fill a cocktail shaker with crushed ice. Add half a measure each of gin and Campari. Squeeze in the juice of ½lemon, add a dash of Angostura bitters, top up with 7-Up and shake. Pour into a fancy glass and decorate with a slice of orange, a whole strawberry and a sprig of mint.

GRAPEFRUIT AND CAMPARI SORBET SLICES

Sharp grapefruit combines with delicate pink Campari in a sorbet which is frozen in the grapefruit shells, then cut into neat wedges. Pieces of pink perfection.

ingredients . . . .

⅔cup water	2 grapefruit
6tbsp sugar	¼cup Campari or grenadine
¼cup medium white wine	

Place the water, sugar and wine in a stainless steel saucepan and bring to a boil, then simmer for 2-3 minutes. Pour the syrup into a metal bowl and cool over ice.

Cut the grapefruits in half from top to bottom and spoon out the flesh into a strainer. Set the grapefruit skins to one side ready for filling later. Squeeze the juice into a measuring cup to make 9floz, adding a little water if necessary.

Stir the grapefruit juice and the Campari into the syrup and freeze for 30 minutes. (Sorbets and ice cream will freeze more quickly in a metal container, ideally of stainless steel or enamel.) Remove the sorbet from the freezer and break up the ice crystals with a balloon whisk. Return to the freezer, then beat every 30 minutes to break up large ice crystals until pink and slushy.

Fill the grapefruit shells with the mixture and return them to the freezer for about 60 minutes until firm. Cut each grapefruit shell into 6 wedges and keep in the freezer until needed.

CHINESE-STYLE PORK BALLS

ingredients . . . .

1cup   long-grain rice
¾lb   lean boneless pork, cut into
  equal-sized pieces
1 egg
1tbsp   light soy sauce

1tsp   chopped fresh ginger root
  or ground ginger
2   scallions, chopped
6   water chestnuts, roughly
  chopped

Cover the rice in a saucepan with 2cups boiling water, add a pinch of salt, cover and simmer for 17 minutes. Spread the rice out on a metal pan and allow to cool.

Place the pork, egg, soy sauce, ginger and scallions in a food processor and chop until quite smooth. Stir in the water chestnuts by hand. Shape the pork mixture into little balls no bigger than a gooseberry and roll them in the cooked rice. Place the pork balls in a steamer and set aside until ready to cook. Steam them for 20 minutes and serve warm, with a shallow bowl of soy sauce for dipping.

Makes about 24 balls.

PUFF PASTRY BUTTERFLIES

ingredients . . . .

½lb   puff pastry
½cup   freshly grated Parmesan
  cheese

1   egg, beaten
butter for greasing

Roll the pastry out on a floured work surface to a rectangle ⅛inch thick. Sprinkle the cheese over the pastry and roll over lightly with the rolling pin. Cut the pastry into three equal strips 2½inches wide. Brush the center of two of the strips with beaten egg. Stack the strips one on top of the other, finishing with the unmoistened strip, and press down gently in the middle to stick them together. Wrap the strip in a plastic bag and leave in the refrigerator to rest for 30 minutes.

When ready to bake, preheat the oven to 400°F and lightly grease two baking sheets. Lay the pastry strip on a chopping board and cut crosswise into¼inch sections. To form the butterfly, twist the center of each piece of pastry and lay on the baking sheet two fingers' width apart. Bake near the top of the oven for 20-25 minutes until the butterflies open out. Allow to cool before serving.

BLACK OLIVE STRAWS

Use leftover puff pastry to make these. Roll it out to a thickness of ⅛inch, place on a floured baking sheet and chill in the refrigerator for 30 minutes or so. Spread with black olive paste, available in jars from gourmet food shops, or with ⅔cup pitted black olives pasted in a liquidizer.

Preheat the oven to 400°F. Cut the pastry into thin strips and place on a baking sheet. Bake in the oven for 15-20 minutes or until crisp. Serve the straws standing up in glasses.

SALTED COCKTAIL ALMONDS

ingredients . . . .

1½cups   blanched almonds
2tsp   egg white

½tsp   chili powder (optional)
1tbsp   table salt

Preheat the oven to 400°F. Place the almonds in a bowl and moisten with enough egg white to coat them lightly. (There should not be any egg white left in the bottom of the bowl.) Blend the chili powder if used with the salt and stir into the nuts, or just use the salt if you prefer.

Spread the almonds out on a baking sheet and roast them on the top shelf of the oven for 15-20 minutes, turning them over once or twice to make sure they color evenly.

TANGY AVOCADO DIP

❧

ingredients . . . .

2 large ripe avocados
1 small onion, finely chopped
1 garlic clove, minced
3 tomatoes, skinned, de-seeded
   and finely chopped
juice of 1 small lemon
½tsp hot pepper sauce
1 pinch salt

To serve
½lb carrots, cut into sticks
1 celery stalk, cut into sticks
½ cucumber, cut into sticks
1 small cauliflower, broken into
   small florets
3 sweet peppers, red, green and
   yellow, cut into strips

Cut the avocados in half, discard the seeds and scrape the soft flesh into a bowl. Rub the avocado to a paste with the back of a spoon and stir in the onion and garlic. Add the tomatoes, lemon juice and hot pepper sauce. Season with salt, cover and chill in the refrigerator until needed. Serve with the fresh vegetables plus potato or tortilla chips, if liked.

Serves 8-10

NEW POTATO TRUFFLES

❧

ingredients . . . .

1lb small new potatoes
⅞cup thick plain yogurt
2tsp lemon juice

2oz (¼cup) caviar
lemon slices and chervil sprigs for
   garnish

Bring the potatoes to a boil in plenty of salted water and simmer for 20 minutes. Drain the potatoes in a colander and leave to cool, then slice off the tops and scoop out the insides with a teaspoon. Place the potatoes in little brown paper cases, such as are used for chocolates, and line them up on a kitchen pan to make finishing easier.

Place the yogurt in a bowl, add the lemon juice and season with pepper but no salt as the caviar is usually quite salty enough. Spoon a little of the yogurt on top of each case of potato, top with a little caviar and decorate each with a tiny lemon slice and chervil sprig. Chill the potato truffles in the refrigerator until needed.

Makes about 30

SAVORY NUTS AND SEEDS

❧

ingredients . . . .

⅔cup blanched hazelnuts
   (filberts)
⅔cup cashew nuts
½cup roughly chopped blanched
   almonds
⅔cup sunflower seeds

½cup walnut pieces
⅔cup pine nuts
2tsp yeast extract
2tbsp soy sauce
2tsp flour
vegetable oil for greasing

Place all the nuts and seeds in a bowl. Stir the yeast extract into the soy sauce and blend in the flour. Pour the mixture over the nuts and seeds to coat them evenly.

Lightly grease a baking sheet with vegetable oil, spread the nuts out in a single layer and toast them under the broiler, or roast them on the top shelf of the oven preheated to 425°F. Turn the nuts once or twice so that they brown evenly. Serve in little bowls.

July

ife in England is at all times dependent on the whims of the weather, but July is normally the month when it is warm enough to light the barbecue and get busy with some real outdoor cooking. Although the occasional shower is inevitable, the month of July is usually a sunny one, bringing a seemingly infinite variety of soft summer fruits. Strawberries are everywhere and, although no longer at their best, are ideal for jam-making. A second crop of strawberries will appear between September and October. Raspberries come into their own during July, as do sharper-flavored loganberries and tayberries, a cross between the two. The price of red currants reaches rock bottom toward the end of the month and if you can get one or two pans on the cheap they are well worth freezing or making into a jelly to last the year round. Clusters of red currants frosted with egg white and sugar make delightful decorations for chilled creamy desserts. Black currants, at their best this month, make superb sorbets and ice cream, and a mouthwatering cheesecake topping.

July sees the beginning of the English bean season. Although im-

ported beans have been around during May and June, home-grown have the best flavor. Zucchini and other summer squash will increase in size and ripen if the weather is favorable, as will sweet peppers, eggplant and fennel. Again providing there is enough sun, we are often treated to an early crop of corn from the Isle of Wight. And greengrocers' shops and stalls are abundant with fresh English herbs, a blessing if, like myself, you use them faster than you can grow them.

By July we are well into the flat fish season and prices should begin to fall as the month progresses, so look out for lemon and Dover soles which, although never cheap, are more reasonable now than at any other time of the year. Mackerel and herring are also worth buying as are their fry, sold as whitebait. If you are planning a special treat, crabs and lobsters are full of flavor at this time and worth every penny. Cockles are in season for most of the year but combine marvelously with the increasingly popular samphire (a succulent seashore plant), now arriving at most fishmongers.

JULY INGREDIENTS IN SEASON

FRUIT & NUTS

British at their best:
Black Currants
Blueberries
Cherries
Damsons
Elderberries
Gooseberries
Greengages
Loganberries
Pears
Raspberries
Red Currants
Rhubarb
Strawberries
Tayberries

Also available:
Apples
Blackberries
Hazelnuts (Filberts)
Walnuts

Imported in season:
Almonds
Apricots
Bananas
Brazil Nuts
Figs
Grapefruit
Grapes
Kiwi Fruit
Lemons
Limes
Mangoes
Melons
Nectarines
Oranges
Papaya
Peaches
Watermelons

VEGETABLES & HERBS

British at their best:
Aubergines (Eggplant)
Basil
Beets
Broad (Fava) Beans
Carrots
Cherry Tomatoes
Chervil
Chives
Courgettes (Zucchini)
Corn
Cucumbers
Dill
Fennel
French (Green) Beans
Garlic
Globe Artichokes
Horseradish
Lavender
Lettuce
Mange tout (Snow Peas)
Marrows and other Large
  Summer Squashes
Marjoram
Mint
Mustard and Cress
Nasturtiums
Parsley
Peas
Pickling Cucumbers
New Potatoes
Radishes
Rosemary
Runner (Italian Green) Beans
Sage
Samphire
Savory
Spring Onions (Scallions)
Sorrel
Spinach
Sweet Peppers
Tarragon, Thyme
Tomatoes

Also available:
Asparagus
Broccoli
Cabbages
Cauliflowers
Celeriac
Celery
Jerusalem Artichokes
Leeks
Shallots
Turnips

Imported in season:
Aubergines (Eggplant)
Avocados
Chicory (Belgian Endive)
Sweet Peppers

FISH & SHELLFISH

British at their best:
Brill
Cockles
Conger Eel
Crabs
Dover Sole
Freshwater Crayfish
Hake
Halibut
Herring
John Dory
Lemon Sole
Lobsters
Mackerel
Monkfish
Plaice
Prawns
Red Mullet
Salmon
Sea Trout
Scampi (Langoustines)
Shrimp, Squid
Trout, Turbot
Whitebait
Winkles

Also available:
Cod, Coley (Pollock)
Gray Mullet
Haddock, Huss
Sea Bass, Skate
Whiting

Imported in season:
John Dory
Red Mullet
Sardines
Squid

POULTRY & GAME

British at their best:
Guinea Fowl
Pigeon
Quail

Also available:
Chicken, Duck
Goose
Rabbit, Turkey
Venison

MEAT

Beef
Lamb
Offal
Pork
Veal

Starters

ICED MELON AND RASPBERRY SOUP

elon and raspberry soup is colorful and designed to stimulate the taste buds. Serve it ice-cold with sprigs of fresh mint before a main course of lamb or fish.

ingredients......................

2 cantaloupe or similar-sized melons
2½cups fresh raspberries
2tsp raspberry or wine vinegar
½tsp ground ginger

1 pinch ground coriander
salt and pepper
4 mint sprigs, for garnish

Cut the melons in half and discard the seeds. Using a small melon baller, scoop out as many balls as you can from one of the melons. Place them in a small bowl and chill in the refrigerator until they are needed.

Scoop out the flesh from the remaining melon and place in a blender or food processor. Add all but 20 of the raspberries and blend until smooth. Add the vinegar, the spices, and seasoning and blend once more until well mixed.

Strain the soup into a tureen to remove the seeds, add the melon balls and reserved raspberries and chill until ready to serve.

SQUASH AND TOMATO SOUP

arge summer squashes can be watery if overcooked, and are inclined to be bland. To impart a little flavor to this vegetable, I have put together this delicious cold soup. Mature squashes, with tough skin and seeds, are particularly suitable.

ingredients......................

2tbsp olive oil
1 large onion, chopped
1 clove garlic, minced
1½lb summer squash, peeled and seeded if necessary, and grated
2tsp oregano or marjoram (fresh or dried)

2tsp tomato paste
1¼cups tomato juice
1lb ripe tomatoes, skinned, deseeded and roughly chopped
salt and pepper

Heat the oil in a large saucepan, add the onion and soften over a gentle heat without allowing it to color. Add the garlic, followed by the squash, herbs, tomato paste and juice. Cover and simmer for 10 minutes. Add the tomatoes and simmer for a further 10-15 minutes until the squash has softened completely. Season to taste with salt and pepper and allow to cool. The soup can be served as it is or, if the occasion is a little more formal, can be liquidized until smooth.

POTTED CRAB

*T*he two best-known crab centers in England are Cromer on the north Norfolk coast and Brixham in Devon. Brixham crabs are known for their monster proportions, whereas Cromer crabs are smaller. For my money, Cromer crab has a sweeter more delicate flavor than his big brother. Most crabs are sold ready-cooked. If you are buying whole cooked crab, the beast should feel heavy in proportion to its size, indicating a larger proportion of meat. As a rule one-third of the weight of the crab is edible.

(The species of crab caught in British waters does not occur on the American side of the Atlantic, but the meat from American crabs can be used to make this dish, just omitting the brown crabmeat.)

ingredients . . . .

three ¾lb cooked crabs	¼tsp ground mace
juice of 1 large lemon	1 pinch cayenne
salt and pepper	1½ sticks unsalted butter

To dress the cooked crabs: hold the crab face down on a chopping board and give its back a sharp thump with the heel of your hand, to loosen its underside. Twist off the legs and claws and set aside. Remove the head in one piece.

Scoop out the brown meat from inside the shell onto a small plate. The white meat is found in and around the center of the body. First discard the gray gills, known as "dead man's fingers" which lie on either side of the center piece. Cut the center piece into a V pointing toward the back of the crab, to release the internal cavities which contain a considerable amount of meat. Removing the meat from the center piece does take time but is worth the effort.

To remove the white meat from the claws and legs, crack the shell with a small hammer or pair of nut crackers and loosen the meat with a small skewer.

When you have separated the white from the dark meat, season each with lemon juice, salt, pepper, mace and cayenne. Place the butter in a small measuring cup and stand in a saucepan of boiling water to melt. Preheat the oven to 300°F.

Meanwhile, distribute the crab meat in alternating layers among four 3inch ramekin dishes. Stand the dishes in a shallow roasting pan and pour the melted butter over each dish. Pour in boiling water to come halfway up the sides of the dishes and cook in the oven for 20-25 minutes. Although the crab is already cooked, heating it through gently will bring out the flavor of the spices. Allow the potted crab to cool, then chill in the refrigerator until needed. Serve the crab with a simple green salad and melba toast or buttered brown bread.

To make melba toast:
Toast slices of ready-cut white or brown bread on both sides under a high heat. Remove the crusts and split each slice of toast in half horizontally with a serrated bread knife. Rub the two halves together to loosen the crumbs and place toasted side down on the grill rack. Turn the grill down to low and finish the toast until crisp and golden. Serve the melba toast in a basket lined with a white napkin.

STUFFED PATTYPAN SQUASH

*T*he pattypan squash is an attractive member of the cucurbitas family, which also includes melons and cucumbers. The pattypan squash is prized for its creamy whiteness and is at its best stuffed and served as a vegetable appetizer.

ingredients . . . .

salt and pepper	¼ hothouse cucumber, cut into
4 pattypan squashes	short batons
1 large pinch sugar	¾lb ripe tomatoes
2tbsp olive oil	1tsp tomato paste
1 onion, chopped	2tsp wine vinegar
1 garlic clove, minced	1tbsp chopped marjoram or
½lb zucchini, quartered and	savory
sliced	1tbsp chopped black olives
1 small eggplant, diced	(optional)

Bring a large saucepan of salted water to a boil. Meanwhile, slice the tops from all the pattypan squashes and scoop out the insides with a spoon. Cut the flesh into equal-sized pieces and set aside.

Place the hollow squashes in the boiling water and simmer for 6-8 minutes to soften. Remove from the pan, immerse in cold water and drain.

To prepare the filling: heat the oil in a large skillet, add the onion and garlic and soften over a gentle heat without allowing to color. Add the zucchini, eggplant, cucumber and squash flesh, cover and soften gently for 4-5 minutes.

Pierce the tomatoes with a small knife and place them in a bowl. Cover them with boiling water to loosen the skins.

Discard the skins and chop the tomatoes roughly. Add the tomatoes, tomato paste, vinegar, marjoram or savory, olives and seasoning to the pan, cover and simmer for a further 12 minutes. If the mixture seems a little wet, remove the lid and allow the moisture to evaporate. Preheat the oven to 350°F.

Pile the mixture into the prepared squash cases, place on a baking sheet and bake in the oven for 25 30 minutes, until tender. Serve as a starter, or sprinkle with grated cheese and serve as a light main course. This recipe can be adapted for other varieties of summer squash such as spaghetti squash, large zucchini and yellow crookneck or straight squash as well as winter squashes such as acorn and butternut.

NASTURTIUM LEAF SALAD WITH WARM FILLETS OF RED MULLET

Both the leaves and flowers of the nasturtium plant can be used in this slightly unconventional salad. The leaves have a delicate peppery flavor not unlike watercress. This dish makes a colorful special-occasion starter or main course.

ingredients . . . .

1½-2cups nasturtium leaves
1 handful of nasturtium flowers
1 head curly endive
3cups young spinach leaves
4 fillets red mullet or trout (1lb)
salt and pepper
2tbsp olive oil

Dressing
6tbsp olive or walnut oil

1tbsp raspberry or red wine
  vinegar
1tbsp lemon juice
½tsp English mustard
1 garlic clove, minced
1tbsp chopped capers
2tbsp chopped gherkins
  pepper

To prepare the dressing: place all the ingredients in a screw-top jar and shake until well mixed. Season with pepper but no salt, which will not dissolve in oil. It is far better to season the salad with a little salt before adding the dressing.

Trim the stems from the nasturtium leaves. Pick the flowers over to remove any uninvited insects and set aside. Place the nasturtium leaves, lettuce and spinach in plenty of cold water and leave them there for a few minutes to crisp up nicely, then place in a large salad bowl ready for dressing.

Just before serving, season the fillets of fish with salt and pepper, heat the olive oil in a non-stick skillet and cook the fillets for 3 minutes on each side. Pour the salad dressing over the leaves, toss and arrange on 4 serving plates. Lay the fillets of fish over the top of the salad, garnish with nasturtium flowers and serve immediately.

RED WINDSOR SALAD

Red Windsor is one our finest English cheeses. It is at its best served with a summer salad of fine lettuce, red currants, sliced gooseberries and a dressing made with raspberry vinegar.

ingredients . . . .

1 head crisp lettuce
3oz (1-2 cups) field lettuce
½lb Red Windsor cheese
¾cup red currants
⅔cup sweet gooseberries, thinly
  sliced

6tbsp walnut or olive oil
2tbsp raspberry vinegar
1 egg yolk
2tbsp chopped parsley
1tbsp Worcestershire sauce
2tsp sugar

Wash and dry the lettuce leaves and place them in a large salad bowl. Crumble the Red Windsor cheese over the leaves, add the red currants and gooseberries and set aside.

To prepare the dressing: measure all the ingredients into a screw-top jar and shake thoroughly until blended. (The egg yolk will thicken the dressing slightly and help it adhere to the leaves.) Pour the dressing over the salad just before serving and toss well. Arrange the salad on 4 serving plates and serve as an appetizer or light lunch main course.

Main Courses

A SALAD OF SMOKED TROUT WITH FRESH HORSERADISH

Spicy horseradish need not only be enjoyed with roast beef. Smoked trout is especially delicious if it is flaked off the bone into a crisp salad and tossed in a horseradish dressing. If you cannot obtain fresh horseradish, ready-grated horseradish is available in jars; after opening it will keep for up to 12 weeks in the refrigerator.

ingredients . . . .

1 hard red-leaf lettuce	½tsp English mustard powder
1 small head Bibb lettuce	1tbsp sugar
2oz (1-1½cups) field lettuce	2tbsp white wine vinegar
½ cucumber	¼cup peanut oil
½lb small tomatoes	⅔cup plain yogurt
three ½lb smoked trout	salt and pepper

Sauce
¼cup finely grated horseradish
   root

Wash the salad leaves in plenty of cold water. Dry and place in a large salad bowl. Peel the cucumber and slice into neat little fingers; add to the salad bowl and set aside. Cut the tomatoes into thin wedges and set aside on a small plate: if they are put into the salad too early, the lettuce will lose its crispness.

Remove the skin from the trout and flake the fish from the bone onto another plate, making sure you discard all the small bones.

To prepare the sauce: place the horseradish in a bowl. Add the mustard powder and sugar and stir in the vinegar, oil and yogurt until smooth. Season to taste with salt and pepper. (If you prefer a hotter flavor, stir in a little more mustard powder.)

To assemble the salad: pour the horseradish dressing over the salad leaves and toss evenly. Divide the leaves among 4 plates, distribute the flaked trout over the top and lastly add the wedges of tomato. Season each salad with a grinding of black pepper, garnish with lemon wedges and serve with whole wheat toast.

FILLETS OF SOLE WITH A DELICATE GREEN SAUCE

Make the most of the subtle flavor of sole by poaching it gently and serving it with a sauce of fresh sorrel and mushrooms stuffed with garden herbs.

ingredients . . . .

8 sole fillets (ask the fishmonger for the bones)	Mushroom stuffing
8 button mushrooms	1 small onion, chopped
1 shallot, roughly chopped	1 garlic clove, minced
2 parsley stems	3tbsp butter
1 thyme sprig	1tbsp chopped parsley
salt and pepper	2tbsp chopped thyme
¼cup dry white vermouth	1tsp finely grated lemon zest
⅔cup shredded sorrel leaves	1cup fresh bread crumbs
2tbsp butter	

Place the fish bones in a stainless steel or enamel saucepan and cover with cold water. Trim the stems from the mushrooms and place the trimmings in the saucepan with the shallot, parsley stems and thyme. Bring to a boil as slowly as you can, then simmer for 20 minutes to make a basic fish bouillon. Strain into a bowl and set aside.

Season the sole fillets with salt and pepper and lay them in a shallow skillet. Pour over the vermouth and ⅞cup of the fish bouillon. Cover and simmer as gently as possible over a low heat for 12 minutes. Lift the fish fillets onto a warm serving dish. Allow the cooking juices to simmer until they have reduced by two-thirds. Add the shredded sorrel, cover and simmer for 6-8 minutes.

Pour the contents of the skillet into a liquidizer. Add the butter and blend until smooth. Season to taste with salt and pepper.

Place the mushrooms in a small saucepan, cover with the remaining fish bouillon and simmer for 3-4 minutes.

Meanwhile, prepare the mushroom stuffing: soften the onion and garlic in the butter and stir in the fresh herbs, zest and crumbs. Arrange the mushrooms on a baking sheet and stuff them with the herb mixture. Broil gently until golden-brown.

Serve the fillets of sole with the sauce poured over and the mushrooms to one side. Offer a bowl of buttered new potatoes and a simple green salad to finish.

EAST END COCKLES WITH BACON AND SAMPHIRE

C ockney people in the East End of London would argue that cockles are one of the tastiest shellfish to be found along our coastal waters. To get the best flavor, buy them in their shells and cook them as you would mussels in a large saucepan. Small clams can be prepared in the same way.

ingredients . . . .

3lb cockles in their shells or	2tsp tomato paste
2½cups cooked cockles	2tbsp chopped parsley
2tbsp lard	1tsp chopped marjoram
1 onion, chopped	1tbsp malt vinegar
½lb slab bacon, roughly	¾cup stout or brown ale
chopped	3oz samphire tips
1tbsp flour	pepper
1lb ripe tomatoes	

If you are using live cockles in their shells, leave them in plenty of salted water – fresh sea-water is ideal – for 3-4 hours to flush out any sand or grit. This done, place the cockles in a large saucepan and add 2½cups cold water. Cover and bring to a boil, then simmer for 4-5 minutes until all the shells have opened. Drain the cockles and spread them out on a kitchen pan to cool. Shell the cockles and set the meats aside.

Melt the lard in a large heavy skillet, add the onion and bacon and fry until lightly browned. Stir in the flour until absorbed and remove from the heat.

Pierce the tomatoes with a small knife and place them in a bowl. Pour over boiling water to loosen their skins. Cool the tomatoes under cold running water, remove the skins, chop them and add to the pan. Stir in the tomato paste, herbs and vinegar. With the pan still off the

heat, add the stout or ale a little at a time and stir until thoroughly blended. Add the samphire tips, if using, and simmer for 6-8 minutes, stirring occasionally.

Just before you are ready to serve, add the cockles and warm them through in the sauce. Do not cook them any more or else they will shrink and become rubbery. Serve with mashed potato, in true Cockney style, or with freshly cooked tagliatelle.

CRISPY WHITEBAIT WITH FRIED PARSLEY AND LEMON

B etween May and August the fry of mackerel and herrings are netted in enormous quantities in river estuaries around Britain and appear on the table as whitebait.

ingredients . . . .

2cups fresh whitebait or	⅔cup milk
1lb frozen whitebait	oil for deep frying
¼cup flour	4 parsley sprigs
¼tsp cayenne	1 lemon, cut into wedges, for
salt	garnish

If you are using frozen whitebait, allow them to thaw slowly at room temperature. Put the flour, cayenne and a large pinch of salt into a plastic bag. Moisten the whitebait in the milk and shake them in the flour until evenly coated. If you have been able to get fresh whitebait, they are often covered with a delicate layer of their own moisture: for the best flavor, they should not be washed and will not need moistening with milk before shaking in flour.

Heat a deep-fat fryer to 400°F and fry the whitebait one handful at a time in a wire basket for 2-3 minutes until half cooked. Drain on paper towels and continue frying until they are all cooked. Just before serving, crisp again in the oil for 1-2 minutes, until golden.

Fry the parsley sprigs in the hot oil for 1½-2 minutes, then drain on paper towels. Garnish the whitebait and serve with slices of brown bread and butter and lemon wedges for squeezing.

LOBSTER FOR TWO IN A SEA OF GREEN NOODLES

S *ummer is the season for fresh lobster. Like so many delicacies from the sea, lobster is expensive, but ideal for a special occasion. Before buying a lobster, there are a few things worth knowing. Cock lobsters have firmer flesh and meatier claws, while the hens are appreciated for their more delicate flavor. The hen often carries a cluster of coral beneath her slightly broader tail which is suitable for the enriching of bisques and sauces.*

ingredients..............................

two ¾lb cooked hen lobsters with coral	1 thyme sprig
3tbsp butter, softened	3 tomatoes, roughly chopped
1tsp flour	2tbsp brandy
2tbsp olive oil	⅓cup dry white wine
2 shallots or 1 small onion, roughly chopped	1cup fish bouillon or water
1 small carrot, roughly chopped	⅓cup heavy cream
1 celery stalk, roughly chopped	1 pinch salt
2 tarragon sprigs	1 pinch cayenne
2 parsley stems	½lb spinach noodles, to serve

Remove the coral from beneath the tail of both lobsters and place in a small bowl. Add the butter and flour and stir until smooth. Set aside until you are ready to finish the sauce.

Twist the tails from both lobsters. Cut along the underside of each tail with a pair of kitchen scissors and remove the flesh in one piece. Remove the claws and crack them gently with a small hammer or the back of a heavy knife and try to remove the claw meat in one piece as well. Cut the body in half down the middle and discard the white gills found in both halves near the top of the head, as these can be bitter. The creamy green tomalley, or liver, has a good flavor, so scrape it out and stir together with the butter and coral ready for the sauce. Slice the body meat into even-sized medallions. Set aside. Preheat the oven to 350°F.

Place the lobster shells on a baking sheet and roast them in the oven for 25 minutes, to bring out their full lobster flavor. Place the shells in a heavy bowl or saucepan and pound them finely with one end of a rolling pin.

Heat the oil in a heavy skillet and add the shallot or onion, carrot and celery. Stir over a moderate heat until the vegetables are just beginning to brown. Add the crushed lobster shells, the tarragon, parsley and thyme and the tomatoes. Pour in the brandy, wine and fish bouillon or water, cover and simmer for 8-10 minutes. Remove the pan from the heat and stir in the heavy cream.

Strain the contents of the pan through a fine sift into a clean saucepan. To finish the sauce: stir the coral mixture into the pan and simmer for 2-3 minutes. Place the lobster tail, claw and body meat in the sauce to warm through. Season with a little salt and cayenne pepper and serve with buttered green noodles.

STEAMED FILLETS OF JOHN DORY WITH TARRAGON AND ORANGE

J *ohn Dory, or Saint Pierre as it is called in France, is an extraordinary looking fish with cartoon-like features. The distinctive brown spot found on each side is said to be where Saint Peter once picked the fish out of the sea with his hand, hence the French name. Despite appearances John Dory is a delicious fish of remarkable flavor and texture. Here it is wrapped in blanched lettuce leaves and gently steamed with tarragon and orange. Fillets of pomfret or porgy (scup) can be prepared in the same way.*

ingredients..............................

1 head romaine lettuce	2tbsp chopped tarragon
finely grated zest and juice of 1 orange	4tbsp unsalted butter, softened
	1tsp grainy mustard
1½lb John Dory fillets, skinned	salt and pepper

Remove the outer leaves of the lettuce and blanch them in a large saucepan of boiling water for 1 minute, then transfer to a bowl of cold water to cool. Put the orange zest into a small bowl and the juice into a shallow dish. Lay the fish in the orange juice and set aside.

Add the tarragon to the orange zest and stir in the butter. Add the mustard and season well with salt and pepper.

Lay two of the blanched lettuce leaves on a work surface so that they overlap slightly. Place 3 John Dory fillets on the leaves, spread with one-quarter of the flavored butter and wrap into a neat parcel. Repeat with the other fillets to make parcels.

Place the parcels in a steamer, cover and steam for 15 minutes. Serve with buttered new potatoes, carrots and snow peas.

ables, cover again and cook for a further 2-3 minutes. Taste one or two of the vegetables. If they are to your satisfaction, serve immediately as they will continue to cook if left to stand.

If your family is particularly hungry, prepare a bowl of egg noodles or buttered new potatoes to go with the vegetables. Otherwise serve the stir-fry by itself with a sprinkling of Worcestershire sauce.

STIR-FRIED CHICKEN BREAST WITH CRISPY VEGETABLES

If you have access to a variety of garden fresh vegetables and, like me, enjoy them only just cooked and in abundance, try this simple stir-fry as a weekday supper idea.

ingredients . . . .

three 5oz chicken breast halves, skinned and boned	¼lb Italian green beans, stringed and cut into diamonds
salt and pepper	¼lb broccoli, divided into florets, with the stems sliced diagonally
2tbsp vegetable oil	1 bunch of scallions, trimmed to 2inch lengths
1tbsp sesame oil	
1tbsp sesame seeds	¼lb zucchini, halved and sliced
1 garlic clove, cut in half	⅔cup beansprouts
¼lb young carrots, scraped and cut into fingers	
¼lb whole baby corn, halved down the middle	
3 celery stalks, cut into 2inch batons	

Slice the chicken into equal-sized strips and season with salt and pepper. Heat the vegetable and sesame oils in a wok or large skillet until beginning to smoke. Add the sesame seeds, garlic and chicken. Stir-fry until evenly browned. Plain bamboo chopsticks are very useful for this.

Remove the garlic and add the carrots, corn, celery, green beans and broccoli stems. Cover and steam the vegetables in the chicken juices for 3-4 minutes, shaking occasionally. Add the remaining veget-

SLICED DUCK BREAST WITH A BLACK CURRANT SAUCE

ingredients . . . .

two 7oz duck breast halves	1⅓cups fresh black currants
1tbsp salt	2tbsp black currant preserve
1tbsp goose fat or olive oil	1tbsp cornstarch
2 shallots, finely chopped	2tbsp butter, softened
⅓cup full-bodied red wine	salt and pepper
⅛cup chicken bouillon	4 black currant clusters
2tsp wine vinegar	

Pierce the skin of the duck several times with a fork. This will allow some of the fat to melt away during cooking. Rub the skin with salt.

Heat the goose fat or olive oil in a heavy skillet. Lay the duck breasts in the pan skin side down and cook for 12 minutes. Turn the duck breasts over and cook for a further 5 minutes. The fashion in many restaurants is to serve duck breasts so that they are pink inside and if your duck is really fresh, this is by far the best way to enjoy them. Transfer the duck breasts to a warm plate and allow to rest, to ensure that the pinkness of the meat will spread evenly inside.

To make the sauce: pour off as much of the cooking fat as you can from the pan without losing any of the sediment. Add the shallots and soften over a low heat. Increase the heat and pour in the wine. Loosen the sediment with a flat wooden spoon, add the bouillon, vinegar, blackcurrants and preserve. Bring to a boil then simmer until reduced by half. Mix the cornstarch with 2tbsp cold water and stir into the sauce to thicken. When ready to serve, stir in the butter until melted and season to taste with salt and pepper.

Slice the duck breasts diagonally into thin strips and arrange on the serving plates. Pour over the sauce and serve with Basmati rice, young carrots and zucchini.

A WARM SALAD OF ARTICHOKES, NEW POTATOES AND BACON

ome-grown globe artichokes make a first appearance in July and are delicious if properly prepared. In this recipe the spiny leaves are trimmed to reveal the tender heart at the base. If you are unable to get artichokes at a reasonable price, look out for bottled artichoke hearts in your supermarket or specialty food store. Serves 4 as a main course or 6 as a starter.

ingredients...........

4 globe artichokes	3tbsp peanut oil or lard
1 lemon	½lb Canadian bacon, cut into
salt and pepper	strips
1lb small new potatoes	2tbsp wine vinegar
1 head crisp new lettuce	2tsp grainy mustard
1-1½cups field lettuce	1tsp chopped lemon thyme
1 head Belgian endive, sliced	
⅔cup sliced button mushrooms	

To prepare the artichokes: snap the stem away from the base and draw out the fibers from the heart. Slice the bottom very thinly with a stainless steel knife so as to reveal the underside of the heart. Rub the cut edge with lemon juice to prevent discoloration. Peel away any loose leaves from around the base and trim away three-quarters of the leaves, cutting across the artichoke to reveal the pink choke inside.

Bring a large stainless steel or enamel saucepan of salted water to a boil. Add the lemon juice and boil the artichokes for 12-15 minutes until the outside leaves pull away easily. Immerse the artichokes in cold water to prevent them from overcooking. Peel off the leaves and scrape away the fibrous choke with a teaspoon. Trim the bases neatly with a small knife and cut diagonally into slices.

Bring the potatoes to a boil in a saucepan of cold salted water and simmer for 20 minutes. Wash the lettuce leaves and combine with the endive and mushrooms.

Heat the oil or lard in a skillet and crisp the bacon over a moderate heat. Add the vinegar, mustard and thyme and heat gently. When ready to serve, add the sliced artichokes to the pan and warm with the bacon. Add the potatoes and toss together with the salad leaves. Season with freshly ground pepper and serve immediately.

Barbecue Party

*I*t is not often that we English get the chance to venture into the great outdoors for a barbecue feast. But when we do, we certainly know how to go about it. Weather permitting – and we do have some good weather in July – we like to invite all our friends round for an outdoor barbecue party A great variety of foods can be cooked over the barbecue: quite ordinary foods take on an appetizing smoky flavor. Sausages, chops and chicken have never tasted better. Ribs and steaks are cooked to perfection. In fact, virtually everything tastes better when cooked on the barbecue and eaten outside, accompanied by a simple green salad and washed down with a bottle of inexpensive wine.

SPECIAL BARBECUE SAUCE

ntil now, this barbecue sauce has been one of my best kept secrets. I use it both to marinate and baste chicken pieces, lamb kabobs, steaks and spareribs. The secret of the sauce is, among other things, the addition of fresh mango, which contains a special enzyme that will tenderize the meat before it is cooked. Once over the coals, the sauce will begin to glaze the meat and help it cook to perfection.

ingredients...........

1 ripe mango	1tbsp spicy brown mustard
6tbsp peanut oil	2tbsp tomato paste
6tbsp wine vinegar	1tbsp chopped oregano or
2tbsp Worcestershire	marjoram
sauce	salt and pepper

To remove the mango flesh from the seed, cut down either side of the seed with a serrated bread knife. Peel the 2 side pieces and cut into elegant slices ready to be served as a garnish. Remove the flesh still adhering to the seed and rub through a fine sift to make a smooth paste. Blend in the remaining ingredients until evenly combined. Pour the sauce over the meat to be barbecued and leave to marinate and tenderize for as long as you have time: overnight is ideal.

CHARCOAL-BAKED MACKEREL WITH LEMON AND GARDEN HERBS

C ould there ever be a better way of preparing fresh mackerel than simply dressed with lemon and fresh herbs? Take them and a party of hungry people down to the beach for a barbecue, and you will enjoy mackerel at their very best. Burn a few sprigs of thyme, bay or rosemary among the glowing embers and the flavor of the herbs will impart a special magic to the fish.

ingredients . . . .

6 equal-sized mackerel, cleaned and trimmed, heads removed	1tbsp chopped fresh tarragon
juice of 4 lemons	1tbsp chopped fresh sage
1 stick butter, softened	2 garlic cloves, minced
¼cup chopped parsley	6 bay leaves
2tbsp chopped thyme	salt and pepper

Score the mackerel 3 times on each side and lay them in a shallow dish. Squeeze lemon juice over the fish and leave for 1½-2 hours in the refrigerator to marinate. The lemon juice will counteract the oiliness of the fish and will whiten the color of the flesh.

To prepare the herb butter: place the butter in a bowl and stir in the chopped herbs and minced garlic.

When the mackerel has marinated sufficiently, place each fish on a piece of heavy-duty foil. Spread the fish with a portion of the herb butter, add a bay leaf and season with salt and pepper. Pour a little of the lemon juice used in the marinade over the fish and seal into parcels.

To barbecue the mackerel, make sure that the embers have died down enough so that the fish does not burn. Line the mackerel parcels up on the grid and allow them to cook for 15-20 minutes.

Serves 6

BARBECUED FISH KABOBS WITH FENNEL AND HERBS

I f fish is your fancy, look out for pieces of salmon, halibut, turbot and monkfish. A combination of these fish will remain moist and firm on the barbecue. Skewer them together with fennel and herbs and leave them in a specially prepared marinade until your guests arrive. The marinade can also be used for basting the fish while it is cooking.

ingredients . . . .

1½lb salmon, halibut, turbot or monkfish fillet, cut into 1inch cubes	1 fennel bulb
	salt
	1 large onion
	3 small zucchini
Marinade	1cup cherry tomatoes
⅓cup dry white wine	
3tbsp Pernod	
1tbsp chopped thyme	
1tbsp chopped fennel herb	
1tbsp chopped marjoram	
3tbsp olive oil	
freshly ground black pepper	

Place the fish cubes in a bowl and pour over the wine and Pernod. Add the herbs, oil and plenty of pepper, toss the fish in the marinade, cover and leave in the refrigerator for 1½-2 hours.

Meanwhile, cut the fennel into pieces a little larger than the fish and blanch them in a saucepan of salted boiling water for 4-5 minutes, to prevent the fennel from drying out over the barbecue. Cut the onion into similar shapes and slice the zucchini diagonally.

When the fish has marinated sufficiently, thread it alternating with the fennel, onion, zucchini and tomatoes onto 8 metal skewers. (If you only have wooden skewers, they can be used if they are first soaked in boiling water for 10-15 minutes.)

To cook the kabobs: brush them well with the marinade and place them over a gentle heat. If the embers seem to be too hot, keep the kabobs to the edges where the heat is less intense. Cook the kabobs for 5 minutes on each side, and serve on a bed of rice cooked ahead of time, cooled under running water and reheated in a steamer when ready to serve.

CHARCOAL-GRILLED SALMON STEAKS WITH VERMOUTH AND GINGER

almon is one of the most popular fish in the British Isles. The finest salmon are landed during the summer as they swim upstream in search of quiet still waters. It is these wild specimens that have the best flavor – although wild salmon is also wildly expensive! A little less romantic but costing a lot less are the salmon reared on special farms. If you are having an informal barbecue, I would suggest that farmed salmon might be a more practical choice as the marinade will enhance the flavor of the fish.

ingredients......................

four 6oz salmon steaks
⅓cup dry white vermouth
¾inch piece fresh ginger
  root

1tbsp finely chopped coriander
  (cilantro)
salt and pepper

Place the salmon steaks in a shallow dish and pour over the vermouth. Peel the ginger, grate it finely and add to the salmon with the coriander, salt and pepper. Cover the dish closely and refrigerate for 2½-3 hours.

Wrap each of the salmon steaks in heavy-duty foil with a little of the marinade. Cook the salmon on the edge of the barbecue for 10-12 minutes. Serve straight from the foil with a simple salad and a small baked potato.

SPATCHCOCK CHICKEN IN A PIQUANT SAUCE

patchcock is a colloquial term used to describe the preparation of a whole bird, in this case a small chicken, for grilling. The technique is to remove the backbone, enabling the bird to be opened out flat. The spatchcock method can also be applied to squabs, guinea fowl and duckling.

ingredients......................

two 2lb chickens (ask the
  butcher to remove the
  backbones)
½tsp salt

Sauce
6tbsp wine vinegar

2tbsp black peppercorns
3 shallots, finely chopped
¼cup peanut oil
1tsp ground cumin
1tsp ground coriander
1tsp tomato paste

If you have been unable to find a butcher to prepare the chickens, you can remove the backbone yourself by cutting down either side of the bone with a pair of poultry shears. Press the birds out flat and skewer them twice in a criss-cross. Pierce the skin several times with a fork, season well with salt and set aside. The salt will help the skin to crisp evenly during cooking.

To prepare the sauce: place the vinegar in a non-aluminum saucepan. Place the peppercorns on a chopping board and crush them under a heavy saucepan; one sharp movement will crush them. Add the crushed peppercorns and the shallots to the vinegar and reduce until there is only enough vinegar to coat the bottom of the pan. Strain through a fine sift into a shallow dish suitable for marinating. Add the remaining ingredients and stir well to mix.

Place the spatchcocked chickens in the marinade and leave them for as long as you can – overnight is ideal.

When you are ready to barbecue the birds, place them straight on the grid and cook for 10-12 minutes on each side.

Remove the skewers, cut the birds in half down the breastbone, using poultry shears or a sharp knife, and serve half a chicken to each person.

Iced Melon and Raspberry Soup; Nasturtium Leaf Salad with Warm Fillets of Red Mullet;
Red Currant Meringue Tart.

SMOKY BAKED POTATOES WITH SOUR CREAM AND CHIVES

*B*aked potatoes finished on the barbecue are delicious topped with sour cream and chives. But do spare a thought for your guests if they are standing. How many times have you been defeated by an enormous potato on a wobbly paper plate? Smaller potatoes are much more convenient.

ingredients . . . .

2lb small baking
  potatoes
1 small bunch of chives, finely
  chopped

⅔cup sour cream
salt and pepper

Lightly scrub the potatoes, cover with cold water, add a good pinch of salt and parboil for 15 minutes. Cool the potatoes under running water and wrap in squares of heavy-duty foil.

Cook the potatoes by placing them directly in the coals. If they seem to be too hot, keep to the edges where the heat is less likely to burn them.

To prepare the topping: combine the chives with the cream and season well with salt and pepper.

To serve: score a deep cross in each potato and pinch firmly at the base to open the top. Spoon on the sour cream topping and serve immediately.

GOLDEN CORN-ON-THE-COB WITH MELTED BUTTER

*C*orn is not one of my favorite vegetables unless it is barbecued on the cob with plenty of melted butter. Only then does it taste as it should. The first English crop of corn comes up from the Isle of Wight, weather permitting, during early July. There will be another crop later on.

ingredients . . . .

4 ears of corn
sugar

4tbsp salted butter

Remove the husks and silk from the corn. Bring a large saucepan of water to a boil, add a large pinch of sugar and boil the corn for 2 minutes. Cool under running water, then wrap each ear loosely in heavy-duty foil. Place a tbsp of butter on each and enclose with the foil. (All this can be done several hours before your guests arrive.)

To finish the corn, line them up on the grid and barbecue for 10-12 minutes. Serve in the foil, with the buttery juices.

Puddings

SOFT SUMMER FRUITS

July boasts the most colorful display of soft berry fruits; with so much color and flavor to be had, ideas for desserts abound. Mouthwatering homemade sorbets and ice creams, smooth custards and fools, yogurt ices, fruit salads, soufflés and mousses, tarts and cakes can be enjoyed throughout the summer. Any surplus can be made into jams, jellies and home-prepared fruit vinegars to stock the larder for the winter months.

HOT BLUEBERRY PANCAKES WITH VANILLA ICE CREAM

ingredients..........................

1¼cups self-rising flour
2tbsp sugar
1cup milk
1 egg

2tbsp salted butter
1cup blueberries or
    blackberries

Sift the flour and sugar into a mixing bowl. Pour the milk into a pitcher and beat in the egg. Heat the butter in a saucepan until it begins to brown and stir into the milk. Make a well in the center of the flour, pour in all the liquid and stir to make a thick batter. Lastly add the blueberries and leave to stand for 10-15 minutes.

Heat a large non-stick skillet over a steady heat: non-stick pans do not need additional fat. Spoon the batter into small heaps in the pan and let them spread into 3inch rounds. As soon as bubbles begin to break out on the surface (after about 1 minute), turn them over and give them a further 30 seconds on the other side. To keep the crêpes warm, fold a dish towel on a large plate, cover and keep in a warm oven (325°F) until needed.

Serve with vanilla ice cream for dessert, or with plenty of butter and syrup for breakfast.

BLUEBERRY AND LAVENDER TARTLETS

ingredients..........................

Pastry
1⅔cups flour
1 stick cool butter, diced
2tbsp sugar
1 egg, beaten
a little extra soft butter for
    greasing

1¼cups milk
2 egg yolks
2tbsp sugar
5 lavender flower stems
1½cups blueberries

Filling
3tbsp cornstarch

To make pastry: sift the flour into a large mixing bowl. Add the butter and sugar and cut in or rub together with your fingers until the mixture resembles large crumbs. Or make the pastry in a food processor. Stir in the egg to make a dough: avoid overworking the pastry or it will become difficult to handle. Wrap in plastic wrap and refrigerate for 30 minutes.

To prepare the filling: place the cornstarch in a mixing bowl, mix with 3tbsp of the milk and stir in the egg yolks and sugar. Bring the remaining milk to the boil and infuse the lavender flowers in it for 3 minutes to release their flavor. Pour the boiling milk over the egg mixture and stir until thoroughly mixed. Strain the custard back into the saucepan and stir over a low heat to thicken.

Preheat the oven 375°F.

Lightly grease 8 individual tartlet pans with soft butter and set on a baking sheet. Divide the pastry in half and roll out one half on a floured work surface. (It is best to roll out pastry a little at a time as it is much easier to manage in small quantities.) Cut out as many circles as you can, a little larger than the pans, and line the pans evenly. Add the trimmings to the second half of the pastry and roll out as before.

Line each tartlet case with an opened out paper cup cake case and fill with dried beans or rice. Bake the tartlet cases unfilled in the oven for 15-20 minutes. When they are cooked, lift out the paper cases and fill each tartlet with lavender custard. Top with a layer of blueberries and chill. Decorate with sprigs of fresh lavender and serve two tartlets per person as an elegant dessert or teatime fancy.

GOOSEBERRY AND RED CURRANT TEA CAKE

ingredients . . . .

1½ sticks butter, softened
½cup sugar
2 eggs, at room temperature
¾cup self-rising flour
⅔cup ground almonds

½tsp ground mace
1tsp orange-flower water
1cup sweet gooseberries, trimmed
½cup red currants, stringed

Lightly grease a 9×5×3inch loaf pan with butter and line with parchment paper. (There is no need to grease the paper.)

Preheat the oven to 375°F.

Place the butter and sugar in a mixing bowl and cream until pale. Beat the eggs lightly and add them a little at a time to the creamed mixture. Beat until smooth. (Using the eggs at room temperature helps prevent the mixture from curdling.)

Stir in the flour, ground almonds, mace and orange-flower water and beat until smooth. Stir in the gooseberries and red currants and turn the mixture into the prepared loaf pan. Smooth the surface and bake for 40-45 minutes until well risen and golden. Most cakes of this sort will improve if they are kept for a least a day before slicing.

BLACK CURRANT YOGURT ICE

ingredients . . . .

1pint ripe black currants
juice of 2 lemons

¼cup sugar
2cups plain yogurt

Strip the black currants from their stems and place them in a stainless steel or enamel saucepan with the lemon juice. Bring to a boil, then simmer for 6-8 minutes. Add the sugar and stir until dissolved. Pass the black currants through a nylon sieve to make a paste and allow to cool, then stir into the yogurt.

Turn the black currant yogurt into a metal bowl and freeze for

about 45 minutes. Plastic is not suitable – the yogurt ice will take three times as long to freeze as in metal. Stir the ice to break up any large crystals, then return to the freezer. Stir every 20 minutes or so until firm. Depending on your freezer, the ice will take up to 1¾ hours to freeze.

A FROZEN MOUSSE OF GOOSEBERRIES AND CARDAMOM

ingredients . . . .

1½pints sweet gooseberries
finely grated zest and juice of 2
  large oranges
6 green cardamom pods
⅓cup sugar
2 eggs
⅔cup heavy cream

Cardamom Custard
1¼cups milk
1tbsp cornstarch
3 egg yolks
2tbsp sugar
4 green cardamom pods

Trim the gooseberries and place them in a stainless steel or enamel saucepan. Add the orange zest and juice. Split the cardamom pods open to release their flavor, tie them in a piece of cheesecloth and bury in the gooseberries. Add 2tbsp of the sugar and bring to a boil, then simmer for 2-3 minutes. When the berries are beginning to turn a milky green color, remove 12 of them for decoration. This will happen very quickly, so watch them carefully. Continue to simmer the berries for 6-8 minutes until they fall apart, then let them cool. Discard the cardamom pods.

Line a 9×5×3inch loaf pan with a single layer of plastic wrap and set aside. Crack the eggs into a mixing bowl, add the remaining sugar and beat until a thick ribbon can be drawn across the surface. Softly whip the cream and fold into the cold gooseberries. Fold in the beaten eggs with a spatula, then stir in the whole gooseberries. Turn the mixture into the prepared pan and freeze for 6-8 hours. Well-wrapped, the frozen mousse will keep in the freezer for up to 6 weeks.

To prepare the cardamom custard, measure 2tbsp of the milk into a bowl and stir in the cornstarch. Add the egg yolks and sugar and stir until well mixed. Place the remaining milk in a saucepan, split open the cardamom pods and add to the milk. (Do not add the cardamom pods from the gooseberries as the acidity may curdle the milk.) Bring the milk to a boil and stir into the cornstarch mixture in the bowl. Strain the custard back into the saucepan and simmer to thicken – about 2-3 minutes. The custard is not intended to be any thicker than light cream. Allow to cool, then chill before serving.

To serve the mousse, unmold it onto a chopping board, remove the plastic wrap and cut into ¾inch slices. Serve on individual plates and hand the sauce separately.

RED CURRANT MERINGUE TART

*T*he most simple dessert recipes are often the best. Try this easy-to-put-together tart of sharp red currants and sweet meringue: beautifully light and quite delicious.

ingredients.........................

6oz frozen puff pastry, thawed, or 1⅓cups graham cracker crumbs
5tbsp unsalted butter

3 egg whites
½cup superfine sugar
1pint red currants, stringed

Lightly grease a 9inch tart pan with butter. Roll out the puff pastry on a floured work surface as thinly as you can. Working at speed is the best way to prevent the pastry from sticking to the table if your kitchen is warm. Lift the pastry on a rolling pin and position over the tart pan. Lift the edges of the pastry into the pan and trim the edges with a small knife.

Alternatively, instead of pastry use a crumb crust, which is much easier. Melt the butter in a small saucepan and stir in the graham cracker crumbs. Press the mixture into the bottom and up the sides of the tart pan, using the back of a large spoon, and leave in the refrigerator for about 15 minutes to set.

To prepare the filling: beat the egg whites with 2tbsp of the sugar until peaks are formed. Add the remaining sugar a little at a time, beating all the while. Fold in the red currants, using a large spoon, and turn the mixture into the prepared tart case. Sprinkle the top with extra sugar and brown under a broiler.

Chill the tart in the refrigerator before serving.

A BRÛLÉE OF SOFT FRUITS

*T*he ubiquitous crème brûlée has appeared on virtually every dinner and restaurant menu since its arrival in the late 1970s. As with so many trends, only the best examples survive.

ingredients.........................

1¼cups heavy cream
2tsp cornstarch
2tbsp milk
4 egg yolks

2tbsp sugar
1½pints fresh raspberries, blueberries, blackberries, etc.
⅔cup raw brown sugar

Rinse the inside of a heavy saucepan with cold water, add the cream and bring to a boil. (Rinsing the pan with water is an old trick that will prevent the cream from burning on the bottom.) Contrary to popular belief, cream will boil quite happily providing it is fresh.

Place the cornstarch in a bowl, mix smoothly with the milk and stir in the egg yolks and granulated sugar. Pour the boiling cream into the mixture and stir until thoroughly combined. Return the contents of the bowl to the saucepan and return to a boil, stirring. As soon as the custard begins to boil, return it to the bowl and cool.

A small amount of cornstarch or starch in the custard containing eggs will prevent it from curdling: however, just as a precaution, I would only boil the sauce for 15-20 seconds, enough to cook out the starch.

Distribute the soft fruits among 4 ovenproof dishes, pour the custard over the tops and leave to set. To glaze the brûlées, sprinkle an even layer of raw brown sugar over the tops and place under the broiler until the sugar is melted and bubbling. Allow to cool and harden, then refrigerate until needed.

PEACHES AND RASPBERRIES IN BEAUJOLAIS WINE

The smooth character of Beaujolais wine goes perfectly with this stunning combination of fruits to create one of my all-time favorite desserts.

ingredients . . . .

2pints fresh raspberries	8 ripe peaches
¾cup Beaujolais wine	½cup sliced almonds, toasted
3tbsp confectioners' sugar	

Reserve 18 of the raspberries for decoration. Place the remainder in a liquidizer and paste. Rub the paste through a fine sift into a glass or porcelain bowl. Add the wine and stir in the sugar to sweeten.

Plunge the peaches into boiling water for 2-3 minutes to loosen their skins, then peel. Slice the peaches into the sauce and leave in the refrigerator to macerate for 1½-2 hours. (The peaches will keep in their sauce for up to 3 days.)

To serve: spoon the peaches into a serving dish and decorate with the reserved raspberries and toasted sliced almonds. A good-quality vanilla ice cream goes particularly well with this dish.

Preserves

This is the month for raspberries, strawberries, tayberries, loganberries, red, white and black currants, blueberries, bilberries, blackberries, whortleberries and gooseberries in great abundance. Pick-your-own farms offer excellent value, especially for fruit for preserving. Ever since I can remember, jam and jelly making has signified the very peak of summer – hard work, but always a pleasure to see the day's labor captured in rows of gleaming glass jars.

To ensure a good seal, and to prevent spoilage, you can process your jars of jam in a boiling water bath for about 10 minutes. In this case, use canning jars with lids and leave a little headroom when filling with the jam.

HOME-MADE STRAWBERRY JAM

ingredients . . . .

3½lb (5½pints) strawberries	2 lemons
2pints red currants	4½lb (10cups) sugar

Pick the strawberries over, discarding any that are moldy. Hull them, then place them with the red currants in a large preserving kettle. The fruit should not reach more than halfway up the side, to leave room for when it boils. Pare the zest from both lemons and squeeze the juice into the fruit. Tie the zest and the pith into a piece of cheesecloth and bury in the fruit.

Bring the fruit to a boil and allow the juice to run. Continue to boil the fruit until the juices have reduced by one-quarter. Meanwhile, place the sugar in a large heatproof bowl and warm through in a moderate oven 350°F) for 10-15 minutes. At the same time wash your jam jars in plenty of hot soapy water, rinse and dry thoroughly, then place in the oven to warm. This will kill any bacteria and also prevent the jars from cracking when they are filled.

When the fruit has reduced by one-quarter, remove the cheesecloth bag containing the lemon and stir in the warm sugar. Bring the jam back to a boil and simmer until the jell point is reached – about 20-25 minutes depending on the quantity. On a candy thermometer the temperature for jell point is 220°F. The jell point can also be determined by chilling a white plate or saucer in the refrigerator, then spooning a little of the jam onto one side. Let it cool, then push your fingernail across the plate into the jam. If the surface wrinkles, the jam has reached jell point.

Line up the hot jars on a kitchen tray and fill them right to the top. This is best done by two people, one filling and the other sealing the jars. There are a number of cellophane products on the market especially made for sealing preserves. Allow the jams to cool, then label and date. Home-made strawberry jam will keep almost indefinitely, although it is best eaten within a year.

Makes about 6lb.

RED CURRANT JELLY

ingredients........................

4quarts red currants   sugar

Wash the red currants and place them in a large enamel, copper or stainless steel saucepan, not more than half full. (There is no need to remove the stems from the berries as they contain extra pectin.) Bring the berries to a boil with 5cups water and simmer for about 30 minutes, mashing occasionally with a large wooden spoon.

Strain the berries and juice through a scalded jelly bag. It is best to suspend the bag between the legs of an upturned kitchen stool and let the juice drip into a bowl. This procedure can take up to 2 hours. Do not force the debris through the bag or the jelly will become cloudy.

When you have obtained all the juice, measure it into a clean saucepan and add 2¼cups sugar for each 2½cups of juice. Bring back to a

boil and simmer for 4-5 minutes. Test the set by spooning a little of the jelly onto a cold plate. Allow to cool, then run your fingernail along the plate and into the jelly. When the surface wrinkles, the jelly is ready for packing into jars.

Smaller jars are preferable for red currant jelly so collect as many as you can find, wash them well and heat them in a moderate oven for 10-15 minutes. Line up the jars on a kitchen tray, fill them and seal while still warm with cellophane.

Makes about 4lb

RASPBERRY VINEGAR

ingredients........................

2quarts deep red raspberries
5cups white wine vinegar

Pick the raspberries over, removing any leaves and stems, and place them in an earthenware casserole. Bruise the berries lightly with the end of a rolling pin without reducing them to a purée. Pour the vinegar over the berries and cover with a clean dish towel. Leave to steep for 24 hours in a warm place. I find the best way is to leave them out in the sunshine during the day, or keep the vinegar at room temperature.

Strain the vinegar through a piece of cheesecloth into attractive bottles. Avoid using metal sifts and utensils as they will blacken and taint the vinegar. Add a few whole raspberries to each bottle, then seal the bottles with corks as screwtop lids may corrode in time, and store in a cool, dry place.

August

August is the month when summer recedes gently toward the beginning of autumn. Since the gradual ebbing of the tides, subtle changes have been taking place in the countryside. Before the month is over farmers will have started their harvest of oats, barley and wheat and the fields will be ready for burning or ploughing. The weather is often unsettled during August, although we are promised one or two weeks of sunshine to ripen the last of the summer fruits. The uncertainty of the weather has led many of us to take off on our summer vacation in search of more reliable weather.

Attempts to keep the vegetable gardens in order during August are made impossible since nearly everything has become overgrown. Many varieties of green beans and broad or fava beans are at their most plentiful at the moment. Cooking should be as brief as possible to capture their full flavor. Fresh peas in their pods and flat snow peas are still sweet and tender, delicious in salads or blanched briefly to retain their crispness. Corn on the cob is becoming more widely available since supplies have been arriving from the southern counties. Broccoli and cauliflower are available in the shops although prices are likely to remain high until September-October. Carrots are still young and tender and are at their best if their tops are left on until ready to eat. New season's parsnips and rutabaga are worth looking out for since they have not a hint of bitterness. Zucchini and other squashes, eggplant, sweet peppers and tomatoes are all plentiful at the moment and are delicious baked into a light vegetable stew. Cucumbers, scallions, Chinese or Napa cabbage, celery and fennel are all useful ingredients for summer salads. Fresh herbs are also in good supply at the moment and should last well into next month.

The fruit season is at its most colorful during August when the summer berries reach their peak. Raspberries, loganberries and tayberries flood onto the market at the beginning of the month and are often sold cheaply if they are soft. The English strawberry season has just about finished now although we can expect a second harvest in early autumn. Black currants, red currants and Dorset blueberries are in good supply at the moment and challenge us for dessert ideas. The last of the English cherries arrive during August when prices are at their lowest. Melons are sweet and plentiful throughout the summer months; look out for ripe ones to chill and serve with fresh raspberries or black currants softened with a little sugar. Watermelons are also available and make a thirst-quenching treat on a hot summer's day. Peaches, nectarines and apricots are in good supply at the moment, although their prices usually fall towards the end of the month. Large sweet gooseberries are a common sight at most greengrocers and can be combined with ripe elderberries into a creamy huff. New arrivals for August are the long-awaited plums, particularly greengages, to be baked in a crumble or eaten as they are. The English apple season kicks off just in time for the coming blackberry season: apple and blackberry must be the most popular – and traditional – combination of fruits.

There is plenty on offer at the fishmonger during August with attractive displays of Dover and Torbay soles, brill, turbot, flounder and halibut. Mackerel and herring are doing well at the moment and are best enjoyed wrapped in foil with a few herbs on the barbecue. Fresh salmon is one of the best buys of the month since prices usually reach their lowest in the year. There are often one or two unusual fish on offer during August. Look out for red mullet, John Dory, monkfish and dogfish. Fresh tuna and swordfish steaks are often available and are worth trying if you haven't already. Freshwater crayfish are becoming more popular although they are an expensive treat. Crabs and lobsters are at their best and should be enjoyed while their prices are low.

The glorious 12th marks the beginning of the game bird season with the arrival of Highland grouse and snipe. Early supplies of grouse are usually snapped up by restaurants at silly prices, while the humble gourmet is advised to wait a few weeks until the excitement has died down. Squabs and quails are often available throughout the summer and require little cooking to secure their delicate flavor.

AUGUST INGREDIENTS IN SEASON

FRUIT & NUTS

British at their best:
Apples
Blackberries
Black and Red Currants
Blueberries
Cherries
Cooking Apples
Damsons
Elderberries
Gooseberries
Greengages
Loganberries
Pears
Raspberries
Rose Hips
Tayberries

Also available:
Hazelnuts (Filberts)
Strawberries
Walnuts

Imported in season:
Almonds
Apricots
Bananas
Brazil Nuts
Dates
Figs
Grapefruit
Grapes
Kiwi Fruits
Lemons, Limes
Mangoes
Melons
Nectarines
Oranges
Papaya
Passion Fruit
Peaches
Peanuts
Pecans
Pineapples
Pistachio Nuts
Watermelons

VEGETABLES & HERBS

British at their best:
Aubergines (Eggplant)
Basil
Beets
Broad (Fava) Beans
Brussels Sprouts
Carrots
Cauliflowers
Cherry Tomatoes
Chervil
Chicory (Belgian Endive)
Chives
Corn
Courgettes (Zucchini)
Cucumbers
Dill, Fennel
French (Green) Beans
Garlic
Globe Artichokes
Horseradish
Kohlrabi
Lavender, Lettuce
Mange tout (Snow Peas)
Marjoram
Marrows and other
 Large Summer Squashes
Mint
Mustard and Cress
Nasturtiums
Onions
Parsnips
Peas
Pickling Cucumbers
Pickling (Pearl) Onions
Radishes
Rosemary
Runner (Italian Green) Beans
Sage, Samphire
Savory
Spring Onions (Scallions)
Shallots
Sorrel, Spinach
Sweet Peppers
Swedes (Rutabaga)
Tarragon, Thyme
Tomatoes
Watercress
Winter Squashes

Also available:
Broccoli
Cabbages
Celeriac
Celery
Leeks
Turnips

Imported in season:
Aubergines (Eggplant)
Avocados
Curly Endive

FISH & SHELLFISH

British at their best:
Brill
Cockles
Coley (Pollock)
Conger Eel
Crabs
Dover Sole
Freshwater Crayfish
Hake, Halibut
Herring
Lemon Sole
Lobsters
Mackerel
Monkfish
Plaice, Prawns
Red Mullet
Salmon
Scampi (Langoustines)
Sea Trout
Sea Bass
Shrimp, Squid
Torbay Sole
Trout, Turbot
Whitebait, Winkles

Also available:
Cod
Gray Mullet
Haddock, Huss
Skate, Sprats
Whiting

Imported in season:
John Dory
Red Mullet
Sardines, Squid

POULTRY & GAME

British at their best:
Grouse from 12th
Guinea Fowl
Pigeon
Quail
Snipe from 12th

Also available:
Chicken
Duck, Goose
Rabbit
Turkey
Venison

MEAT

Beef
Lamb
Offal
Pork
Veal

TOMATO AND RED CURRANT SOUP

T his recipe came to me three-quarters of an hour before some good friends of mine were due to arrive for lunch. As usual things were at fever pitch in the kitchen and as usual the food was far from finalized. There was a row of ripening tomatoes on the window-sill and two punnets of redcurrants in the refrigerator. Within half an hour a rather special soup appeared, which turned out to be the talk of the table.

ingredients ....

2 shallots or 1 medium onion, chopped
2tbsp raspberry vinegar
2tbsp sugar
1pint red currants

2 fresh mint sprigs
2lb ripe tomatoes
¼cup sour cream
1 bunch chives, snipped

Place the shallots or onion, vinegar and sugar in a stainless steel or enamel saucepan and simmer until the shallots or onion have softened and the vinegar reduced by half. Strip the red currants from their stems, add to the pan with the mint, cover and simmer for 6-8 minutes or until the berries have burst. Remove the mint, then liquidize the mixture until smooth. Strain through a nylon sift into a bowl.

Score the tomatoes once with a sharp knife and place them in a large bowl. Pour boiling water over them to loosen their skins, then plunge them into cold water and remove the skins. Cut the tomatoes in half and remove the seeds.

Place the tomatoes in the liquidizer and blend lightly so that there are still pieces of tomato to be seen.

Stir the tomatoes into the red currant purée and chill until ready to serve. If you are in a great hurry to chill the soup, half fill a large bowl with ice, sprinkle over 2tbsp of table salt and chill the soup over the ice. Salt will lower the temperature of the ice.

To serve: ladle the soup into 4 individual bowls, swirl a spoonful of sour cream into each and sprinkle with snipped chives or mint.

ICED CUCUMBER AND MELON SOUP

ingredients ....

1 onion, finely chopped
2tbsp olive oil
½ hothouse cucumber, peeled and finely chopped
½tsp ground ginger

finely grated zest and juice of 1 orange
1 ripe cantaloupe melon
⅔cup sour cream
salt and pepper

Soften the onion in the oil without allowing it to color. Add the cucumber and stir in the ginger followed by the orange zest and juice. Cover and allow the cucumber to soften for 10-12 minutes. It is interesting to note that however long you cook cucumber, it will never disintegrate.

Cut the melon in half, discard the seeds and scoop out as many balls as you can with a melon-baller. Scoop the remaining melon into a liquidizer, add the cooked cucumber and blend until smooth.

Pour the soup into a tureen, add the melon balls and stir in the sour cream. Taste and adjust the seasoning if necessary. Chill well before serving.

NORFOLK COCKLE CAKES

*T*he cockle is one of our best-known and most popular shellfish. For hundreds of years cockles have been gathered in enormous quantities from the north Norfolk coast and around the Thames estuary. Cockles are still sold by the pint measure at coastal resorts up and down the country. Without thinking how else they can be prepared, vacationers douse them with malt vinegar and chase them down with a pint or so of strong ale. By way of a change, I have prepared for you an interesting variation of an old Norfolk recipe in which the cockles are coated in a simple batter and deep-fried. Small clams may be prepared in the same way.

ingredients . . . .

2½cups shucked cockles	½cup cold milk
9tbsp flour	1tbsp Worcestershire sauce
½tsp English mustard powder	1tbsp chopped parsley
1tbsp finely grated Parmesan cheese	oil for deep frying
	extra flour for dusting

Rinse the cockles in plenty of cold water and dry them well on paper towels.

To prepare the batter: sift the flour and mustard powder together into a mixing bowl. Sprinkle the Parmesan cheese over the top and make a well in the center. Add the milk and Worcestershire sauce and gradually stir the flour into the milk with a wooden spoon. Add the parsley and leave the batter to stand for at least 20 minutes at room temperature. Standing batter is not just an old wives' tale. Any mixture of flour and liquid, including pastry, will benefit by allowing time for it to rest properly.

It is best to cook the cockle cakes just before you want to serve them. So have ready a deep-fat fryer heated to 375°F. To test the temperature of the oil, drop in a small piece of bread. If it turns golden brown in under 1 minute, the temperature will be about right. As a word of caution, the fryer should be only half-filled with oil.

Dust the cockles with flour and coat them in the batter. This is best done on a shallow plate. Scatter the cockles into the hot oil, in batches if necessary, and fry for 1½-2 minutes until golden. If you have to keep the fried cockles warm do so in a moderate oven, uncovered so that they will keep their crispness. Serve with a squeeze of fresh lemon and a sprinkling of salt.

BACON AND AVOCADO SALAD WITH A SHARP TOMATO DRESSING

*H*ot crispy bacon and soft avocado tossed into a cold salad has become a favorite of mine both as a starter and as a main course. To improve the salad yet further, I have bound it with a sharp tomato dressing to create a wonderful contrast of flavors.

ingredients . . . .

Tomato dressing
3 shallots, finely chopped
¾cup red currants
¼cup raspberry or red wine vinegar
1tbsp Worcestershire sauce
¾lb ripe tomatoes
2tbsp olive oil

Salad
assorted salad green leaves
1 large ripe avocado
1tbsp lemon juice
1½lb slab bacon, cut into broad strips

To prepare the dressing: place the shallots, red currants, vinegar and Worcestershire sauce in a small stainless steel saucepan and simmer, uncovered, until the vinegar is evaporated.

Pierce the skins of the tomatoes with a small knife and place them in a bowl. Pour boiling water over them to loosen the skins, then plunge into cold water and remove the skins. Cut the tomatoes in half and remove the seeds.

Place the tomatoes, oil and shallot mixture in a liquidizer and blend until smooth, then strain through a fine sift. Season to taste.

Wash the salad leaves and leave them in a bowl of cold water to freshen up. Cut the avocado in half, remove the seed and peel away the skin. Cut the flesh into even-sized pieces, brush with lemon juice and set aside. Cook the bacon in a non-stick skillet until crispy.

Dry the salad leaves, place in a large salad bowl and scatter the bacon and avocado over the top. Pour the dressing down the side of the bowl, then when you are ready to serve the salad, toss well and serve immediately.

a small knife into the center; if it comes away cleanly the quiche is ready. Allow to cool and serve warm or cold with a simple salad or as part of a buffet spread.

A ZUCCHINI AND TOMATO QUICHE MADE WITHOUT PASTRY

If you are one of these people for whom pastry-making is just the last straw, let me relieve you with this delicious quiche recipe. I have used leaf spinach instead of pastry to line the dish and, like all good quiches, there is a good depth of filling.

ingredients ....

¾lb fresh spinach leaves, cooked and dried
3tbsp butter, softened
1 onion, chopped
¼lb Canadian bacon, cut into strips

1½lb zucchini
¼lb tomatoes, skinned and deseeded
2 eggs
⅔cup milk
salt and pepper

Preheat the oven to 375°F. Lightly grease a 9inch porcelain quiche dish with some of the butter. Arrange the spinach leaves over the bottom and up the sides of the dish, ensuring that it is evenly lined to a good thickness.

To prepare the filling: melt the remaining butter in a large saucepan, add the onion and bacon and soften over a gentle heat without allowing them to color. Reserve two of the straightest zucchini for the final decoration and shred the remainder on a coarse cheese grater. Stir the shredded zucchini in with the onion and bacon and remove from the heat. Roughly chop the tomatoes and add to the mixture. Turn the contents of the saucepan into the quiche dish.

To prepare a simple custard: break the eggs into a bowl and beat them lightly with a fork. Add the milk and season well with salt and pepper. Pour the custard over the filling and decorate the top of the quiche with the reserved zucchini, thinly sliced. Bake the quiche in the center of the oven for 25-30 minutes. Test the quiche by inserting the point of

A LIGHT VEGETABLE STEW

There is a time during August when vegetables seem to grow more quickly than we can make use of them. One of the easiest and most delicious ways is to make an enormous vegetable stew. The result is beautifully light and full of flavor. Serve the stew hot or cold as a starter for 8 or a main course for 4. It will keep well in the refrigerator and freezes excellently.

ingredients ....

3 large onions, sliced
1 fennel bulb, roughly chopped
2 garlic cloves, minced
3tbsp olive oil
2½lb ripe tomatoes
2 large eggplants, roughly chopped
1lb zucchini, thickly sliced
1lb yellow squash, thickly sliced

½lb red and green sweet peppers, roughly chopped
6oz button mushrooms, quartered
½ large hothouse cucumber, peeled and cut into short strips
2tbsp tomato paste
2tbsp chopped marjoram or oregano
1 large bay leaf
salt and pepper

Place the onions, fennel and garlic in a large saucepan, add the oil, cover and soften over a gentle heat stirring occasionally.

Score the tomatoes with a sharp knife and place them in a large bowl. Cover with boiling water to loosen their skins, plunge into cold water, then remove the skins. Roughly chop the tomatoes and add to the saucepan with the eggplants, zucchini, yellow squash, peppers, mushrooms and cucumber. Stir in the tomato paste, add the herbs, season with salt and pepper, cover and simmer for 35-40 minutes.

If the stew seems to be a little too liquid at the end of the cooking time, allow to simmer uncovered. Sprinkle with grated cheese such as Parmesan, and serve hot.

Main Courses

STEAMED FILLETS OF SOLE IN GREEN JACKETS

*C*ould there ever be a sweeter, more delicious creature of the sea than sole? English species include lemon sole with its pointed nose and yellowish-brown skin, Dover sole with a more rounded nose and rougher brown skin, and Torbay sole, also known as the witch, recognizable by its beautiful marbled skin of purple and pink. Torbay sole is for my money one of the best tasting fish on the market. To make the most of its subtle flavor, I have wrapped the fillets in blanched lettuce leaves around a filling of muscat grapes. The parcels are then steamed gently and served with a delicate cream sauce. For added color and texture, you may like to garnish the dish with fleurons, *tiny crescents of puff pastry baked until golden.*

ingredients......................

two 14oz sole, filleted and
  skinned, bones reserved
1 head romaine lettuce
2 shallots, finely chopped
2tbsp butter
½cup muscat grapes, sliced
2 firm tomatoes
⅓cup heavy cream
1tbsp chopped parsley
salt and pepper

Stock
1 shallot or small onion, chopped
1 celery stalk, chopped
½ small carrot, chopped
1 thyme sprig
2 parsley stalks

To make the bouillon: place the fish bones in a stainless steel saucepan. Add the shallot or onion, celery, carrot, thyme and parsley stalks. Cover with cold water and bring to a boil as slowly as you can. (It is during this time that the best flavor is extracted from the bones.) As soon as the bouillon comes to a boil, remove from the heat and let it stand for 10 minutes. Strain the fish bouillon through a fine sift into a clean saucepan, bring to a rapid boil and reduce the bouillon to 3-4tbsp.

Meanwhile, bring a saucepan of water to a boil and blanch 8 of the larger lettuce leaves for no longer than 1 minute. Immerse the leaves in a bowl of cold water, then drain and spread out on paper towels.

Place the shallots in a small saucepan with the butter and soften over a gentle heat without allowing them to color. Spread 2 of the leaves out on the work surface. Lay one of the fillets of sole on the leaves, spread with a quarter of the shallots and a quarter of the grapes. Place the second fillet over the filling and enclose in the leaves. Repeat to make 4 parcels.

To prepare the sauce: score the tomatoes with a sharp knife and cover with boiling water to loosen their skins. Cool under running water, then remove the skins. Cut the tomatoes in half, discard the seeds and cut the flesh into neat dice. Set aside. Stir the cream into the reduced bouillon and simmer gently.

About 20 minutes before serving, steam the sole parcels for 15 minutes. To finish the sauce: stir the chopped tomatoes and parsley into the cream mixture, taste and season. Pour onto 4 fish plates and arrange the sole parcels in the centers.

HOME-SOUSED HERRING WITH SOUR CREAM AND CHIVES

*I*f you are faced with more herring than you know what to do with, why not souse them in spiced vinegar and turn them into rollmops? Serve them with rye or pumpernickel bread, sour cream and chives as an open sandwich or in a salad.

ingredients......................

2½cups water
3tbsp salt
6 herrings, filleted and skinned
2½cups cider vinegar
2 thyme sprigs
3 parsley stems
2tsp dill seeds
2tsp black peppercorns

2 blades mace
2 bay leaves
1 small piece of fresh ginger
  root, peeled
½lb pickling cucumbers
1 large onion, sliced

Combine the water and salt in a shallow dish to make a simple brine. Lay the herring fillets in the brine, cover and leave in the refrigerator for 2-3 hours. To make the pickling marinade, place the vinegar in a stainless steel or enamel saucepan and add the thyme, parsley stems, dill seeds, peppercorns, mace, bay leaves and ginger. Bring to a boil as slowly as you can, then remove from the heat and leave to cool.

Meanwhile, cut the pickling cucumbers into 2inch strips and blanch them in boiling water for 2-3 minutes. Rinse the herring fillets under cold running water to wash off the salt and roll each fillet up around pieces of onion and cucumber. Secure each fillet with a wooden toothpick and arrange in a glass or pottery jar. Cover each layer of fish with slices of cucumber and onion and cover with the pickling marinade. Cover the jars and leave in the refrigerator for at least 7 days before eating. Soused herrings will keep 3 months in the refrigerator.

BUTTERED FLATFISH WITH A SAUCE OF VERMOUTH AND ORANGE

*O*t the many flat fish that reach their peak during the summer months, brill with its mixed tweed coloring is one of the most delicious. Smaller in size than the turbot and much less expensive, brill has a similar sweet flavor and softness to its flesh. If brill is not available you can use halibut, flounder, dab, or cod steaks cut from the tail end.

ingredients . . . .

1½lb brill fillets, skinned
salt and pepper
1 large carrot, cut into matchsticks
2 celery stalks, cut into matchsticks

2 large zucchini, halved and sliced
2 shallots, chopped
2 small oranges
6tbsp unsalted butter
¼cup dry white vermouth

Season the brill with salt and pepper and lay each fillet on a square of foil. Distribute the carrot, celery, zucchini and shallots among the fillets. Sprinkle over the finely grated zest of 1 orange.

Squeeze the juice of both oranges into a measuring cup and pour over the brill. Cut the butter into 4 equal pieces and divide among the

brill. Lastly pour on the vermouth and seal the brill into neat parcels ready for cooking. (All this can be done up to 24 hours in advance and the parcels kept in the refrigerator if you are planning ahead.) To cook the brill, place the parcels in a shallow dish and bake in the oven, preheated to 350°F, for 20-25 minutes. Serve the brill with plain boiled Basmati rice.

PAN-FRIED SALMON STEAKS WITH A SAUCE OF CUCUMBER AND TARRAGON

*T*he salmon season is in full swing during the summer when prices are at their lowest in the year. Spoil your friends with rich salmon steaks for the perfect summer dinner.

ingredients . . . .

four 6oz salmon steaks
salt and pepper
2tbsp olive oil
1 onion, finely chopped
2tsp flour
1¼cups fish or vegetable bouillon

1cup grated cucumber
1tbsp tarragon vinegar
2tbsp chopped tarragon
½lb ripe tomatoes
4 tarragon sprigs, for garnish

Season the salmon with salt and pepper and shallow-fry in the oil for 3-4 minutes on each side. Do not overcook, or the salmon will be dry. Transfer the salmon to a plate, cover and keep warm.

To prepare to sauce: soften the onion in the remaining oil without allowing it to color. Stir in the flour until absorbed, remove from the heat and stir in the bouillon until evenly mixed. Add the cucumber, vinegar and tarragon, stir and simmer until thickened. Score the tomatoes with a sharp knife and pour boiling water over them to loosen their skins. Cool under running water, then remove the skins, halve and de-seed.

Just before you are ready to serve the salmon, cut the tomato into a neat dice and stir into the sauce. Season with salt and pepper, pour over the salmon steaks and garnish with tarragon sprigs. Serve with buttered new potatoes.

FRESHWATER CRAYFISH IN A NEST OF ZUCCHINI

*T*he freshwater crayfish is a miniature version of the common lobster. Crayfish measure 3-4inches long and can be found in unpolluted chalk streams and rivers. The people of France, Germany and Scandinavia are very fond of them and look forward to their short season, August to September, when they are eaten at great expense in fancy restaurants. Like so many delicacies gathered on the Continent, freshwater crayfish thrive quite happily in streams in Britain, but they are as yet a rare sight at the fishmonger's – though he may be encouraged to order them if asked often enough to do so. If you cannot find freshwater crayfish, you can substitute Dublin Bay prawns or Norway lobsters (which are also known by their French name langoustine) or jumbo shrimp. This elegant dish serves 8 as a starter, 4 as a main course.

ingredients . . . .

16 live freshwater crayfish
1 small carrot, thinly sliced
⅓cup sliced fennel bulb
1 small onion, sliced
1 garlic clove, minced
2tbsp olive oil
3tbsp brandy
⅞cup dry white wine
1¼cups light fish bouillon or
  water
4 ripe tomatoes

1tsp cornstarch
2tsp tomato paste
⅔cup heavy cream
1½lb large zucchini
salt
cayenne
1tbsp chopped tarragon
4 parsley sprigs

The most humane way to kill live crayfish is to drop them into a saucepan of boiling water to which a few smooth stones have been added. The stones help to maintain the boil after the crayfish have entered the water, thus killing them instantly. Simmer the crayfish for 3-4 minutes, until they turn bright red, then leave them to stand off the heat for 10-12 minutes.

Preheat the oven to 425°F.

Remove the crayfish with a slotted spoon and cool under running water. Twist off the tails and peel off the shells into a roasting pan. Cut each of the tail pieces of meat in half down the middle and remove the intestinal tract that runs down the center. Put the tail pieces aside. Reserve 4 of the bodies for garnish and place the remainder in the roasting pan with the carrot, fennel, onion, garlic and oil. Place the pan near the top of the oven to bake for 10-12 minutes, to bring out the full flavor of the vegetables and crayfish shells. Place the contents of the pan in a food processor and blend until fine. Turn the mixture into a large heavy skillet, add the brandy, wine and bouillon or water, and simmer over a gentle heat until reduced by half. Roughly chop the tomatoes and add them to the pan with the tomato paste. Stir well and simmer for 5 minutes.

To strain the sauce, place two layers of cheesecloth in a large sieve, and strain the contents of the pan into a saucepan beneath. Mix the cornstarch with 1tbsp of cold water and stir into the cream. Add the cream to the strained sauce, bring to a boil and simmer to thicken. (If the sauce seems to be too thick, add a little more bouillon or water.)

To prepare the zucchini, slice them lengthwise on a vegetable slicer and cut the strips into spaghetti lengths. Bring a saucepan of water to a boil, add a pinch of salt and boil the zucchini for no longer than 2 minutes. Drain well. When you are ready to serve, heat the crayfish tails in the sauce, season with salt and cayenne, arrange a nest of zucchini on 4 attractive plates and spoon the sauce into the middle. Sprinkle with tarragon and add a parsley sprig to one side.

BUTTERFLY LAMB CHOPS WITH A RED CURRANT SAUCE

*W*hen two loin chops are left joined together they are known as butterfly chops and make a fairly substantial serving. A sharp red currant sauce makes a delicious accompaniment.

ingredients . . . .

4 butterfly lamb chops
salt and pepper
2tbsp peanut oil

Sauce
2 large oranges
1 large lemon

2tbsp red currant jelly
½inch piece of fresh ginger root,
  peeled and grated
½tsp English mustard powder
¾cup red currants

Season the chops with plenty of salt and pepper. Heat the oil in a large skillet and cook the chops for 6-8 minutes on each side. Transfer to a plate, cover and keep warm.

To prepare the sauce: allow the sediment to settle in the pan and spoon off any visible fat. Remove the zest from one of the oranges with a vegetable peeler and cut into thin strips. Add to the pan and squeeze in the juice of both oranges and the lemon. Bring the juices to a boil and simmer until they have reduced by half. Stir in the red currant jelly, the ginger and the mustard until evenly blended. Just before you are ready to serve the lamb, add the redcurrants to the sauce and simmer for 1 minute. Serve with plain boiled rice and buttered green beans.

STIR-FRIED PORK WITH FRESH FIGS AND RASPBERRY VINEGAR

1½lb pork tenderloin, cut into
  thin strips
salt and pepper
3tbsp peanut oil
2oz fine green beans, trimmed
  and cut in half
2oz snow peas
1 bunch scallions, sliced
  diagonally

1 carrot, cut into thin batons
1 turnip, cut into thin batons
1 zucchini, halved and sliced
1tsp chopped fresh sage
2 ripe figs
2tbsp raspberry vinegar

Season the pork tenderloin with plenty of salt and pepper. Heat the oil in a large wok or skillet until it is beginning to smoke. Add the pork and stir-fry quickly for 3 minutes. Add all the vegetables with the sage,

cover and cook over a steady heat for 6-8 minutes or until the vegetables are only just cooked.

Trim the tops from the figs and cut each one from top to bottom into 6 slices. Add the figs to the pan, stir in the vinegar, cover and cook for a further 3 minutes. Serve the pork with plain boiled rice.

SLICED CHICKEN BREAST WITH A LAVENDER SAUCE

The idea of using lavender as a fragrant herb first occurred to me a few years ago during a trip through central France, when I saw it featured on a restaurant menu. I have since used it successfully both in savory and sweet dishes (see recipe for Blueberry and Lavender Tartlets in July).

1½cups chicken bouillon
4 chicken breast halves, skinned
2tbsp butter
2 shallots, finely chopped
1 garlic clove, minced

2tsp chopped thyme
1tbsp cornstarch
2 fresh lavender flower sprigs
⅓cup heavy cream
salt and pepper

Bring the chicken bouillon to a gentle boil in a wide saucepan and simmer the chicken breasts for 6 minutes. Remove from the heat and let the chicken finish cooking in its own heat for a further 10-15 minutes.

Meanwhile, melt the butter in another saucepan, add the shallots, garlic and thyme and soften over a gentle heat without letting them color. Stir in the cornstarch with a wooden spoon and remove from the heat. Add a little of the bouillon in which the chicken was cooked and stir until completely absorbed. Continue to add the bouillon until evenly mixed, then return to the heat and bring to a boil, stirring until thickened. Add the lavender flowers and simmer for 6-8 minutes. To finish the sauce, stir in the cream and season with salt and pepper.

When ready to serve: slice the chicken breasts diagonally and arrange on 4 plates. Remove the lavender sprigs and pour the sauce over the chicken. Serve with Basmati rice, zucchini and young carrots.

CRISPY DUCK BREAST WITH A PLUM SAUCE

uring August home-grown plums are beginning to ripen on the trees but are still too sharp for most tastes. I have used this sharpness to prepare a sauce that goes wonderfully with the sweetness of duck. Many supermarkets now sell prepackaged duck breasts which are ideal for pan-frying or barbecuing during the summer when it is too hot to turn the oven on. If you cannot obtain breasts only, a whole duck can be cut up and the legs frozen for another meal.

ingredients . . . .

four 6oz duck breast halves, boned
1tbsp salt
watercress sprigs, for garnish

Plum Sauce
3 shallots or 1 onion, chopped
2tbsp peanut oil
½lb sour plums, pitted and chopped

⅓cup blackberries (optional)
finely grated zest and juice of 1 orange
1tbsp Worcestershire sauce
3tbsp sugar
1tbsp cider or wine vinegar
salt and pepper

Pierce the skin of the duck breasts several times with a fork, sprinkle the skin with salt and leave in the refrigerator while the sauce is prepared. The salt will draw out some of the fattiness of the skin and will enable it to crisp properly during cooking.

To prepare the plum sauce: place the shallots or onion and the oil in a stainless steel or enamel saucepan and soften over a gentle heat without allowing them to color. Add the plums and the blackberries if used. Add the orange zest and juice, Worcestershire sauce and sugar. Cover and simmer for 15-20 minutes, until the fruit is quite soft, then stir in the vinegar and season with salt and pepper. Pour the contents of the saucepan into a blender and liquidize into a smooth sauce.

To cook the duck breasts: heat a non-stick skillet without any oil and cook the breasts over a fast heat for 5 minutes on each side until the skin becomes crispy. (It is a mistake to over-cook the duck breasts as they will become quite dry. Instead, aim for the meat to be slightly pink in the center. As with any fried, broiled or roasted meat, it must be allowed to stand to enable the juices to settle inside.)

To serve the duck: slice each breast into 6-8 strips and transfer to each serving plate. Garnish with a watercress sprig and serve with buttered turnips, peas and plain boiled potatoes. Transfer the sauce to a sauceboat and serve separately.

SPATCHCOCK QUAIL SCENTED WITH ENGLISH WINE

n recent years a number of English white wines of notable interest have appeared. The tendency is for these wines to be of a medium sweetness with a flowery bouquet, quite drinkable as an aperitif and useful in certain recipes. This wine blends interestingly with other flavorings in a marinade for spatchcocked quail. This recipe is also worth trying with squab, dove or woodcock.

ingredients . . . .

4 quail
2tsp cornstarch

Marinade
⅞cup English white wine
1 onion, sliced
1 garlic clove, minced

2 blades mace
finely grated zest and juice of 1 orange
2 lavender flower sprigs
¼cup peanut oil
salt and pepper

To prepare the quail for spatchcock cooking, remove the backbone of each bird by cutting either side with a pair of kitchen scissors. Open the quails out flat and secure with 2 metal or wooden skewers. Place the birds in a shallow dish and pour over the wine. Add the onion, garlic, mace, the orange zest and juice, lavender flowers and oil. Turn the quails in the marinade, season with plenty of salt and pepper, cover and leave to marinate overnight.

Broil the quails under a moderate heat for 15-20 minutes until evenly colored. Strain the marinade into a small saucepan and bring to the boil. Mix the cornstarch with 1tbsp cold water and stir into the marinade to thicken. (The sauce should be fairly thin.) Remove the skewers from the quails and serve with buttered new potatoes, green beans and baby carrots, with the sauce handed separately.

ROAST GROUSE WITH ALL THE TRIMMINGS

*T*he 12th of August sees the beginning of the grouse season and in recent years it has become somewhat fashionable, not to say plain silly, to be among the first to feast on the grouse. Fancy restaurants all over England make it their business to place the bird on their menus to meet the requirements of those who do not know any better. The truth is that young grouse need to hang for at least three days for their flavor to develop. So if you are looking for the true qualities of grouse, it is as well to wait a while.

ingredients . . . .

4 grouse, barded with bacon, livers reserved
salt and pepper
6tbsp unsalted butter
4 lovage or thyme sprigs
1cup raspberries

Gravy
2tbsp Cognac
⅔cup game or chicken bouillon
1tsp raspberry vinegar

Garnish
1tbsp Cognac
3tbsp heavy cream
salt and pepper
4 pieces toast
1½cups fresh brown breadcrumbs
1 bunch of watercress

Preheat the oven to 425°F.

Season the grouse inside and out with plenty of salt and pepper. Place a piece of butter the size of your thumb inside each bird followed by the lovage or thyme sprigs and raspberries.

Place the remaining butter in a roasting pan and add the grouse. Roast near the top of the oven for 15 minutes, turning the birds once during this time, until cooked but still slightly pink inside. Transfer to a plate, cover and keep warm. Allow the cooking juices to settle in the roasting pan and spoon the fat into a small skillet.

To prepare the liver croûtons: fry the grouse livers in the fat until they are pink, then transfer to a small bowl. Mash the livers with a fork, add the Cognac and cream and season with salt and pepper. Spread the mixture onto the toast, cut into triangles and keep warm. Fry the bread crumbs in the remaining fat until golden and keep warm.

To prepare the gravy: heat the sediment in the roasting pan on top of the stove until sizzling, add the Cognac and stir to loosen. Stand well clear as there may be a few flames to contend with. When the flames have died down, add the bouillon and vinegar. Bring to a boil and season to taste with salt and pepper.

Serve the grouse garnished with watercress, the liver croûtons and the bread crumbs to soak up the juices. Hand the gravy separately.

SLICED CALVES' LIVER WITH CAPERS AND CREAM

*C*alves' liver is considered by most people to be the finest type of liver. Here is a favorite recipe of mine in which capers and cream are used to a make a sauce along with the cooking juices.

ingredients . . . .

1lb calves' liver, thinly sliced
flour for dusting
salt and pepper
2tbsp butter

1 small onion, finely chopped
⅔cup heavy cream
3tbsp capers
½lb ripe tomatoes
1tsp wine vinegar

Season the calves' liver on both sides with salt and pepper and dust with flour. Heat the butter in a skillet until is It just beginning to turn brown. Cook the liver over a fast heat until the blood begins to appear on the surface, then turn and cook for a further 1 minute. Transfer the liver to a plate to keep warm. Calves' liver is very tender and will spoil if over-cooked.

To prepare the sauce: soften the onion in the remaining cooking juices in the pan without letting it color. Remove the pan from the heat and stir in the cream and capers. Score the tomatoes with a sharp knife and pour boiling water over them to loosen their skins. Plunge into cold water, remove the skins, cut in half and de-seed. Dice the tomato flesh neatly.

When you are ready to serve the liver, bring the cream mixture to the boil and simmer very gently to thicken. (The cream will not curdle if it is really fresh.) Stir in the tomatoes and sharpen with a little vinegar. Return the liver to the sauce and serve with broad (fava) beans and bacon, carrots and parsley potatoes.

A STRING OF BEAN RECIPES

 $\mathcal{A}$ ugust is the month when beans are in their element. If you grow them yourself, you will know what I am talking about, but the problem for most people is not growing them so much as knowing what to do with so many of them. If your freezer is full and your friends have taken as many as they can politely say yes to, here are a few recipe ideas to help you put them to good use.

BROAD BEANS AND BACON

ingredients . . . .

2lb broad (fava) beans in their
  pods
1 onion, roughly chopped
2tbsp peanut oil
¼lb Canadian bacon, cut into
  strips

2tsp cornstarch
⅔cup milk
salt and pepper

Bring a saucepan of water to a boil with a large pinch of salt. Shell the beans and cook for 10-12 minutes. When they are cooked, cool them under cold running water and remove their skins if necessary by pinch-ing them between your thumb and forefinger. This will not be necessary for young, tender beans, but is always advisable for older, tough ones.

Soften the chopped onion in the oil, add the bacon and cook until lightly browned. Remove the pan from the heat and stir in the cornstarch with a wooden spoon. With the pan still away from the heat, stir in the milk until absorbed. Season with plenty of salt and pepper, add the beans and simmer to thicken.

SLICED GREEN BEANS WITH BUTTER AND BLACK PEPPER

 $\mathcal{D}$ oes a recipe have to be a fancy one to appear in a cook book? All too often the answer is yes, and favorites, which are often the simplest, get left out. If your beans are really fresh and your appetite is keen, what more delicious way to enjoy green beans than to sit down in front of a plateful and eat them as they are, with plenty of butter and freshly ground black pepper. If the beans are cooked properly, they will squeak between the teeth.

ingredients . . . .

1½lb Italian green beans
salt and pepper

4tbsp butter

To prepare the beans, run a vegetable peeler down each side of each bean to remove the strings. There are also several gadgets on the market for slicing beans: the simplest is a set of fine blades set into a plastic holder, known in my family as a push me-pull you. The beans are pushed through one end and pulled out the other.

To cook the beans, fill a large saucepan with water, add a large pinch of salt and bring to a boil. The idea of cooking green vegetables is to do so as briefly as possible, so the quicker the water comes back to a boil after the beans have gone in the water the more flavor they will have. As a rule green beans will take between 6-8 minutes to cook depending on their age.

As soon as the beans are cooked, drain them well, stir in the butter and season well with freshly ground black pepper.

Freshwater Crayfish in a Nest of Zucchini; Sliced Chicken Breast with a Lavender Sauce;
Upside-down Summer Fruit Cake.

BUTTERED GREEN BEANS WITH YOUNG PARSNIPS

*D*espite the feeling that this is the height of summer, young parsnips are already beginning to appear on the market to start the winter season. If you find the flavor of mature parsnips too strong, try them when they are young and sweet cut into strips and served with green beans.

ingredients......................................

½lb green beans
½lb young parsnips

salt
2tbsp butter

Trim the ends off the beans and pull off any strings. Peel the parsnips and cut them into neat strips no thicker than the beans. Place the parsnips in a saucepan, cover with cold water, add a pinch of salt, bring to a boil and cook for 15 minutes.

Meanwhile, bring a larger saucepan of water to a boil and cook the beans for 8 minutes. When both vegetables are cooked, toss them together in the butter and serve.

GREEN BEANS WITH TOASTED ALMONDS

ingredients......................................

¾lb thin green beans
2tbsp unsalted butter

salt
½cup sliced almonds

Trim the beans and cook for 6-8 minutes in plenty of salted boiling water. Meanwhile, melt the butter in a non-stick skillet, add the almonds and brown over a steady heat. When the beans are cooked, drain them and toss with the butter and almonds.

A BUMPER CROP OF TOMATOES

*G*ardeners who grow their own tomatoes are often at a loss for ideas when a bumper crop occurs. If, like many people, you are the not-so-proud owner of row upon row of green tomatoes that refuse to ripen, may I suggest a delicious chutney blended with slices of apple and a few lively spices. Red tomatoes have a sweeter flavor and are best married with the sharpness of vinegar and made into a sauce or relish.

TOMATO RELISH

ingredients......................................

3lb ripe tomatoes
4 onions, finely chopped
2 celery stalks, finely chopped
2 carrots, finely chopped
2tbsp salt
2tbsp flour

1tsp English mustard powder
½tsp mild curry powder
2½cups white malt vinegar
1cup sugar

Boil a large saucepan of water and blanch the tomatoes for 30 seconds to loosen their skins. Cool under running water, remove the skins and roughly chop the tomatoes. Place them in a large bowl with the onions, celery and carrots. Sprinkle over the salt, cover with a clean dish towel and leave for 24 hours. Meanwhile, mix the flour, mustard and curry powder together with ⅔cup of the vinegar, to form a paste. Leave this preparation in the refrigerator until the tomatoes are ready.

To finish the relish: place the vegetables in a colander to drain (the salt will have drawn out some of the bitterness in the vegetables into the juices). Place the vegetables in a large non-aluminum saucepan, add the remaining vinegar and the sugar and boil for 10 minutes, stirring occasionally. Lastly, stir in the spicy paste and simmer for 3-4 minutes to thicken. Pour the relish into four 1lb hot clean jars and seal immediately. It will keep for 3-4 months.

Makes about 4lb

GREEN TOMATO CHUTNEY

ingredients . . . .

3lb green tomatoes	8 allspice berries
4 onions, finely chopped	3 cloves
1½cups large raisins, chopped	3 blades mace
1lb tart green apples	1tsp celery seeds
2tbsp salt	12 black peppercorns, lightly
1⅓cups sugar	crushed
3¾cups malt vinegar	2 fresh red chili peppers,
2inch cinnamon stick	chopped (optional)

Wash and chop the tomatoes and place them in a large preserving kettle (aluminum is not suitable). Add the onions, three-quarters cover with water and bring to a boil, then simmer for 8 minutes. Drain in a colander, then return to the pan with the raisins, apples, salt, sugar and vinegar. Add the spices, with the chilis if you like a hot chutney. Bring to a boil and boil, stirring continually, for 1½-2 hours, until the chutney has thickened. Pour the chutney into three 2lb jars and seal immediately. Label and store for 3-4 months before opening.

Makes about 6lb

TOMATO SAUCE

ingredients . . . .

6lb ripe tomatoes	1tbsp chopped tarragon
⅞cup white malt vinegar	2 pinches cayenne
2inch cinnamon stick	1tbsp salt
1tsp allspice berries	¾cup sugar
3 blades mace	

Roughly chop the tomatoes, place them in a large non-aluminum saucepan, cover and cook over a gentle heat until pulpy. Place the vinegar in another saucepan and add all the remaining ingredients. Bring to a boil and stir until the sugar has dissolved. Cover the pan and reduce for 2-3 minutes.

Meanwhile, rub the tomato pulp through a fine sift. Return to the saucepan and strain the vinegar over the tomatoes. Bring to a boil and simmer for 15-20 minutes until the sauce is beginning to thicken.

Place the bottles in a kettle deep enough to reach their necks. Half fill the bottles with sauce, add boiling water to the pan to a level just above the sauce and keep the water simmering for 30 minutes. Seal and label. Keeps for 3-4 months.

Makes about 2½pints

Puddings

UPSIDE-DOWN SUMMER FRUIT CAKE

*L*ate one Saturday afternoon last summer I returned home from the market with the makings of a supper party. I had decided on the starter and the main course, but as far as the pudding was concerned, both time and ideas were running out fast. Out of the blue came this idea that I had been meaning to try out for ages.

ingredients...................

1cup raspberries	Sponge cake
1cup strawberries, hulled	3 eggs, at room temperature
1cup blackberries	1/3cup sugar
1cup blueberries	1/4cup flour
1cup red currants, stringed	6tbsp ground almonds
1/4cup sugar	

Place all the fruits and the sugar in a non-aluminum saucepan. Bring to a boil, stirring, until the juices run, then simmer for 3-4 minutes. Turn the contents of the saucepan into an 8inch soufflé dish.

To prepare the topping, first preheat the oven to 375°F. Crack the eggs into a mixing bowl, add the sugar and beat for 8-10 minutes until they are thick. Sift the flour and almonds over the mixture and with a large spoon or rubber spatula, fold in evenly. Spread the batter over the soft fruit and bake in the center of the oven for 35 minutes or until the top is springy to the touch.

Allow to cool for 5-10 minutes, then invert onto a serving dish. Serve warm or cold with vanilla ice cream or softly whipped cream.

AN ENGLISH SUMMER PUDDING

*E*nglish summer pudding is seen by many people as the culinary highlight of the English summer. However little the sun has shone down on our berry fruits, somehow they ripen in time to make this delicious pudding. Vary the fruits as you wish: the total weight should be 1½lb.

ingredients...................

8-10 thin slices of white bread, crusts removed	1cup strawberries, hulled
1/4cup sugar	1cup raspberries
1cup black cherries, pitted	1cup blackberries
1cup black currants, stringed	2tsp unflavored gelatin
1cup red currants, stringed	extra soft fruits, to decorate

Line the bottom and sides of a 5-cup pudding basin or slant-sided mold with the slices of bread so that they overlap each other, reserving 2 slices for the lid. Make sure there are no cracks. Bring 7/8cup water to a boil in a non-aluminum saucepan, add the sugar and simmer until dissolved. Simmer the cherries in the syrup for 8 minutes, then lift them out with a slotted spoon into a nylon strainer set over a bowl and let drain.

Place the black currants, red currants, strawberries, raspberries and blackberries in the syrup and simmer for 3 minutes, then spoon the fruit into the strainer. Combine the fruits evenly and fill the lined pudding basin to the top. Return the juices that have collected in the bowl to the saucepan. Place the gelatin in a small cup or bowl and soften with 2tbsp cold water. Stir the gelatin into the warm fruit juices to dissolve. Do not boil the gelatin or it will become stringy and lose its setting quality. Pour one-third of the juices over the pudding; save the remainder for a sauce. Cover the top with the remaining bread slices and secure with a saucer. Weight down the saucer with a heavy can and leave the pudding in the refrigerator overnight to become firm. The small amount of gelatin included is not intended to set the pudding firmly, rather just to hold its shape.

To serve the summer pudding, invert a serving dish over the basin

AUGUST *Puddings*

and turn the dish and basin the right way up. Give the basin a shake from side to side and unmold. Moisten the pudding with a little of the sauce, decorate with a variety of whole berry fruits and serve with softly whipped cream or yogurt.

RED CURRANT AND PASSION FRUIT BOMBE

 very summer new ideas come to mind for mouthwatering fruit desserts. This combination of the very English taste of red currants with the more exotic flavor of passion fruit is most unusual.

ingredients...................

2tbsp unsalted butter, softened
3 passion fruits
1½cups red currants, stringed
5 eggs, at room temperature, separated
⅓cup sugar

Sauce
1¼cups milk
1tbsp cornstarch
2tbsp sugar

Lightly grease a 8inch soufflé dish or large casserole with the butter. Scoop the flesh and seeds out of the passion fruits. Preheat the oven to 375°F.

Place the egg whites in a large mixing bowl and the yolks in a smaller bowl. Add 2tbsp of the sugar to the egg whites and beat until stiff. Add the remaining sugar 2tbsp at a time and beat until light and smooth. Fold in the passion fruit and red currants and turn into the prepared dish. Stand the dish in a roasting pan and pour in boiling water to come about 2inches up the sides of the dish. Bake in the center of the oven for 25 minutes.

Meanwhile, make the sauce: bring the milk to a boil in a heavy saucepan. Mix the cornstarch with 2tbsp cold water. Stir the cornstarch into the egg yolks until evenly blended. Pour the boiling milk over and stir with a wooden spoon. Return the custard to the saucepan and bring to a boil, stirring, to thicken: the sauce is not intended to be thicker than light cream. Strain the sauce through a fine sift back into the bowl. Stir in the sugar and leave to cool.

When the bombe is cooked, let it cool for a few minutes, then unmold it onto a pretty serving dish. Serve with the custard sauce.

ETON MESS

ingredients...................

1pint mixed soft berry fruits: raspberries, strawberries, blackberries, black currants, loganberries, etc.

3tbsp medium sherry
1¼cups heavy cream
¼cup confectioners' sugar

Wash and prepare the fruits, removing stems and stalks where necessary. (If you are using black currants and they are particularly sharp, cook them with 2tbsp of sugar until their juices run.)

Place the fruits in a bowl with the sherry and mash them with a fork. Whip the cream softly with the sugar, stir in the mashed fruits and turn into bowls or pretty glasses. Chill well and serve with lady-fingers.

GOOSEBERRY AND ELDERFLOWER HUFF

ingredients...................

1pint sweet gooseberries, trimmed
½cup ripe elderberries
finely grated zest and juice of 1 orange

6tbsp sugar
3 eggs, at room temperature
1¼cups heavy cream

Place the gooseberries and elderberries in a non-aluminum saucepan and add the orange zest and juice. Add 2tbsp of the sugar, cover and soften the berries over a gentle heat for 6-8 minutes. Spread the mixture out on a shallow dish or pan to cool.

Meanwhile, separate the eggs into 2 bowls. Pour the cream into the yolks and whip lightly. Add 1tbsp of the remaining sugar to the egg whites and beat in, then add the remaining sugar a little at a time, continuing to beat, until the mixture forms soft peaks.

When the fruit mixture has cooled, stir it into the cream with a large metal spoon. Fold in the beaten egg whites, turn into 4 pretty glasses and chill before serving, accompanied by lady-fingers.

PEACHES AND RASPBERRIES IN A FLUFFY EGG CUSTARD

In this recipe, the custard is lightened with egg white and the usual quantity of sugar has been reduced, to help make the most of the true flavor of the fruit.

ingredients.................

3 large peaches
1½pints raspberries
2tbsp confectioners' sugar,
  sifted
1¼cups milk

¼cup flour
4 eggs, at room temperature,
  separated
⅓cup superfine sugar

Slice half the peaches into a 1-quart glass serving bowl. Save the remainder for decoration. Divide the raspberries into 3 batches. Scatter one batch over the peaches and save the second for decoration. Purée the remaining raspberries in a blender, stir in the confectioners' sugar and mix with the fruit in the bowl.

To prepare the custard: measure 3tbsp of the milk into a mixing bowl and bring the remainder to a boil in a large saucepan. Mix the flour into the milk in the bowl, add the egg yolks and stir until evenly blended. When the milk has boiled, pour it over the egg yolk mixture and stir until evenly blended. Return the mixture to the saucepan and stir to thicken. Beat the egg whites to a soft snow, adding the superfine sugar a little at a time, and fold them into the hot custard.

Turn the custard into the bowl with the peaches and raspberries and leave to cool. Decorate the top with the remaining peach slices and raspberries. Chill before serving.

RASPBERRY EXTRAVAGANZA

One day of rain and two of sunshine is all that is needed to bring the English raspberry season to a head. Suddenly farmers cannot pick them fast enough and they are sold off at silly prices. If you are lucky enough to have a glut of raspberries, take them home with you and get busy making jams, jellies, sauces and sorbets.

FRESH RASPBERRY SAUCE

Fresh raspberry sauce is perhaps the easiest way to deal with an excess of raspberries. Serve it poured over ice cream, crêpes and pastries. It freezes well.

ingredients.................

4pints fresh raspberries   ½cup sugar

Pick the raspberries over and remove any leaves or stems. Place the berries in a stainless steel or enamel saucepan with the sugar. Stir over a gentle heat until the juice begin to run, cover and simmer for 3-4 minutes. Allow the sauce to cool, then rub through a fine nylon sift.

RASPBERRY SORBET

Fresh fruit sorbet is deliciously refreshing on a hot summer's day. Homemade sorbets need not contain the enormous quantities of sugar found in many commercial varieties. This recipe relies largely on the natural sweetness of the fruit and requires little extra sugar for freezing.

ingredients.................

4pints fresh raspberries   ½cup sugar

Place the raspberries in a non-aluminum saucepan with the sugar and stir over a low heat until the juice begin to run. Bring the raspberries to a boil and simmer for 3-4 minutes. Pour the contents of the saucepan into a shallow dish or pan and leave to cool.

Purée the cooled raspberries in a liquidizer or food processor and pass through a nylon sift to remove the seeds. Freeze the raspberry purée in a metal bowl for 30 minutes. When the mixture is just beginning to freeze around the edges, beat the larger ice crystals until smooth. Return to the freezer for about 1½-2 hours, beating every 30 minutes, until firm. Store in a sealed plastic container until ready to use.

JELLIED RASPBERRY SHAPES

ingredients . . . .

3pints fresh raspberries
½cup sugar

2 envelopes unflavored gelatin
sugar for dusting

Place the raspberries in a non-aluminum saucepan with the sugar, and stir over a gentle heat until the juices begin to run. Bring to a boil, then simmer for 3-4 minutes. Pour the raspberries into a dish or pan and leave to cool, then blend into a purée in a liquidizer or food processor. Pass the purée through a nylon sift to remove the seeds.

Place the gelatin in a small heatproof bowl, add 2tbsp cold water and stand the cup in a saucepan containing enough boiling water to come halfway up the cup. Stir the gelatin until completely dissolved.

Add 3-4tbsp of the raspberry purée to the liquid gelatin and stir evenly. Stir the contents of the bowl into the purée and pour into a 6inch square shallow pan. Chill in the refrigerator for 1½-2 hours until set.

Dip the pan briefly in hot water, then unmold onto a chopping board sprinkled with extra sugar. Cut the jelly into even shapes – squares, diamonds, triangles and circles – chill until required, and roll in sugar again.

RASPBERRY JAM

ingredients . . . .

3½quarts raspberries
2pints red currants

1 lemon
10cups sugar

Pick the raspberries over, removing any leaves or stems. Place the raspberries and red currants in a large preserving kettle (the fruit must not reach more than halfway up the sides of the pan). Remove the zest from the lemon with a vegetable peeler and squeeze the juice into the kettle. Tie the zest and pith in a piece of cheesecloth and bury in the fruit.

Bring the fruit to a boil and allow the juices to run. Continue to boil until the juices have reduced by one-quarter.

Meanwhile, heat the sugar in a moderate oven (350°F) for 10-15 minutes. At the same time wash and prepare your jam jars and place in the oven to warm.

When the fruit has reduced by one-quarter, remove the cheesecloth bag containing the lemon and stir in the warm sugar. Bring the jam back to a boil and simmer for about 25 minutes until jell point is reached. To test, chill a small white plate in the refrigerator, then spoon a little of the jam onto it. Cool, then push your fingernail across the plate and into the jam. If the surface wrinkles, the jam has reached jell point and is ready for packing into jars. If you have a candy thermometer, it is as well to double-check the set. it should read 220°F.

Line the jars up on a kitchen pan and fill each one to the top. This is best done by two people, one filling the jars and the other sealing while the jars are still hot. There are a number of cellophane products on the market especially made for sealing preserves. Allow to cool, then label. Homemade raspberry jam will keep almost indefinitely, although it is advisable to consume it within a year.

Makes about 6lbs

September

September is a month both of endings and new beginnings as summer fades into autumn. Before the month is out, summer will have packed its bags and left us with a definite chill in the air. The nights will begin to draw in although the days are often clear, bright and sunny. The vegetable garden is looking well-worn after a busy summer as many crops will be coming to an end. Harvest time is celebrated during late summer when families give thanks at beautifully decorated church services.

Fruit trees are groaning during September with the sheer weight of apples, pears and plums such as greengages and damsons, all of which are at their best and juiciest both for eating and preserving. The hedgerows are bursting with wild blackberries, full of flavor and waiting for anyone who is prepared to brave their briers. Cultivated varieties are available in the shops but they tend to lack the flavor necessary for a proper blackberry and apple crumble. English strawberries are in for their second season toward the end of the month and there may still be a few raspberries to be had. Peaches are at their cheapest and are worth turning into a pickle to serve with roast pork or ham.

Fresh figs are also available at reasonable prices. Kentish cobs and filberts will appear during September, reminding us that autumn is just around the corner.

Fruit vegetables come into their own during September. These include squashes, eggplant, sweet peppers, cucumbers and tomatoes, all of which combine well together and are full of flavor at this time of year. Young root vegetables – parsnips, rutabaga, turnips, carrots and celeriac – are starting their winter season young and sweet. Winter cabbages are just starting as are Brussels sprouts, although these are not at their best until the first frost.

Cauliflowers and broccoli are still plentiful, and the English onion season will start toward the end of the month, bringing in a good supply of onions, garlic and leeks.

Lovers of shellfish have been waiting since April for that all important R to appear again in the month when oysters, mussels and scallops arrive back in season. The flat fish season is still with us and will be for as long as the weather holds. Mackerel and herring tend to put on weight during September in readiness for winter and are often good value. Crabs and lobsters are still reasonably priced as are squid.

Wild duck and partridge start their season from 1 September joining a host of feathered game for the autumn and winter: look out for guinea fowl, quail, grouse, snipe and pigeon. Most game dealers will pluck and draw them ready for the oven, and these birds are also becoming increasingly available ready-dressed from supermarkets.

SEPTEMBER INGREDIENTS IN SEASON

FRUIT & NUTS

British at their best:
Apples
Blackberries
Black Currants
Blueberries
Cooking Apples
Crab Apples
Damsons
Elderberries
Figs
Greengages
Hazelnuts (Filberts)
Loganberries
Pears
Plums
Quinces
Raspberries
Rose Hips
Strawberries
Tayberries

Also available:
Cherries
Red Currants
Walnuts

Imported in season:
Almonds
Apricots
Bananas
Chestnuts
Cranberries
Dates
Grapefruit
Grapes
Kiwi Fruit
Lemons, Limes
Mangoes
Melons
Nectarines
Oranges
Papaya

Passion Fruit
Peaches
Peanuts, Pecans
Pineapples
Pistachio Nuts
Pomegranates
Watermelons

VEGETABLES & HERBS

British at their best:
Aubergines (Eggplant)
Basil, Beets
Carrots
Cauliflowers
Cherry Tomatoes
Chervil
Chicory (Belgian Endive)
Chives
Corn
Courgettes (Zucchini)
Cucumbers
Dill, Fennel
French (Green) Beans
Garlic
Globe Artichokes
Horseradish
Lavender
Leeks, Lettuce

Mange tout (Snow Peas)
Marjoram
Marrows and other
  Large Summer Squashes
Mint
Mustard and Cress
Nasturtiums and leaves
Onions, Parsley
Parsnips
Peas
Pickling Cucumbers
Pickling (Pearl) Onions
Potatoes, Pumpkins
Radishes
Rosemary
Runner (Italian Green) Beans
Sage, Samphire
Savory, Shallots
Sorrel
Spring Onions (Scallions)
Swedes (Rutabaga)
Tarragon, Thyme
Tomatoes
Watercress
Winter Squashes

Also available:
Broad (Fava) Beans
Broccoli
Brussels Sprouts

Cabbages
Celeriac, Celery
Turnips

Imported in season:
Aubergines (Eggplant)
Avocados

FISH & SHELLFISH

British at their best:
Brill
Cockles, Coley (Pollock)
Conger Eel
Crabs
Dabs, Dover Sole
Freshwater Crayfish
Haddock
Hake, Halibut
Herring
John Dory
Lemon Sole, Lobsters
Mackerel, Monkfish
Mussels
Oysters
Plaice, Prawns
Red Mullet
Salmon
Scallops
Scampi (Langoustines)

Sea Trout
Shrimp
Squid
Torbay Sole
Trout, Turbot
Whitebait
Whiting, Winkles

Also available:
Cod, Gray Mullet
Huss
Skate, Sprats

Imported in season:
John Dory
Red Mullet
Sardines, Squid

POULTRY & GAME

British at their best:
Grouse
Guinea Fowl
Hare
Partridge
Pigeon, Quail
Rabbit
Snipe

Also available:
Chicken, Duck
Goose, Turkey
Venison
Wild Duck

MEAT

Beef
Lamb
Offal
Pork
Veal

Starters

FIFTEEN MINUTE CHICKEN AND PARSLEY SOUP

*A*nton Mosimann, at the Dorchester Hotel in London, introduced me to one or two dishes that he was working on, stressing how much he relied on the freshness of basic ingredients. His advice was to keep ingredients simple and to let their flavors speak for themselves.

ingredients......................

cups homemade chicken
  bouillon
1 skinned, boned chicken breast
  half
²⁄₃cup heavy cream
1 handful parsley, finely chopped
juice of ½ lemon (optional)

Garlic croûtons
2tbsp unsalted butter
1 garlic clove, minced
2 slices of white bread, crusts
  removed and cut into cubes

Bring the chicken bouillon to a boil. Cut the chicken breasts into even-sized pieces and simmer them in the bouillon for 3 minutes. Pour the contents of the saucepan into a liquidizer, add the cream and the parsley and blend until smooth.   Return the soup to the saucepan and season to taste with salt and pepper. Sharpen the soup to taste with lemon juice.

To prepare the garlic croûtons: melt the butter in a skillet, add the garlic and cubes of bread and toss until golden. Sprinkle the croûtons over the soup and serve as soon as possible.

A SALAD OF SMOKED EEL WITH CRISP PEARS

*S*moked eel makes a delicious starter or light main course combined in a salad with slightly tart pears, served in a dressing based on mayonnaise with lemon juice and fresh herbs.

ingredients......................

¾lb smoked eel
1 head leaf lettuce
1 head Bibb lettuce
2oz (1-1½cups) field lettuce
  (mâche)
2 comice pears
juice of ½ lemon
3tbsp olive oil

Dressing
6tbsp mayonnaise
juice of ½ lemon
1tbsp chopped parsley
2tsp chopped thyme
2tsp chopped tarragon
freshly ground white pepper

To prepare the eel, remove the dark skin in one piece and cut the body into 3inch lengths. On each length of eel you will find 4 fillets of meat. To remove these, ease them away from the central bone with a small knife. Set aside.

Place all the salad leaves in a bowl of ice water. Cut the pears in half down the middle, remove the core and slice each half into 5-6 wedges. Place the wedges in a bowl and sprinkle with lemon juice to keep them white.

To prepare the dressing: place the mayonnaise in a bowl and stir in the lemon juice. Stir all the herbs into the mayonnaise with two or three grindings of white pepper.

Just before you are ready to serve: dry the salad leaves thoroughly and toss them with the olive oil. Arrange the leaves on 4 plates, place the fillets of smoked eel in the center with the pears and serve the dressing separately in a sauce-boat. Accompany with brown bread and butter.

OYSTERS ON THE HALF SHELL WITH BLACK PEPPER AND LEMON

I can still remember eating my first oyster at the age of fifteen. It felt like swallowing a mouthful of sea water! For a moment I felt as if I was beneath the waves. Since then I have had plenty of practice and enjoy oysters all the more for it. Some of our finest oysters are situated around Colchester and Whitstable in the south-east of England. Plentiful supplies are also taken from the river Helford in Cornwall. To get the best flavor from oysters, they must first be chilled on ice and opened carefully so as to retain their natural juices. Allow between 6-12 oysters per person depending on the occasion. When you buy oysters, remember to ask your fishmonger for some of the seaweed in which they are often packed. To open the oysters, wrap each one in a folded dish towel and hold it firmly on a work surface with the flatter of the two shells uppermost. Using a special oyster knife, slide the blade firmly into the hinge and twist. Discard the flat shell, retaining the oyster and its juices in the curved under shell.

Arrange the seaweed on serving plates with crushed ice, add the oysters and serve with lemon wedges and a pepper mill.

A SALAD OF BACON, LETTUCE AND TOMATO

I have childhood memories of the most enormous toasted sandwiches filled higher than my mouth would open. My favorite filling was mayonnaise, crispy bacon, lettuce and tomato, but the ingredients are decidedly easier to eat if they are served as a salad. This dish is good as a starter, or for a light lunch.

ingredients . . . .

1 crisp head lettuce
½lb Canadian bacon
3tbsp vegetable oil
3 slices of white bread, cut into
 short fingers
⅓cup mayonnaise

juice of ½ lemon
salt
freshly ground black pepper
¾lb ripe tomatoes, cut into
 wedges

Trim the base from the lettuce, and immerse it in a bowl of cold water. Cut the bacon into broad strips, not too small or it will be lost among the lettuce. Heat 1tbsp the oil in a skillet and crisp the bacon evenly. Remove the bacon from the pan and keep it warm on a plate. Heat the remaining oil in the skillet and toss the bread fingers until they are golden.

Measure the mayonnaise into a bowl, stir in the lemon juice and season to taste with salt and pepper.

When you are ready to serve the salad, dry the lettuce leaves thoroughly and place them in a salad bowl with the bacon and the tomato wedges. Spoon the dressing over the top and toss evenly. Distribute the salad among 4 plates and scatter the crisp bread fingers over the top.

FRESH TOMATO SALAD SCENTED WITH BASIL

W hen tomatoes are at their freshest and are full of flavor, the best way to prepare them is often the most simple. Slice them, dress them and serve them with a sprinkling of fresh basil. If you do not have basil, parsley or chives will also lift the flavor of the tomatoes, but don't use dried basil, which has no flavor at all.

ingredients . . . .

1lb fresh tomatoes
salt and pepper

1tbsp wine vinegar
2 basil sprigs, chopped

Dressing
¼cup olive oil

Slice the tomatoes as thinly as you can, using a serrated knife, and arrange them in an attractive dish. Season with salt and pepper and set aside.

To prepare the dressing: place the oil and vinegar in a jar and shake them together. Pour the dressing over the tomatoes, sprinkle with chopped basil and serve as a starter with buttered brown bread or as a side salad to accompany grilled fish or meat.

ICED MELON WITH WILD BLACKBERRIES

*T*here are still some delicious melons on the market during September. A ripe melon should have a delicate but assertive fragrance and the stalk end should yield to slight pressure when pressed with the thumbs.

Melon is best served cold and fresh as you would enjoy a good bottle of white wine. Cut the melon in half, spoon out the seeds and fill each cavity with ½-¾cup slightly tart wild blackberries. (Raspberries, blueberries, loganberries and tayberries are also delicious.) Chill well before serving.

LATE SUMMER FIGS WITH GOAT'S CHEESE

*I*n some gardens in the south of England you can find mature fig trees, and the chances are that during September it will be full of ripening fruit. I have prepared them here as an unusual starter sitting in a nest of shredded buckwheat crêpes with just a taste of goat's cheese – preferably English – which I find has a more delicate flavor than many of the French varieties.

ingredients ....

4 ripe figs, peeled
¼lb mild goat's cheese
4 parsley sprigs, for garnish

salt and pepper
1tbsp chopped parsley
1tsp chopped thyme

Crêpe batter
2tbsp buckwheat flour
2tbsp all-purpose flour
½cup milk
1 egg

Dressing
2tbsp walnut or olive oil
2tsp raspberry or white wine
      vinegar

To prepare the crêpe batter: sift the buckwheat and all-purpose flours into a mixing bowl. Add half the milk and stir to a firm, lump-free batter.

Gradually add the remaining milk and stir until smooth. Add the egg, seasoning, parsley and thyme and leave to stand for 10-15 minutes. Meanwhile, place the oil and vinegar in a screwtop jar and shake together.

To make the crêpes: heat a small non-stick crêpe pan over a gentle heat and spoon enough batter into the pan to coat the bottom as thinly as you can. Cook the crêpe for 15-20 seconds, then turn it over and brown on the other side. Turn the crêpes onto a clean dish towel and leave to cool. To shred the crêpes, roll each one into a sausage and slice crosswise into ribbons.

Toss the shredded crêpes in the dressing and arrange in the center of 4 plates. Cut a cross in the top of each fig and ease them apart into star shapes. Place the figs in their nests of crêpe ribbons and flake the goat's cheese over the top. Decorate with parsley sprigs.

If you are planning ahead, the crêpes and the dressing can be prepared well ahead of time.

147

Main Courses

MUSSELS WITH WHITE WINE AND PARSLEY

One of the pleasures of September is the arrival of the long-awaited mussel season. As they appear in great bags on the fish stalls, I am always reminded that absence really does make the heart grow fonder. Smaller varieties of mussels have the most delicate flavor.

ingredients

4lb mussels, scrubbed
⅓cup dry white wine
1 onion, chopped
2 garlic cloves, bruised

2 parsley stems
pepper
chopped parsley, for garnish

Pick over the mussels and discard any that may be open. Place the wine in a large non-aluminum saucepan. Add the onion, garlic, parsley stems and 5 grindings of freshly ground black pepper. Add the mussels, cover and cook over a fast heat for 5-6 minutes or until all of them have opened. Discard any that remain closed.

Divide the mussels among 4 bowls and ladle the juices over the top. Sprinkle with parsley and serve with hot crispy bread. It is a good idea to place a large bowl in the middle of the table for the empty shells.

SQUID WITH TOMATOES AND FRESH HERBS

We English tend to associate squid with sun-drenched vacations in faraway places, where admirers of these spineless creatures can't seem to get enough of them. Many of us have developed a passion for squid and cannot wait until our next visit to Spain, Portugal or Greece. But, in fact, squid are also netted in English waters. Why then don't we enjoy them more in our own country? Cleaning them could be the problem, but ask your fishmonger nicely and he will often do this for you, leaving you with little white pouches which can be stuffed or cut into rings. Squid must either be cooked very quickly – deep-fried for instance – or very slowly: anything in between and they will become rubbery. In this recipe I have stuffed them with ripe tomatoes and herbs ready for slow cooking in the oven.

ingredients

8 squid, about 5inches long, skinned and gutted
3tbsp olive oil
1 onion, chopped
2 garlic cloves, minced
1lb ripe tomatoes, skinned, deseeded and chopped
½cup dry white wine

1tsp oregano or marjoram
1 pinch cayenne
salt
1cup fresh white bread crumbs
⅓cup mayonnaise
1tbsp lemon juice
flat parsley or dill, for garnish

Wash the prepared squid and dry on paper towels. Preheat the oven to 375°F.

Heat the oil in a skillet, add the onion and garlic, cover and soften without letting them color. Add the tomatoes, wine, herbs and seasoning, cover and simmer for 6-8 minutes. Transfer one-third of the sauce to a shallow casserole into which the squid will fit in a single layer. Stir the bread crumbs into the remaining sauce, stuff the squid with the mixture and secure the opening with thread.

Arrange the squid in the casserole, cover and bake in the preheated oven for 25-30 minutes. To finish the sauce: transfer the squid to a plate and keep warm. Pour the sauce into a blender, add the mayonnaise and blend until smooth. Add the lemon juice and season to taste with salt and pepper. Warm the sauce through by simmering gently.

Slice 4 of the squid into sections. Serve the sliced and whole squid with crusty bread as a starter or with Basmati rice as a main course.

NORTH SEA HERRING WITH MUSTARD AND OATMEAL

T his recipe is one of my favorite midweek ideas. Ask your fishmonger to fillet the herrings for you and most of the preparation will be out of the way before you begin.

ingredients . . . .

4 herrings, filleted
salt and pepper
3tbsp spicy brown mustard
1tsp rubbed sage
1cup rolled oats, coarsely
  ground in a food processor

4tbsp bacon fat or butter

Garnish
lemon wedges
parsley sprigs

Season the fillets with salt and pepper, spread both sides with mustard and sprinkle with the sage. Spread the oatmeal out on a plate and coat the herring fillets, pressing it on firmly with the fingers to secure.

Heat the fat or butter in a large skillet and cook the herring fillets for 4 minutes on each side, until crisp and golden. Transfer to a warm serving dish and serve with wedges of lemon and parsley. Mashed rutabaga with butter and freshly ground black pepper are well suited to this dish.

ROLLED FILLETS OF SOLE ON A BED OF CREAMY LEEKS

N ew-season leeks are full of flavor at the moment and combine beautifully with button mushrooms to make this delicious midweek fish dish. If you are keeping to a family budget, fillets of a less expensive flatfish can be used instead of sole.

ingredients . . . .

4 sole or other flatfish, filleted
  and skinned
salt and pepper
2 parsley stems
1 bay leaf
1cup milk
½lb new potatoes, peeled and
  chopped
4tbsp butter
¾lb leeks, halved, washed and
  shredded

¼cup heavy cream
4 parsley sprigs

Stuffing
2tbsp butter
1 onion, finely chopped
¼lb button mushrooms,
  chopped
3tbsp dry white wine
2tbsp heavy cream

Season the fish fillets with salt and pepper and set aside. To make the stuffing: melt the butter in a non-aluminum saucepan and soften the onion over a gentle heat without letting it color. Add the mushrooms and wine, simmer and allow the moisture to evaporate, then stir in the cream and season to taste.

Lay the fish fillets on a work surface skinned side up. Spoon a little of the mushroom filling onto each fillet, roll up and secure with a wooden toothpick. Arrange the rolls in a shallow saucepan and add the parsley stems and bay leaf. Pour in the milk and simmer over the lowest possible heat for 12 minutes. Transfer the fish rolls to a plate, cover and keep warm.

Discard the parsley stems and the bay leaf from the pan, add the chopped potatoes and simmer for 12-15 minutes or until the potatoes are very soft. Meanwhile, melt the butter in the pan in which the mushrooms were cooked, stir in the leeks, cover and soften for 8-10 minutes. Stir in the cream and season to taste.

When you are ready to serve, stir the milky potatoes into the soft leeks and spoon over the bottom of a heated serving dish. Arrange the fish rolls on top and decorate with parsley sprigs. Serve with buttered carrots.

PINK TROUT WITH CUCUMBER, SHRIMP AND TOMATO CREAM

*N*ot to be confused with sea trout, farmed trout with pink flesh are much less expensive: one fish will make a single serving. To complement their delicate flavor, I have put together a sauce of cucumber, shrimp, tomato and a hint of tarragon.

ingredients . . . .

four ¾lb pink trout, cleaned
salt and pepper
4tbsp butter
1tbsp peanut oil
1 onion, chopped
½ hothouse cucumber, peeled
  and cut into 1inch strips

2tsp white wine or tarragon
  vinegar
⅔cup heavy cream
½lb peeled cooked bay shrimp
4 firm tomatoes, skinned,
  de-seeded and diced
1tbsp chopped tarragon

Season the trout inside and out with salt and pepper. Heat the butter and oil in a large non-stick skillet and cook the trout for 6-8 minutes on each side. Drain the trout on paper towels and keep warm.

To prepare the sauce: soften the onion and cucumber in the cooking juices in the pan without letting them color. Stir in the vinegar and cream and simmer for 2-3 minutes. Just before you are ready to serve add the shrimp, tomatoes and tarragon and simmer briefly. Do not overcook the shrimp or they will shrink and become tough. Season the sauce with salt and pepper to taste.

To serve the trout: remove their skins with a table knife, transfer to a serving dish and pour the sauce over the top. Serve with parsley potatoes, snow peas and cauliflower.

BONED SHOULDER OF LAMB WITH MARJORIE PRYOR'S TOMATO CRUMBLE

*S*houlder of lamb is one of the least expensive roasts because it contains a large blade bone and is therefore more difficult to carve. Ask your butcher to remove the bone and you will have an ideal pocket which you can fill with your favorite stuffing. This is my mother-in-law's recipe, and one of the reasons why I visit her so often.

ingredients . . . .

one 3lb lamb shoulder roast,
  boned
salt

1tbsp fresh oregano or marjoram
2tbsp chopped parsley
salt and pepper

Stuffing
8 slices stale bread, crisped in a
  low oven
6 ripe tomatoes, cut into
  quarters

Gravy
⅓cup red wine
⅔cup chicken bouillon
1tbsp cornstarch

Prick the skin of the lamb with a fork and rub with plenty of salt.

To prepare the stuffing: place the crisp bread in a large bowl and break it into small pieces. Add the tomatoes, herbs and seasoning and stuff the shoulder. Press the remainder into a small roasting pan. Secure the opening of the lamb with thread or fine string. If you are planning the meal in advance, the lamb can be prepared up to 24 hours in advance.

Preheat the oven to 450°F.

Stand the roast on a rack in a roasting pan and roast near the top of the oven for 20 minutes, to brown. Transfer the roast to the middle of the oven, reduce the heat to 350°F and continue to cook for a further 1 hour until pink and tender. Cook the pan of stuffing in the oven at the same time.

Lift the lamb roast onto a carving board, cover and keep warm.

To prepare a delicious gravy: allow the meat juices to settle in the roasting pan and spoon off the layer of fat. Bring the juices to a boil on top of the stove and pour in the wine and bouillon. Mix the cornstarch with 2tbsp cold water and stir into the gravy to thicken. Season to taste.

Serve the lamb with parsleyed potatoes, leeks and a few mushrooms cooked in butter and thyme.

*Salad of Smoked Eel with Crisp Pears; Pan-fried Pork with Peaches and Green Peppercorns;
Harvest Fruits in a Muscat Jelly.*

PAN-FRIED PORK WITH PEACHES AND GREEN PEPPERCORNS

It is not very often that I can sit down and enjoy my own cooking without wishing I had added this or that to improve it. However, this recipe is a rare exception which gives me as much pleasure as it does my guests.

ingredients...............

2tbsp olive oil
1½lb pork tenderloin or boned
  loin, sliced
3tbsp brandy
1 small onion, finely chopped
1¼cups chicken bouillon

1 pinch ground bay
1tbsp green peppercorns
2tsp cornstarch
3 ripe peaches, skinned, pitted
  and sliced
salt

Heat the oil in a heavy non-stick skillet. Cook the pork quickly over a high heat for 10-12 minutes, then transfer to a warm plate.

Pour the brandy into the pan and stir to loosen the sediment. Add the onion and soften over a gentle heat. Add the bouillon, bay and peppercorns and simmer briskly until the bouillon has reduced by two-thirds. Mix the cornstarch with 1tbsp cold water and stir into the sauce to thicken. Return the pork to the pan, add the peaches and simmer to warm through. Check the sauce for seasoning and add a little salt if necessary.

Serve the pork with Basmati rice, broccoli and carrots.

SWEET AND SOUR PORK CHOPS WITH CRAB APPLE AND ORANGE

Crab apples have such a wonderful flavor when cooked that it surprises me how so often they are left to rot on the tree. In this recipe I have made good use of their sharpness by blending them with one or two herbs and a hint of orange. The resulting sauce will give a special lift to the everyday pork chop.

ingredients...............

4 pork chops
pepper
2tbsp lard
3tbsp medium sherry
½lb crab apples, cut into
  quarters

2 oranges
1tsp rubbed sage
1 lemon thyme sprig
3tbsp sugar
2tbsp salted butter

Season the pork chops on both sides with freshly ground pepper. I have chosen not to add salt because it has a tendency to draw out the moisture from lean meat during cooking.

Melt the lard in a large skillet. When it is nice and hot seal the chops on both sides and cook for 15-20 minutes over a moderate heat. Transfer the chops to a plate, cover and keep warm. Allow the sediment to settle in the pan and pour off the excess fat. Heat the juices over the heat without letting them burn. Add the sherry and loosen the sediment with a wooden spoon.

Add the crab apples, the finely grated zest of one of the oranges and the juice of both. Stir in the sage, thyme and sugar, cover and soften the apples over a gentle heat for 10-12 minutes. Allow to cool, then rub the mixture through a vegetable mill into a non-aluminum saucepan. Warm the sauce gently, stir in the butter and season with freshly ground pepper.

Serve the chops with sliced new cabbage, carrots and mashed potatoes. You will find that at about this time of the year large potatoes are almost impossible to cook without them falling apart.

STUFFED WILD MUSHROOMS WITH CHICKEN, BACON AND HERBS

*S*ome of the largest and finest wild mushrooms are gathered during September. I often serve them stuffed as a main course with buttered potatoes and zucchini.

ingredients . . . .

8 large wild or large, open
 cultivated mushrooms
4tbsp butter or oil
2 boneless chicken breast
 halves, roughly chopped
1 onion, chopped
3 bacon slices, cut into strips

1 thyme sprig
2tbsp flour
1cup milk
salt and pepper
1tbsp chopped parsley
parsley and thyme sprigs, for
 garnish

Wipe the mushrooms, break off their stems, chop them and set aside. Arrange the caps on a baking sheet. Heat the butter or oil in a skillet with a lid and fry the chicken gently without letting it color. Transfer the cooked chicken to a plate and keep warm.

Add the onion, bacon, thyme and mushroom stems to the cooking juices in the pan, cover and soften. Stir in the flour until absorbed, then remove the pan from the heat and stir in the milk a little at a time until evenly absorbed. Return to the heat and simmer to thicken. Add the chicken and the parsley and season to taste with salt and pepper.

Preheat the oven to 350°F. Spoon the filling into the mushroom caps and bake in the oven for 25-30 minutes. Decorate with parsley and thyme sprigs and serve 2 per person as a supper dish, or 1 per person, to serve 8, as a starter.

ingredients . . . .

one 3lb roasted chicken
salt
¼cup vegetable oil
4 bacon slices, cut into
 strips
1 onion, chopped
1tbsp Worcestershire sauce
1½cups fresh white or brown
 bread crumbs
3tbsp chopped parsley

1tbsp rubbed sage
1 rosemary sprig, chopped
3 thyme sprigs, chopped
herbs sprigs, for garnish

Gravy
⅓cup red wine
¼ chicken bouillon cube
2tsp cornstarch
salt and pepper

Preheat the oven to 425°F. Prick the skin of the chicken all over and season inside and out with salt. Heat 2tbsp of the vegetable oil in a skillet and brown the bacon, then add the onion and soften over a moderate heat. Stir in the Worcestershire sauce, the bread crumbs and the herbs until evenly mixed. Stuff the chicken in the front and rear cavities and truss with fine string.

Heat the remaining oil in a heavy roasting pan on top of the stove. Turn the chicken in the oil, transfer to the oven and roast for 1 hour or until cooked through.

Transfer the chicken to a warmed serving dish and keep warm. Let the juices in the roasting pan settle, then spoon off the fat and bring the sediment to a boil on top of the stove. Pour in the wine and stir with a wooden spoon to loosen. Add ⅓cup water together with the bouillon cube. Mix the cornstarch with 3tbsp cold water and stir into the gravy to thicken, then season well. Serve the chicken decorated with sprigs of fresh herbs, with creamed potatoes, carrots and peas, accompanied by the gravy.

ROAST CHICKEN AT SCARBOROUGH FAIR

*A*re you going to Scarborough Fair? Well, this chicken certainly did! Stuffed with parsley, sage, rosemary and thyme and roasted to a crisp, it will satisfy even the hungriest of families.

153

Puddings

PLUM AND ALMOND TART

nglish plums are at their sweetest and most delicious during September. For this recipe I have baked the plums with a handful of ground almonds to absorb any excess moisture. When the plums are cooked, a simple egg custard is poured over the fruit and baked until set. Apricots and cherries could also be used.

ingredients

Pastry
1⅓cups flour
1 stick firm butter, diced
¼cup sugar
1 egg
a little soft butter for greasing

Filling
⅔cup ground almonds

1½lb sweet purple plums, halved and pitted
1 egg
1tbsp sugar
2 drops almond extract
⅓cup heavy cream

To make the pastry: sift the flour into a large mixing bowl and add the butter and sugar. Rub the butter into the flour with the fingertips until the mixture resembles large bread crumbs. Add the egg and mix to a firm dough. Roll into a ball, cover with plastic wrap and leave to rest in the refrigerator for 15-20 minutes.

Preheat the oven to 375°F.

Lightly grease a 9inch metal tart pan with soft butter. Roll out the pastry on a floured work surface to a thickness of ¼inch and line the tart pan evenly. Sprinkle the ground almonds into the bottom of the pastry case and arrange the plums so that they stand up around the edge in a flower pattern. Continue with the remaining plums until you have reached the center. (If the plums are tart, sprinkle them with a little sugar before baking.)

Bake the tart in the center of the oven for 45-50 minutes. Meanwhile, beat the egg, sugar and almond extract into the cream. Strain the custard over the plums, return the tart to the oven and continue to bake for a further 10-12 minutes or until the custard has set. Serve warm or cold with vanilla ice cream.

SPICED GINGER PEARS WITH A CHOCOLATE INTERIOR

utting a dessert recipe together is a bit like making a large firework: you fit in as many hidden surprises as possible before lighting the blue touchpaper. Spiced ginger pears look harmless enough, but when your guests discover the dark chocolate interior they will be delighted.

ingredients

¾cup sugar
1 orange
3 pieces preserved stem ginger, cut into matchsticks
¼cup stem ginger syrup
1inch fresh ginger root, bruised (optional)
2 cloves
8 allspice berries
1 cinnamon stick

juice of ½ lemon
4 small pears
1tbsp cornstarch

Filling
3oz semisweet chocolate
2tsp clear honey
2tbsp heavy cream
¼cup broken macaroons

Measure 5cups water into a large saucepan, add the sugar and simmer until dissolved. Remove the outer zest of the orange with a vegetable peeler, cut into thin strips and add to the syrup. Squeeze in the orange juice and add the ginger, ginger syrup, spices and lemon juice. Allow the spices to infuse for a few minutes.

Peel the pears, leaving them whole, and remove the cores from the bottom with a melon baller. Place the pears in the syrup and simmer for 20-25 minutes, then leave to cool.

Drain the pears and measure 1¼ cups of the syrup into a small saucepan. Bring to a boil. Mix the cornstarch with 2tbsp cold water and stir into the syrup to thicken.

To prepare the filling: break the chocolate into a small heatproof bowl and melt over a saucepan of boiling water. Stir in the honey, the cream and the macaroons. Stuff the pears with the mixture and chill.

To serve: stand the pears on individual serving plates and pour the sauce around the edge.

WILD BLACKBERRY, APPLE AND ALMOND CRUMBLE

❦

Have you noticed the hush that comes over the table when your guests are enjoying dessert? I have learned to take it as a compliment: what else could bring momentary silence to a table of noisy guests? This effect is guaranteed with a crumble of wild blackberries, apples and almonds.

ingredients . . . .

2lb tart baking apples, peeled, cored and chopped
1½pints wild blackberries
½tsp ground cinnamon
1 pinch ground cloves
3tbsp sugar

Topping
6tbsp flour
⅔cup ground almonds
⅔cup rolled oats
¼cup sugar
4tbsp cool butter, diced

Preheat the oven to 375°F. Place the apples and blackberries in a deep 5-cup baking dish. Stir the cinnamon and cloves into the sugar and sprinkle over the fruit. Add 3tbsp of water and set aside.

To make the crumble topping: place the flour, ground almonds, oats and sugar in a mixing bowl. Add the butter and rub the mixture together with the fingertips until even.

Spread the crumble topping over the fruit and bake in the oven for 50 minutes.

Serve hot with pouring cream or custard sauce.

BRANDIED PEACHES IN A BURNT CUSTARD CREAM

❦

Peaches and custard must be one of the earliest memories of childhood. For this recipe I have poached the peaches in brandy and covered them with a glazed creamy custard to turn the dish into a truly adult affair.

ingredients . . . .

3 ripe peaches
3tbsp brandy
2tbsp unsalted butter
1 heaped tbsp cornstarch
⅔cup milk

4 egg yolks
1tbsp granulated sugar
⅔cup heavy cream
½ vanilla bean, split
½cup raw brown sugar

Pour boiling water over the peaches to loosen their skins. Peel, cut into slices and place in a small saucepan with the brandy and butter. Cover and simmer over a gentle heat for 3-4 minutes. Spread the peaches in four individual or one large flameproof dish and set aside.

To prepare the custard: mix the cornstarch with 2tbsp of the milk in a bowl and stir in the egg yolks and granulated sugar. Bring the remaining milk and cream to the boil with the vanilla bean. Whisk the boiling milk over the eggs, return to the saucepan and stir over a gentle heat to thicken. Strain the custard over the brandied peaches and leave to cool. Sprinkle the brown sugar over the top of the custard to cover completely. Caramelize the sugar by placing under the broiler for 8-10 minutes. Allow to cool, then chill before serving.

HARVEST FRUITS IN A MUSCAT JELLY

❦

ingredients . . . .

1cup fragrant English wine
4tsp unflavored gelatin
2 ripe figs, cut into sections
1cup muscat grapes, seeds removed

1 small fragrant melon, scooped into balls
4 strawberries
⅔cup heavy cream, whipped

Place the wine in a non-aluminum saucepan, and bring to a simmer. Soften the gelatin in 2tbsp cold water. Stir the liquid gelatin into the wine and continue to stir over ice until it is just beginning to set. Place enough figs and grapes in 4 stem glasses to quarter fill them, cover with wine jelly and chill until set. Continue with a layer of melon and figs set in more jelly, followed by a layer of grapes, again topped with jelly and left to set. Crown with strawberries and rosettes of cream.

THE LAST OF THE SUMMER FRUITS AND VEGETABLES

*O*ne of the best ways of dealing with September's abundance of late summer fruit and vegetables is the age-old tradition of preserving them for the coming winter.

PICKLED MIXED VEGETABLES

A colorful way of preserving a glut of garden vegetables is to pickle them in vinegar with a few spices. The best vegetables to use include carrots, zucchini, green beans, cauliflower and celery.

Cut the vegetables into neat fingers and blanch in plenty of boiling salted water until only just cooked. Plunge into cold water, then drain and pack into clean jars. Cover with distilled malt vinegar and add a tablespoon of mixed pickling spices: dill seeds, fennel seeds, blades of mace, coriander seeds, peppercorns and a bay leaf. Cover and store in a cool place for at least 3 weeks before opening.

PICKLED ONIONS

ingredients . . . .

3lb pearl onions, peeled	12 allspice berries
⅔cup salt	2inch cinnamon stick
8 peppercorns	5cups distilled malt vinegar
4 blades mace	

Place the onions in a bowl. Prepare a brine by combining 2½quarts water and the salt. Pour over the onions, cover with a plate to keep them submerged and leave for 24-36 hours. Drain the onions, rinse well and pack into clean jars. Add the spices, top up with vinegar, seal and leave for at least 3 months before opening.

PICCALILLI

*H*omemade piccalilli is a wonderful concoction of cauliflowers, which are plentiful now, cucumbers, green beans and a few tart apples all bound in a pickled mustard sauce.

ingredients . . . .

2 cauliflowers, trimmed and cut into florets	6tbsp salt
	3tbsp cornstarch
1 hothouse cucumber, peeled, de-seeded and cut into chunks	5cups white malt vinegar
	3tbsp English mustard powder
1 summer squash, de-seeded and cut into chunks	2tbsp ground ginger
	1tbsp ground turmeric
½lb green beans, trimmed and cut in half	6tbsp sugar
½lb tart green apples, peeled, cored and cut in chunks	

Place the vegetables in a bowl and sprinkle over the salt. Cover with a clean dish towel and leave in a cool place for 24 hours. (Salting the vegetables is necessary to draw out the bitterness before pickling.) Rinse the vegetables well under cold running water and leave to drain.

Place the cornstarch in a large non-aluminum saucepan and mix with ⅔cup of the vinegar. Stir in the mustard powder, ginger, turmeric and sugar, followed by the remaining vinegar. Bring to a boil, stirring occasionally. Add the drained vegetables and simmer for 5 minutes. Pack the vegetables into clean hot jars and seal immediately. Label and store for at least 8 weeks to allow the spice to mingle.

Makes about 6lb

PICKLED PEACHES

*M*ake the most of the peach season by turning a pound or two into a pickle which will be ready in time to eat with the Christmas ham.

ingredients ....

2lb ripe peaches
1tsp coriander seeds
5 allspice berries
2inch cinnamon stick

3 cloves
1cup packed light brown sugar
cups white wine vinegar

Pour boiling water over the peaches to loosen their skins, then peel and cut the fruit into quarters, removing the pits. Measure ⅔cup water into a non-aluminum saucepan. Add the spices and the sugar, simmer and stir until the sugar has dissolved. Add the vinegar and the peaches and simmer for 4-5 minutes until the peaches are beginning to soften. Transfer the peaches to clean jars, pour over the cooking liquid, cover and store for 2-3 months before eating.

FIG JAM

I have included this recipe for the benefit of those who at this time of year find themselves with a tree full of unripened figs, which offer the best flavor for jam-making.

ingredients ....

4lb unripe figs, stalks removed
  and sliced

juice of 3 lemons
7cups sugar

Place the figs in a large preserving kettle and add 1cup water and the lemon juice. Add 3 of the squeezed lemon halves, bring to a boil and simmer for 15 minutes. Remove the lemon halves, add the sugar, and boil for about 25 minutes or until jell point is reached – 220°F on a candy thermometer, or until the jam sets on a cold saucer.

  Have ready six 1lb warmed jam jars. When the jam has reached jell point, fill the jars, place circles of wax paper on top of the jam and cover with cellophane, then label.

Makes 6lb

PLUM JAM

ingredients ....

3lb plums, pitted

7cups sugar

Place the plums in a large preserving kettle, add 1¼cups water and cook the fruit until tender. Add the sugar, bring to a boil and cook for about 25 minutes or until the temperature reaches 220°F on a candy thermometer, or until the jam sets on a cold saucer.

  Have ready five 1lb warmed jam jars. Fill the jars with the jam, place circles of wax paper on top of the jam and cover with cellophane, then label.

Makes 5lb

APPLE AND ROSE HIP JELLY

ingredients ....

3lb tart apples
2lb rose hips
juice of 1 lemon

2inch cinnamon stick
2 cloves
sugar

Wash the apples, chop them roughly and place in a large preserving kettle with the rose hips. Add the lemon juice and 5cups water and bring to a boil, then simmer for 20 minutes.

  Pour the contents of the pan into a jelly bag tied over a bowl and leave to drain. Do not force the fruit through the bag or the jelly will turn cloudy. Measure the juice back into the preserving kettle and add 2¼cups of sugar per 2½cups of juice. Bring to a boil, then simmer for about 35 minutes until jell point is reached – 220°F on a candy thermometer, or until the jelly will set on a cold saucer. Pour the jelly into warmed jars, cover and label.

Makes 2½lb

October

$a$utumn arrives good and proper during October, often bringing crisp blue skies and brilliant sunshine. The evenings grow darker but the daylight that is left seems to grow more intense. As the dark green leaves of summer gradually spill into shades of autumn red, yellow and gold and the woodlands become scented with heavy dew, wild mushrooms find perfect conditions among the wet leaves and grasses for their short season.

The saddest moment for the gardener is the damage brought on by the first frost. From this moment, the last of the summer fruits and vegetables are doomed. However, Brussels sprouts that have been around since the beginning of September will benefit from a good frost as will new season cabbages, leeks, parsnips and rutabaga.

Cauliflowers are looking as bright as ever and are still good value for money. Try them baked in a creamy Stilton and walnut sauce. Broccoli is in good condition although it can be quite expensive at this time of the year. Oak leaf lettuces with their russet hue are popular during the autumn and give a seasonal lift to fancy salads. Home-grown onions, garlic and shallots are ready for stringing if they are to last the winter. Small onions are still available for pickling should they take your fancy. Bright orange pumpkins make a special appearance toward the end of October in time for Halloween. The flesh can be steamed in butter and served as a vegetable or sweetened and spiced ready for a traditional pumpkin pie.

If you are having problems boiling your potatoes without them falling apart, you are not alone. At this time of the year many potato varieties are caught between old and new. During this short time they are best suited to mashing with melted butter or cream.

Apples, pears and plums are gathered in and packed away before the frosts can do their worst. The blackberry season has just about finished now although there may still be a few wild berries hiding in the hedgerows.

Children will enjoy breaking open the first pomegranates of the season in search of their juicy red beads of sweetness. Fresh figs are still in good supply and usually fall in price toward the end of the month. New walnuts are available at many greengrocers along with clusters of Kent cobs, chestnuts and pecans. Arrange them in a basket with a few autumn leaves to make an attractive centerpiece for the table.

Fishermen are usually happy with their catch during October and so should we be as it appears glistening at the fishmonger's. Flat fish – lemon and Dover sole, flounder and brill – are still plentiful and reasonably priced. Herrings are showing signs of fattening up and are always a good buy during the colder months. Ask your fishmonger to fillet them for you before you take them home. Fresh scallops in their familiar shells are appearing on the market now to join oysters and mussels for the winter. Crabs and lobsters are still in good supply and not always as expensive as you might imagine. Less expensive still are cockles, winkles, prawns and shrimp. Sold by the pint, they make for rich pickings over a few drinks at the weekend.

The pheasant season opens on October 1. After a few days' hanging the birds will be good and ready for the oven. Wild duck, quail, snipe, grouse, partridge and woodcock are still young enough to roast and make fine eating with a characterful wine.

$\mathcal{O}$CTOBER INGREDIENTS IN SEASON

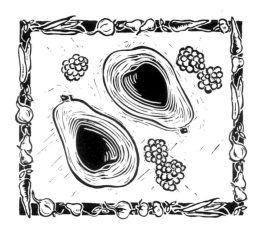

FRUIT & NUTS

British at their best:
Apples
Blackberries
Cooking Apples
Crab Apples
Damsons
Figs
Greengages
Hazelnuts (Filberts)
Pears, Quinces
Rose Hips
Strawberries
Walnuts

Also available:
Loganberries
Raspberries
Tayberries

Imported in season:
Almonds, Apricots
Bananas, Brazil Nuts
Chestnuts
Clementines
Cranberries
Dates, Figs
Grapefruit, Grapes
Kiwi Fruits
Lemons, Limes
Lychees (Litchis)
Mangoes, Melons
Nectarines
Oranges
Papaya
Passion Fruit
Peaches
Peanuts, Pecans
Pineapples
Pistachio Nuts
Pomegranates
Satsumas
Watermelons

VEGETABLES & HERBS

British at their best:
Beets
Brussels Sprouts
Cabbages, Carrots
Cauliflowers
Celeriac, Celery
Chicory (Belgian Endive)
Cucumbers
Corn
Fennel, Garlic
Globe Artichokes
Horseradish
Kohlrabi
Leeks, Lettuce
Mange tout (Snow Peas)
Mustard and Cress
Onions, Parsley
Parsnips
Pickling Cucumbers
Pickling (Pearl) Onions
Potatoes
Rosemary
Sage, Salsify
Samphire, Shallots
Sorrel, Spring Greens
Spring Onions (Scallions)
Swedes (Rutabaga)
Sweet Peppers
Thyme
Tomatoes, Turnips
Watercress
Winter Squashes

Also available:
Basil
Broad (Fava) Beans
Broccoli
Cherry Tomatoes
Chervil, Chives
Courgettes (Zucchini)
Dill
French (Green) Beans
Lavender, Marjoram
Marrows and other
  Large Summer Squashes
Mint, Peas
Radishes
Runner (Italian Green) Beans
Sage, Spinach
Tarragon

Imported in season:
Aubergines (Eggplant)
Avocados, Garlic
Globe Artichokes
Lettuce
Sweet Peppers

FISH & SHELLFISH

British at their best:
Brill, Cockles
Cod, Coley (Pollock)
Crabs
Dabs, Dover Sole
Gray Mullet
Haddock, Hake
Halibut, Herring
Lemon Sole
Lobsters
Mackerel, Monkfish
Mussels, Oysters
Plaice, Prawns
Red Mullet
Scallops
Scampi (Langoustines)
Sea Bass
Sea Trout, Shrimp
Skate, Sprats
Squid
Torbay Sole
Trout, Turbot
Whiting, Winkles

Also available:
Conger Eel
Huss
Salmon

Imported in season:
Freshwater Crayfish
John Dory
Red Mullet
Sardines, Squid

POULTRY & GAME

British at their best:
Grouse
Guinea Fowl
Hare
Partidge
Pheasant from 1st
Pigeon
Quail
Snipe
Venison
Wild Duck
Woodcock

Also available:
Chicken
Duck
Goose
Rabbit
Turkey

MEAT

Beef
Lamb
Offal
Pork
Veal

Starters

SMOKED HADDOCK IN PARSLEY SAUCE

❦

his is one of my favorite midweek standbys because it can be served either as a chunky fish stew or blended into a deliciously creamy soup. Smoked cod can be used instead of haddock.

ingredients ....

4tbsp butter
1 large onion, sliced
2cups milk
1½lb smoked haddock (finnan haddie)
2 parsley stems

¾lb potatoes, peeled and chopped
salt and pepper
2tbsp chopped parsley

Melt the butter in a shallow saucepan and soften the onion without letting it color. Pour in the milk and bring to a boil. Add the smoked haddock, parsley stems and potatoes, cover and simmer for 10-15 minutes.

Transfer the haddock to a plate and leave to cool. Continue to boil the potatoes until they begin to fall apart. Discard the skin and bones of the haddock and flake the flesh between the fingers back into the pan. Season with salt and pepper, sprinkle with parsley and serve as a stew, or blend in a liquidizer to make a creamy soup.

CAULIFLOWER AND WATERCRESS SOUP

❦

s white and beautiful as cauliflowers are at this time of the year, they can have a rather boring flavor, but this is transformed by combining cauliflower with one or two other ingredients. I have based this interesting soup around a chicken stock and a bunch of peppery watercress. Serve it hot or cold with a spoonful of cream.

ingredients ....

1 medium head cauliflower
1 onion, sliced
1 lemon thyme sprig
4tbsp unsalted butter
1tsp English mustard powder
2cups chicken bouillon

1 bunch watercress, finely chopped
salt and freshly ground pepper

Garnish
2tbsp heavy cream
4 watercress sprigs

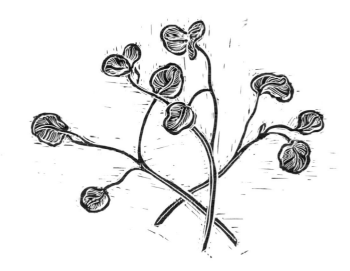

Discard the green leaves from the cauliflower, separate the head into florets and remove the thick stems.

Roughly chop the stems and put them into a large non-aluminum saucepan. Reserve the florets. Add the onion, thyme and butter. Soften over a gentle heat without letting the onion color. Stir in the mustard powder followed by the chicken bouillon. Bring to a boil, then simmer for 15-20 minutes.

Add the cauliflower florets and the watercress and simmer for a further 5 minutes. Pour the soup into a blender and liquidize until smooth. Return the soup to a clean pan, reheat gently and season with salt and pepper.

Serve the soup in pretty bowls with a spoonful of cream stirred into each, garnished with watercress sprigs.

AN OLD-FASHIONED DUCK BROTH WITH PORT WINE

One of the best-tasting warming broths I know is made with leftover duck carcasses. It is a good idea to store them away in your freezer until you need them. Older birds give the best flavor for broth-making.

ingredients . . . .

1 mature duck or 4 duck legs or	1 celery stalk, roughly chopped
2 duck carcasses	1 thyme sprig
1 veal bone, chopped	1 bay leaf
1 onion, roughly chopped	4 juniper berries
½cup roughly chopped leeks	½cup port wine
1 carrot, roughly chopped	salt and pepper

If you are using a whole duck, preheat the oven to 400°F, prick the breast well with a fork and roast for 1 hour. If using duck legs, roast them for 35 minutes.

Place the cooked duck or duck carcasses in a large saucepan and add the veal bone and the vegetables, herbs and spices. Cover with cold water and bring to a boil. Skim the surface, then simmer uncovered for 2½-3hours.

Strain the broth into a clean saucepan. Remove the surface fat with a ladle, add the port wine and season with salt and pepper. If there is any meat left, cut it into thin strips and use to garnish the broth.

POTTED SALMON WITH TOASTED WALNUTS

Before the days of modern factory processing, fresh meats and fish were often potted at home to last through the cold winter. Potted meats and fish are coming back into fashion and can be enjoyed in some of our finest restaurants. I have adapted this recipe from a book of old English cookery and like to serve it at home with a handful of toasted walnuts and a salad.

ingredients . . . .

10oz fresh salmon tail	salt and pepper
1tsp chopped dill	mixed salad leaves
½tsp dried sage	olive oil
1 pinch ground mace	lemon.juice
7tbsp unsalted butter	½cup broken walnuts, toasted
finely grated zest and juice of	
½ lemon	

Preheat the oven to 350°F. Place the salmon tail on a square of foil and cover with the chopped dill, sage and mace. Add 1tbsp of the butter in small pieces with the lemon zest and juice and season with salt and pepper. Wrap the salmon in the foil, place in a shallow dish and bake in the oven for 25-30 minutes.

Allow to cool, then remove the skin and flake the flesh from the bone. Press the flesh into 4 ramekin dishes. Melt the remaining butter, pour over the salmon and leave to set. (Potted salmon will keep in the refrigerator for up to 7 days.) To serve: arrange a simple salad dressed with oil and lemon juice on 4 plates. Unmold the potted salmon onto the salads, sprinkle with toasted walnuts and serve.

ARTICHOKES WITH MUSHROOM STUFFING

I remember watching two French children in a restaurant tackling artichokes. The fun they had lasted for nearly half an hour. It is difficult to hurry an artichoke, as the leaves must be nibbled clean one by one to reveal the all-important base and filling.

ingredients . . . .

salt and pepper	3 shallots, finely chopped
4 large globe artichokes	6oz button mushrooms,
1 lemon, sliced	chopped
	½tsp dried thyme
Stuffing	¼cup heavy cream
2tbsp butter	

Bring a large saucepan of water to a boil with a large pinch of salt. Snap off the stem from the base of each artichoke and draw out the long fibers. Trim the bottom with a stainless steel knife to expose the white base. Rub the base immediately with lemon to prevent it from discoloring. Trim the artichoke one third from the top, tie a slice of lemon to the base with string and boil for up to 30 minutes until tender, depending on size. To test, remove one of the outer leaves: if the flesh at the base of the leaf is tender the artichoke is cooked. Immerse the artichokes in cold water and leave them to drain upside down.

To prepare a cavity for the stuffing: pull out the center leaves to reveal the fibrous choke inside. Scrape away the fibers with a teaspoon and set the artichoke aside.

To prepare the mushroom stuffing: melt the butter in a small saucepan and soften the shallots without letting them color. Add the mushrooms and thyme and cook, uncovered, until their moisture has evaporated. Stir in the cream, season with salt and pepper and fill each of the artichokes. If you are planning ahead the artichokes can be kept in the refrigerator for 24 hours.

When you are ready to serve, preheat the oven to 350°F. Place the artichokes in an ovenproof dish, cover and heat through in the oven for 20 minutes.

Line a 9×5×3inch loaf pan with plastic wrap or strips of wax paper. Place the cheese, mayonnaise, 1 avocado, lemon juice and seasoning in a food processor and blend until smooth.

Beat the eggs until a thick trail can be drawn across the surface. Soften the gelatin in 2tbsp cold water in a small heatproof bowl and dissolve by standing in a saucepan of boiling water. Whisk the liquid gelatin into the eggs and fold into the cheese mixture. Chop half the walnuts and add to the mixture. Spoon half the mixture into the prepared pan and place the 2 remaining avocado halves along the center, cut side up.

Halve the hard-cooked and arrange in the cavities of each avocado. Leave the terrine to set in the refrigerator for 30 minutes.

Cover with the remaining mixture and chill for 1½-2 hours until completely set. Serve as a starter or as a light main course with a tomato salad.

AVOCADO AND WALNUT TERRINE

During October the first walnuts are gathered in for the winter season. If you are quick you will catch them at their best before they dry out. When walnuts are fresh their shells are supple in the hand and have a delightful smell of autumn leaves. When the nut is broken a latex skin is carefully peeled away to expose the milky white interior.

ingredients . . . .

1cup packed pot cheese	2 eggs, at room temperature
¼cup mayonnaise	4tsp unflavored gelatin
2 ripe avocados, halved and peeled	½lb fresh walnuts, cracked and peeled
2tbsp lemon juice	1 egg, hard-cooked (12 minutes)
salt and pepper	

Main Courses

DEEP SEA SCALLOPS IN A FOREST OF WILD MUSHROOMS

This recipe does full justice to the delicate flavor and texture of fresh scallops. If the scallops are absolutely sea-fresh, I would recommend eating them raw with a squeeze of lemon, but most people would probably prefer them served as they are here: warmed through so that they do not toughen, then combined with a handful of wild mushrooms bound in a light butter sauce and presented between two pieces of flaky pastry.

ingredients

½lb puff pastry, thawed if frozen
1 egg
salt and pepper
2tbsp unsalted butter
¾lb sea scallops, sliced
6oz wild mushrooms, such as
   chanterelles, oyster mushrooms
   and cèpes

Sauce
2 shallots, finely chopped
1 thyme sprig
¼cup tarragon vinegar
3 egg yolks
1½ sticks unsalted butter,
   melted
1tbsp chopped tarragon

Roll out the pastry on a lightly floured surface to a thickness of ¼inch. Cut out 4 rectangles measuring 3×6inches and arrange them on a lightly greased baking sheet. Beat the egg with a large pinch of salt, brush the pastry evenly to glaze, and allow to rest for at least 1 hour.

To prepare the sauce: place the shallots and thyme in a non-aluminum saucepan, add the vinegar and reduce by half. Remove the thyme, transfer the contents of the pan to a heatproof bowl or double boiler add the egg yolks and beat over a saucepan of simmering water until pale and fluffy. Gradually add the melted butter, beating until the sauce thickens. Do not overheat or it may curdle: to be on the safe side, remove the saucepan from the heat halfway through beating. Add the chopped tarragon, season to taste with salt and pepper, cover and keep warm.

Preheat the oven to 400°F. Brush the pastry rectangles once more with beaten egg glaze and bake near the top of the oven for 25-30 minutes. When you are ready to serve, melt the butter in a non-stick skillet, season the scallops and cook them for no longer than 30 seconds. Transfer them to the butter sauce and soften the mushrooms in the cooking juices.

To serve: split the pastry rectangles in half horizontally and arrange the lower halves on 4 plates. Spoon over the scallops in the sauce, scatter the mushrooms over the top and replace the pastry tops.

A KEDGEREE OF SALMON WITH SMOKED HADDOCK AND CUCUMBER

Traditional kedgeree has undergone a number of changes since it first became popular with the Victorians as a breakfast specialty. Since our appetites for large breakfasts have declined somewhat, kedgeree has become an informal supper dish. Here I have included a taste of fresh salmon and a few strips of cucumber.

ingredients

1lb smoked haddock (finnan
   haddie)
½lb salmon tail, filleted and
   skinned
1¼cups milk
2tbsp butter
1 onion, finely chopped
2tsp mild curry powder
1tbsp flour

½ hothouse cucumber, cut into
   batons
2cups long-grain rice
salt
1 pinch saffron or 2 drops yellow
   food coloring
4 hard-cooked eggs (12
   minutes), roughly chopped
2tbsp chopped parsley

Place the haddock and salmon in a shallow saucepan with the milk, bring to a boil and simmer gently for 8-10 minutes. Transfer the fish to a plate and leave to cool.

Melt the butter in another saucepan and soften the onion without letting it color. Stir in the curry powder and flour and remove from the heat. Add the milk used to cook the fish a little at a time, stirring until completely absorbed, then add the cucumber, return to the heat and simmer to thicken. Place the rice in the saucepan that contained the milk, add 3cups boiling water, a large pinch of salt and the saffron and boil for 17 minutes.

Flake the fish between your fingers to remove any bones and add to the sauce with the hard-cooked eggs. When the rice is cooked, spoon the fish over the top, sprinkle with chopped parsley and serve with peas or a salad.

A WHITE FISH STEW WITH LEEKS AND MUSHROOMS

One of the advantages of including fish dishes on the midweek menu is the speed with which they are put together. I have devised this recipe for those of us who have a thousand and one better things to do in the evening than to slave over a hot stove.

ingredients

1½lb cod, haddock or whiting, skinned	1 garlic clove, minced
salt and pepper	3tbsp cornstarch
2cups milk	¼lb button mushrooms, quartered
4tbsp butter	
1lb leeks, split and finely sliced	

CIDER-BAKED MACKEREL WITH A YOGURT AND MUSTARD DRESSING

It is always a challenge to find new and exciting ways to prepare these tasty fish. One of my favorite recipes involves baking the mackerel briefly in a little cider before preparing a delicious yogurt and mustard sauce with the cooking juices.

ingredients

	Dressing
2tbsp butter	1tbsp cornstarch
1 onion, sliced	⅔cup plain yogurt
2 firm apples, peeled, cored and sliced	2tsp English mustard
1¼cups dry hard cider	1tsp cider or white wine vinegar
four 7oz mackerel, filleted	salt and pepper
½tsp rubbed sage	

Preheat the oven to 375°F. Melt the butter in a flameproof casserole, add the onion and apple and brown evenly. Remove from the heat and add the cider followed by the mackerel and sage. Cover and bake in the preheated oven for 20-25 minutes. Transfer the mackerel fillets to a warm plate.

To make the dressing: mix the cornstarch with 2tbsp cold water and stir into the yogurt. (This will prevent the yogurt from curdling.) Stir the yogurt into the cooking juices, bring to a boil and thicken. Add the mustard and vinegar and season. Serve with plain boiled potatoes, carrots and broccoli.

Season the fish with salt and pepper. Place the milk in a saucepan, add the fish and cook gently for 6-8 minutes. Melt the butter in another saucepan, add the leeks and garlic, cover and soften over a gentle heat. Stir in the cornstarch, gradually add the hot milk from cooking the fish and stir to thicken. Add the button mushrooms and simmer for 5 minutes. Flake the fish into the sauce, reheat and serve with creamed potatoes and carrots.

PORK CHOPS WITH APPLE SLICES AND SAGE

If you are entertaining figure-conscious friends, and who isn't these days, allow me to introduce you to the pork chop, neatly trimmed of fat, served with apples and sage.

ingredients ....

2tbsp vegetable oil
4 pork chops, trimmed of all fat
2 apples
1tbsp lemon juice

2tbsp sugar
salt and pepper
4 sage sprigs

Heat the oil in a non-stick skillet and cook the pork chops for 8 minutes on each side. Transfer to a warm plate and set aside.

Slice the apples thinly, trim away the cores, brush them with lemon juice and dip each side in sugar. Reheat the cooking juices in the skillet and brown the apple slices on both sides. Season the pork chops with salt and pepper and serve with the apple slices, garnished with sage sprigs.

CHICKEN CASSEROLE WITH PORT WINE AND GREEN FIGS

ingredients ....

4 unripe figs, trimmed and peeled
⅓cup port wine
2 bay leaves
2tbsp vegetable oil
one 3½lb chicken, cut into portions
1 onion, sliced
2 celery stalks, cut into batons

2tbsp flour
1tsp tomato paste
½tsp ground coriander
2½cups chicken bouillon
salt and pepper

Place the figs in a small non-aluminum saucepan, cover with the port wine, add the bay leaves and simmer for 10-15 minutes. Meanwhile, heat the oil in a large skillet, season the chicken pieces and fry them quickly until they are well browned on the outside. Transfer the chicken to a casserole and set aside.

Preheat the oven to 375°F.

Soften the onion and celery in the cooking juices in the pan. Stir in the flour, tomato paste and the coriander. Remove the pan from the heat, and stir in the bouillon a little at a time until absorbed by the flour. Strain the port wine from the figs over the chicken, cover and cook in the oven for 1½ hours. Add the figs 15 minutes before serving to warm through. Serve with plain boiled rice and broccoli.

WARM CHICKEN IN A SALAD OF AUTUMN LEAVES

When at the end of my day I have neither time nor energy to spend on an elaborate supper, I often put together a salad based on one or two of our more interesting lettuces and warm chicken breast sliced and bound in a favorite dressing.

ingredients ....

3tbsp olive oil
1 garlic clove, cut in half
3 chicken breast halves, skinned and boned
1tbsp white wine vinegar
1tsp grainy mustard

1tbsp chopped tarragon
various lettuce leaves: red leaf, curly chicory, radicchio, field lettuce
salt and pepper

Heat the oil in a non-stick skillet, add the garlic and cook the chicken for 6-8 minutes on each side. Transfer the chicken to a warm plate and set aside.

Discard the garlic from the pan and add the vinegar, mustard and tarragon to the cooking juices. Wash and dry the lettuce leaves. Just before serving, pour the warm dressing over the salad leaves arranged on 4 plates. Slice the chicken thinly, season with salt and pepper and scatter over the salad. Serve as a light main course or a starter.

*Artichokes with Mushroom Stuffing; Roast Pheasant with Pomegranates;
Butterscotch Pecan Pie*

ROAST WILD DUCK WITH A SHARP PLUM SAUCE

*T*he two most common forms of wild duck to be found at the English table are the mallard and the widgeon, the female of both species being more tender than the drake. Wild ducks tend to be smaller than domestic varieties although their flavor is far superior. When you are choosing wild ducks for roasting, the lower beak should break easily in the hand and their feet should be scale-free and supple.

When roasting the ducks it is necessary to protect the delicate breast meat with pork fat or bacon and then cook quickly in a hot oven. (It is a mistake to overcook wild duck as it will lose its succulence.) Perfectly cooked duck should have a crisp skin and slightly pink flesh. To complement the duck's gamey flavor and to lift away any greasiness, I have prepared a deliciously sharp plum sauce that has a hint of fresh orange.

ingredients...

2 young wild ducks, such as
    mallards or widgeons
salt and pepper
4tbsp butter

Sauce
½lb dark plums, pits removed
    and roughly chopped
finely grated zest and juice of 1
    orange

2tsp wine vinegar
1tbsp light brown sugar
½tsp ground cinnamon
1 pinch ground cloves
1 pinch cayenne

watercress sprigs, for garnish

Preheat the oven to 450°F.

Season the birds inside and out with salt and pepper, pierce the skin several times with a fork and dot with pieces of butter. Place the ducks in a roasting pan and roast in the oven for 25 minutes.

Meanwhile, place the plums in a non-aluminum saucepan together with the orange zest and juice, vinegar, sugar and spices. Cover and simmer for 15 minutes until the plums are soft, then rub them through a sieve to make a purée.

When the ducks are cooked, transfer them to a warm plate and leave to rest. Let the sediment settle in the roasting pan, then spoon off the layer of fat and keep for another use. Stir the plum paste into the pan and adjust the consistency with bouillon or water.

To serve: carve the ducks, garnish with watercress sprigs and serve the sauce separately. Creamed potatoes, carrots and peas are well suited to this dish.

ROAST PHEASANT WITH POMEGRANATES

*A*bout this time of the year pomegranates are imported from Eastern Mediterranean countries and can be found piled up at the greengrocer's like so many golden cannon-balls. Inside is to be found a honeycomb of seeds like glassy red beads. The flavor of the juice is well-balanced, with a bittersweet acidity, and is suited to many savory dishes. This favorite of mine has a wonderfully rich sauce.

ingredients...

2 young pheasants, with
    giblets
salt and pepper
4tbsp butter
1 onion, roughly chopped
1 celery stalk, roughly chopped
2 small carrots, roughly chopped

½cup red wine
2 pomegranates, split open
1¼cups game bouillon, made
    from the pheasants giblets,
    excluding the liver
2tsp cornstarch

Preheat the oven to 425°F. Season the pheasants inside and out with salt and pepper. Melt the butter in a large flameproof casserole or roasting pan on top of the stove and brown the pheasants on all sides.

Remove the pheasants and brown the onion, celery and carrots. Pour in the wine and boil to reduce to half its volume. Rub the seeds of one pomegranate through a nylon sift to extract the juice and add to the casserole with the game bouillon.

Return the pheasants to the casserole, cover and roast in the oven for 20 minutes. Reduce the oven temperature to 350°F, cover and cook for a further 45 minutes.

Transfer the pheasants to a warm plate and strain the cooking juices into a small saucepan. Mix the cornstarch with 2tbsp cold water, stir into the sauce and simmer to thicken. Add the remaining pomegranate seeds and season to taste with salt and pepper.

To serve: carve the breasts as thinly as you can and serve the sauce separately. The legs can be eaten but are usually too tough. Save them for making game pies and soups. Serve the pheasant with buttered cabbage, carrots and Fondant Potatoes.

BRAISED SQUABS WITH LITTLE ONIONS, MUSHROOMS AND PEAS

❀

 uccessful attempts have been made to rear squabs (young pigeons) for their agreeably beefy flavor. I often see them neatly packaged in my local supermarket. If you shoot your own or buy them locally, younger birds make the best eating; look out for scale-free, supple feet. Older, tougher birds are best made into stews or pies.

ingredients . . . .

4 squabs, barded with
  bacon
2tbsp butter
1tbsp peanut oil
1 small carrot, halved
1 celery stalk, chopped
⅔cup red wine
2cups light beef or chicken
  bouillon
¾lb pearl onions,
  peeled

½lb (1½cups) frozen peas
6oz large wild or cultivated
  mushrooms, thickly sliced

Bouquet garni
1 leek leaf, wrapped and tied
  around:
1 thyme sprig
1 bay leaf
4 juniper berries
3 whole allspice

Preheat the oven to 375°F.

Season the squabs inside and out with salt and pepper. Heat the butter and oil in a flameproof casserole on top of the stove and brown the squabs two at a time. Scatter the carrot and celery into the bottom, add the bouquet garni and place the squabs on top. Pour in the wine and bouillon, cover and braise in the oven for 2 hours. Remove the carrots and the celery as their flavor will now be in the sauce. Add the onions, peas and mushrooms, cover and return to the oven to cook for a further 15-20 minutes.

Serve the squabs with carrots and potatoes creamed with an equal quantity of celeriac. Rowan jelly goes very well with this.

TWENTY-MINUTE CAULIFLOWER WITH A STILTON AND WALNUT SAUCE

❀

ingredients . . . .

1 large head cauliflower, trimmed
  and left whole

Sauce
4tbsp butter
1 onion, chopped

3tbsp flour
2cups milk
¾cup grated Stilton cheese
½cup chopped walnuts
2tsp rubbed sage
salt and pepper

Cook the cauliflower in salted boiling water for 8 minutes; drain well. Meanwhile, make the sauce: melt the butter in a separate saucepan, add the onion and soften over a gentle heat. Stir in the flour until absorbed by the butter and draw away from the heat. Warm the milk in another saucepan and stir it into the roux a little at a time, making sure that the mixture is smooth before each addition. Add the Stilton, walnuts and sage and bring to a boil, then simmer for 5-10 minutes. Season to taste with salt and pepper, pour the sauce over the cauliflower and finish under the broiler. Serve with a salad of ripe tomatoes and crisp lettuce.

FONDANT POTATOES

❀

ingredients . . . .

2lb equal-sized potatoes
6tbsp butter

1¼cups light chicken or
  vegetable bouillon

Preheat the oven to 425°F.

Peel the potatoes and shape them evenly.

Melt the butter in a roasting pan on top of the stove and toss the potatoes in it until they begin to brown. Pour in the bouillon and continue cooking in the oven for 35-40 minutes, shaking the pan occasionally, until all the bouillon is absorbed. Serve with roast meats or game.

Mushroom Gatherer's Breakfast

While most of England is busy complaining about yet another wet autumn, the rewards for anyone prepared to get up bright and early to search through wet woods and fields for a mushroom breakfast can be truly amazing. A far cry from the ubiquitous button mushroom of the supermarket, wild mushrooms with names like horn of plenty, shaggy caps, oyster mushrooms, cèpes and chanterelles have special characteristics before and after they are cooked. The trumpet-shaped chanterelle, for instance, has a delicate scent of apricots while the firm-fleshed cèpe has a decidedly meaty flavor. It is advisable to pick wild mushrooms with an experienced person prepared to show you how to identify the edible varieties, if you are not familiar with these.

BUTTERED OYSTER MUSHROOMS WITH LEMON THYME

Oyster mushrooms are one of the few varieties of wild mushrooms now often available at larger supermarkets and greengrocers. The delicate flavor and texture of the oyster mushroom is best enjoyed at breakfast-time gently stewed in butter and lemon thyme.

ingredients

4tbsp unsalted butter
6oz oyster mushrooms, trimmed
1 small onion, sliced

1 lemon thyme sprig
1tbsp lemon juice
salt and pepper

Melt the butter in a small saucepan and add the mushrooms, onion and thyme. Cover and simmer gently for 3-4 minutes. Add the lemon juice and season to taste with salt and pepper. Serve on slices of hot buttered toast.

SCRAMBLED EGGS WITH CHANTERELLES

ingredients

¼lb chanterelle or oyster mushrooms, peeled and trimmed
¼cup light cream or half-and-half

5 eggs, at room temperature
salt and pepper
2tbsp chopped parsley

Place the mushrooms in a small saucepan, cover with the cream and simmer gently for 3-4 minutes.

Break the eggs into a glass bowl, season with salt and pepper, add the cream from the mushrooms and beat lightly with a fork. Stand the bowl in a saucepan of boiling water so that the water is touching the bottom of the bowl. Stir the eggs with a wooden spoon, loosening them as they cook, the slower the better, although the eggs shouldn't take more than 6-8 minutes. When the eggs are beginning to set, remove from the heat and allow them to continue to cook in their own heat. Stir in the mushrooms, sprinkle with chopped parsley and serve on slices of hot buttered toast.

WILD MUSHROOM PANCAKES WITH CODDLED EGGS

ingredients

4tbsp unsalted butter
½lb wild mushrooms, such as chanterelles, oyster or cèpes, peeled and trimmed

Pancake batter
¾cup self-rising flour
½cup whole wheat flour

1 egg
1cup milk
salt and pepper

Coddled eggs
4tbsp butter, melted
4 eggs

Melt the butter in a small saucepan, add the mushrooms and soften over a gentle heat.

To make the pancake batter: sift both flours into a mixing bowl. Beat the egg into the milk with a fork and add the buttery juices from the mushrooms. Make a well in the center of the flour, add all the liquid and stir into a thick batter. Season with salt and pepper and leave to stand for 10-15 minutes before using.

Preheat the oven to 350°F. Pour half the melted butter into 4 ramekin dishes, arrange on a baking sheet and heat in the oven for 3-4 minutes. Break an egg into each dish, season with salt and pepper, cover with the remaining butter and bake the eggs for 4-5 minutes until they are just beginning to firm.

To make the crêpes: stir the stewed mushrooms into the pancake batter. Heat a non-stick skillet over a steady heat and spoon in the batter in small heaps, letting them spread to a diameter of 3inches. As soon as bubbles appear on the surface, turn the crêpes over and cook for a further 15-20 seconds. Keep the crêpes warm under a clean dish towel until you are ready to serve. The coddled eggs may be served straight from their ramekin dishes or unmolded and served with the crêpes.

Dill, parsley, chives, garlic and sorrel can be blended with butter, allowing 5tbsp chopped herbs per stick of butter, then shaped into a sausage in a sheet of freezer paper or foil and frozen. Cut the butter into rounds as you need it and melt over baked potatoes, broiled fish and meat, or stir into soups and sauces for an extra lift.

Tarragon is best stored in jars with wine vinegar and used for sauces and salad dressings. Mint can be chopped and preserved in the same way with malt vinegar for use in mint sauce.

HERBS FOR WINTER KEEPING

It is as well to gather the last summer herbs before an early frost takes us by surprise. There are three basic methods of preserving them: drying, freezing and pickling in vinegar. Herbs for drying include thyme, sage, bay, rosemary, basil and marjoram. These should be hung up in a warm, well-ventilated place.

171

Puddings

APPLE AND HAZELNUT TART

*T*o make the most of both autumn clusters of hazelnuts and russet red apples, I have encased the apples in a pastry tart with toasted nuts and cinnamon. Serve warm or cold with cream.

ingredients . . . .

Pastry
1⅓cups flour
⅓cup ground hazelnuts (filberts),
  toasted
1tsp ground cinnamon
¼cup sugar
1 stick cool butter, diced
1 egg

Filling
2lb firm, sweet apples
1tbsp lemon juice
1 pinch ground allspice
2tbsp sugar
2tbsp butter

To make the pastry: sift the flour into a large mixing bowl, add the hazelnuts, cinnamon, sugar and butter, and rub the mixture with the fingertips to resemble large bread crumbs. The pastry can also be made in a food processor. Add the egg and mix into an even dough, then cover and allow to rest in the refrigerator for 30 minutes.

Preheat the oven to 400°F. Lightly grease a 9inch tart pan with butter. Roll the pastry out fairly thickly on a floured work surface and line the pan.

Peel and core all but three of the apples, chop them and cook in a non-aluminum saucepan with the lemon juice and allspice until soft. Add the sugar and spread in the pastry case. Core the remaining apples, halve them and slice thinly. Arrange the slices attractively in the tart, dot with butter and bake in the oven for 45-50 minutes.

STEAMED BLACKBERRY AND APPLE PUDDING

*T*he English steamed pudding, if properly made, is one of our best-loved warming winter desserts. Its attraction centers around the all-important topping which can include any number of winter fruits: apples, pears, plums, fresh figs and apricots. Equally important is the moist sponge which serves to support the topping as the pudding is unmolded. The fruit may be replaced with ⅓cup golden syrup, jam or treacle (light molasses).

ingredients . . . .

1lb tart baking apples, peeled,
  cored and chopped
1½cups blackberries
¾cup sugar
1 pinch ground allspice or
  cloves

1 stick butter, softened
grated zest of ½ lemon
2 eggs, beaten
1¼cups self-rising flour
soft butter for greasing

Place the apples, blackberries, 2tbsp of sugar and the spice in a saucepan, cover and simmer until soft.
 Cream the butter with the remaining sugar and lemon zest until pale. Add the eggs a little at a time and beat until smooth. Lastly stir in the flour until the mixture is evenly blended. Liberally grease a 5-cup pud-

ding basin or deep round baking dish with butter, spoon the fruit into the bottom and the batter over the top. To cover, cut out a large square of old linen such as a clean dish towel, and tie around the rim of the basin with string. Bring the corners of the cloth up over the top and tie into a large granny knot. The pudding will keep in the refrigerator for up to 2 days.

To steam the pudding: preheat the oven to 350°F. Place the pudding in a deep roasting pan, pour in boiling water to come halfway up the sides of the basin and cook in the oven for 1½ hours.

To serve: untie the cloth, loosen the sides of the pudding with a table knife, invert onto a serving dish and serve with of hot custard sauce.

BLACKBERRY AND PEAR MOUSSES

It has always been a mystery to me why two fruits appearing at the same time of the year often go together so well. Blackberries and pears are no exception and are quite delicious set into a delicate mousse with a hint of lemon.

ingredients . . . .

6tbsp sugar
finely grated zest and juice of 1
  lemon
4 small pears, peeled, halved
  and cored

1pint blackberries
2tsp unflavored gelatin
1¼cups whipping cream
2 egg whites

Place ⅔cup water in a small saucepan with 4tbsp of the sugar. Bring to a boil, add the lemon zest and juice with the pears and simmer for 15-20 minutes. Drain the pears; reserve one half pear for decoration, and set the remainder aside. Simmer the blackberries in the pear syrup for 5 minutes. Reserve half the berries for decoration, place the remainder into a liquidizer with the pears and blend to a purée.

Soften the gelatin in 1tbsp cold water, stir into the warm purée and leave to cool. Softly whip the cream and fold into the purée. Beat the egg whites, adding the remaining sugar a little at a time, until smooth, then fold into the setting mousse.

Unmold the mousse into 4 pretty glasses or one large bowl and chill

in the refrigerator for 1-1½ hours until set.

To decorate: thinly slice the reserved pear half and arrange in a fan shape at the edge of the mousse. Place the reserved blackberries in the center.

PLUM AND ALMOND SHUTTLE

When our English plums are at their sweetest, they are best eaten raw. However, if the plums are a little too sharp for this, their full flavor can be brought out by baking them with an almond frangipane between layers of puff pastry.

ingredients . . . .

½lb puff pastry, thawed if
  frozen
½lb tart plums, halved and
  pitted
1tbsp sugar
1 egg, beaten, to glaze

Almond frangipane
4tbsp butter, softened
¼cup sugar
1 egg
⅔cup ground almonds
2 drops almond extract

Roll out the puff pastry to a 10×8inch rectangle and cut it in half down the middle. Flour one of the strips and fold it in half lengthwise. Make a series of even cuts into the pastry two-thirds of the way toward the open edge so that when the pastry is opened out, vents are formed. Leave the 2 pieces of pastry to rest in the refrigerator for 1 hour.

Preheat the oven to 400°F.

To make the frangipane filling: cream the butter and sugar together with a wooden spoon, beat in the egg and stir in the ground almonds and the extract.

To assemble the shuttle, lay the uncut piece of pastry on a moistened baking sheet, spread the frangipane over the pastry to within 1inch of the edge, arrange the plums over the top, sprinkle over the sugar and brush the edges of the pastry with beaten egg. Open out the slatted pastry, lay it over the filling and secure the edges firmly. Brush the pastry all over with beaten egg and bake near the top of the oven for 45 minutes.

BUTTERSCOTCH PECAN PIE

ingredients...................

Pastry
1½cups flour
1 stick firm butter
¼cup sugar
1 egg
soft butter for greasing

Filling
6tbsp caster sugar
2tbsp clear honey
2tbsp maple syrup
¼cup heavy cream
4tbsp butter
2cups pecan or walnut
halves

To prepare the pastry: sift the flour into a mixing bowl, add the butter and sugar and rub together between the fingertips until the mixture resembles large bread crumbs. Add the egg and mix into an even dough. Or make the pastry in a food processor. Cover the dough and rest in the refrigerator for 30 minutes.

Lightly grease a 9inch tart pan with soft butter. Roll out the pastry on a floured work surface to a thickness of ¼inch and line the pan evenly. Preheat the oven to 375°F.

To prepare the filling: place the sugar, honey and syrup in a saucepan and melt over a steady heat. Increase the heat and boil rapidly for 5 minutes until lightly caramelized. Remove from the heat and stir in the cream and the butter until evenly blended. Allow the butterscotch mixture to cool for a few seconds, then stir in the nuts and spread into the pastry case. Bake in the oven for 35-40 minutes. Take care when removing the pan from the oven as the filling will be very hot. Allow to cool, then serve with softly whipped cream.

SPICED PUMPKIN PIE

ne of the highlights of autumn is the appearance of bright orange pumpkins, which have become a symbol of Halloween. Hollowed out and carved into ugly faces, they are supposed to frighten away the evil spirits of the night. Pumpkin flesh makes a classic pie filling. Try the seeds toasted and sprinkled with salt and spices such as cayenne as a tasty snack.

ingredients...................

Pastry
1⅔cups flour
1 stick cool butter
2tbsp sugar

Filling
¾lb raw pumpkin, peeled and
chopped (3-4cups)
2tbsp butter
1tsp ground cinnamon

½tsp ground ginger
1 pinch grated nutmeg
1 pinch ground cloves
finely grated zest and juice of 1
orange
1 large pinch salt
2tbsp golden or light corn syrup
⅔cup milk
3 eggs

To make the pastry: sift the flour into a mixing bowl, add the butter and sugar and rub in with the fingertips to form large bread crumbs. Add about 4tbsp cold water and mix to an even dough without overworking. Allow the pastry to rest in the refrigerator for 30 minutes, then roll out thickly and line an 8inch pie pan.

Preheat the oven to 375°F.

To prepare the filling: place the pumpkin in a saucepan with the butter and spices. Add the orange zest and juice with the salt, cover and soften over a steady heat for 10-12 minutes. Add the golden syrup and blend to a smooth paste. Add the milk and beat in the eggs.

Line the pastry case with parchment paper and beans and bake unfilled for 20 minutes. Remove the paper and beans, spoon in the filling and bake for 50-55 minutes. Serve warm or cold with softly whipped cream. A few pieces of chopped preserved stem ginger added to the cream will make a pleasant surprise.

PUMPKIN AND WALNUT TEA BREAD

ingredients...................

soft butter for greasing
¾lb piece raw pumpkin
1⅔cups self-rising flour
1cup light brown sugar
1tsp ground cinnamon
½tsp ground ginger

1 pinch ground cloves
1 pinch salt
¾cup vegetable oil
2 eggs
¾cup roughly chopped walnuts

Lightly grease a 9×5×3inch loaf pan and line with parchment paper. Preheat the oven to 375°F.

Wrap the pumpkin in a piece of foil and bake in the oven for 25 minutes. Allow to cool, then scrape the flesh into a mixing bowl. Add the flour, sugar, spices and salt followed by the oil, eggs and walnuts. Stir together until evenly mixed, then spread in the prepared loaf pan and bake in the oven for 50-55 minutes. Allow the bread to cool in the pan before unmolding onto a wire rack.

WHITE CHOCOLATE AND CHESTNUT CHEESECAKE

*W*hite chocolate has recently become highly fashionable in desserts. It combines beautifully with smooth chestnut purée in this spectacular cheesecake, which should serve up to 10 people.

ingredients . . . .

2cups graham cracker crumbs	¼cup sugar
6tbsp butter, melted	½lb whole chestnuts in syrup,
¼cup milk	drained
3oz white chocolate	
1lb pot or cream cheese	Decoration
⅔cup heavy cream	3tbsp sugar
2 eggs	candied angelica

Mix together the graham cracker crumbs and butter and press over the bottom of a well-greased 9-inch springform cake pan. Chill for 10 minutes. Preheat the oven to 350°F.

Bring the milk to a boil in a small saucepan, add the chocolate and stir off the heat until melted. Place the cheese, cream, eggs and sugar in a mixing bowl. Reserve 4 whole chestnuts for decoration, rub the remainder through a sift and beat into the cheese until smooth. Turn the mixture into the cake pan and bake in the oven for 50 minutes.

To decorate, cut the reserved chestnuts in half and roll them in the sugar. Arrange the chestnuts around the edge of the cheesecake and finish with strips of candied angelica.

HAZELNUT MERINGUE CAKE WITH FLAKED CHOCOLATE

ingredients . . . .

Meringue	Filling
½cup blanched hazelnuts (filberts)	2cups whipping cream
4 egg whites	1tbsp sugar
1cup superfine sugar	3oz semisweet chocolate, flaked
1tbsp cocoa powder	confectioners' sugar, to decorate
1tsp ground cinnamon	

Grind the hazelnuts in a coffee mill or food processor until fine. Spread the nuts out on a baking sheet and toast them under the broiler.

Preheat the oven to 300°F. Line 2 baking sheets with parchment paper. Draw three 7inch circles on the paper and set aside.

To prepare the meringue: place the egg whites in a clean mixing bowl, making sure that they are free from any traces of yolk. Add 2tbsp of the sugar to the whites and beat until stiff. (You should be able to turn the bowl upside down at this stage.) Continue to add the sugar 2-3tbsp at a time, beating well to maintain the stiffness. When all the sugar has been incorporated, sift the cocoa and the cinnamon over the egg whites, add the hazelnuts and fold in with a rubber spatula. Divide the meringue among the three circles marked on the baking sheets and spread out evenly.

The secret of crisp meringues is to realize that egg whites consist of mainly water and that when the meringues are finished in the oven the water must be able to escape as vapor. Some ovens are better ventilated than others, while some are inclined to trap the moisture, causing the meringues to steam and soften rather than dry out. If you feel your oven may not be up to scratch, wedge the door open just slightly with a dish towel so as not to lose the heat. Dry the meringues out in the preheated oven for 2-2½ hours. If you do not require them immediately, they can be stored away in an airtight container.

To finish the cake: lightly whip the cream with 1tbsp of sugar. Put the layers of meringue together with the cream, saving enough to cover the top. Sprinkle the top with flaked chocolate and dust with confectioners' sugar before serving.

The meringue will have a tendency to soften after it is assembled, making it easier to cut and all the more delicious.

A SPOOKY HALLOWEEN PARTY

*D*eviled drumsticks, spareribs, lamb burgers and corn on the cob will be a big attraction at a children's Halloween party with popcorn, a wickedly gooey chocolate cake, plenty of fruit juices and possibly a spiced apple toddy. Round off the festivities with blind man's bluff and dunking for apples.

SPICED APPLE TODDY

ingredients . . . .

2quarts apple juice
1quart orange juice
2 lemons, halved and sliced
2 oranges, halved and sliced
3 apples, cored and chopped

¾cups sugar
2 cinnamon sticks
4 cloves
2 bay leaves
6 allspice berries

Measure the apple juice, orange juice and 2quarts water into a large saucepan. Add the lemons, oranges, apples and spices. Bring to a boil, then simmer for 10-15 minutes. Strain before serving. Since hot toddies are usually popular at children's parties, it is as well to have a supply of fruit juices for the occasional replenishment.

Serves 8

LAMB BURGERS IN BUNS

ingredients . . . .

1½lb ground lamb
1 onion, chopped
1cup fresh bread crumbs

1tsp dried thyme
1 egg
flour for dusting

Place the lamb, onion, bread crumbs, thyme and seasoning in a bowl, add the egg and mix until evenly combined. Divide the mixture into 8 portions, dust with flour and shape into patties.

Cook under the broiler or in a skillet for 6-8 minutes on each side. Serve on split toasted buns with a mixed salad.

Serves 8

DEVILED CHICKEN DRUMSTICKS

ingredients . . . .

8 chicken drumsticks
3tbsp vegetable oil
2tsp English mustard
1tsp tomato paste
2tsp paprika

2tbsp Worcestershire sauce
2 shakes hot pepper sauce
2tbsp wine vinegar
1tbsp clear honey

Combine all the ingredients except the chicken in a bowl. Score the drumsticks several times with a sharp knife and marinate in the sauce for up to 8 hours.

Cook the drumsticks under the broiler for 15-20 minutes or bake them in the oven, preheated to 400°F for 35 minutes.

Serves 8

A WICKEDLY GOOEY CHOCOLATE CAKE

❧

ingredients . . . .

soft butter for greasing
⅓cup milk
4oz semisweet chocolate
10tbsp soft butter or margarine
1cup soft dark brown sugar
3 eggs
1cup self-rising flour
2tbsp cocoa powder

1tbsp black treacle (molasses), warmed

Filling
2tbsp marmalade
2tbsp butter
7oz semisweet chocolate

Lightly grease two 7inch layer cake pans and line their bottoms with parchment paper. Preheat the oven to 375°F.

Bring the milk to a boil in a small saucepan, remove from the heat, add the chocolate and allow to melt.

Cream the butter and sugar together until pale and fluffy, then gradually beat in the eggs. Sift the flour and cocoa powder together and stir into the mixture. Stir in the melted chocolate and the warm treacle. Divide between the prepared cake pans and bake in the center of the oven for 25-30 minutes.

To prepare the topping: place the marmalade, 1tbsp water and butter in a saucepan, bring to a boil, add the chocolate and stir to melt. Put the two cake layers together with half the filling and spread the rest on the top and sides. Store for up to 1 week in an airtight tin.

Serves 8

November

The weather takes on a definite change in November as the last of the autumn leaves are blown from the trees. Some would say that November is a sad month, bringing cold, frosty mornings and the threat of winter, but despite the cold weather there are many good things to look forward to. Rich warming stews, thick soups and hot spongy puddings become particularly attractive. Somehow chocolate is especially satisfying during the winter months, so I have included it in three of the puddings for November.

If you are looking for an excuse for a party, Bonfire Night on the 5th is an ideal opportunity to meet up with friends for a few fireworks, a knock-out punch and a plate of hot food.

For those who are interested, the just about drinkable but ever-popular Beaujolais Nouveau will be with us again toward the end of the month.

Since the arrival of colder weather the vegetable market has thinned out quite considerably. Main-crop carrots are at their best at the moment and join other root vegetables, parsnips, rutabaga, turnips and celeriac, to make good fillers for stews and casseroles. English celery is becoming firmer now the weather has turned colder, and is good in crunchy salads as well as braised and served hot. Cabbages, too, come into their own during November and can be delicious providing they are not overcooked. I often shred cabbage finely with a few carrots and a stalk of celery, before simmering it briefly in a beef or chicken bouillon. Ripe avocados are often in good supply at this time of the year and are ideal for hot or cold starters and creamy dips. Broccoli is often sold at a good price during November as are cauliflowers and Brussels sprouts. Some fresh spinach may still be around at the moment although it can be a bit stringy. Leeks are in good condition and full of flavor for soups and stews. Pumpkins, still available in some shops, can be served as an accompanying vegetable or puréed with potatoes and leeks to make a wonderful soup. Potatoes are shaping up slowly although many varieties are still inclined to fall apart when boiled. It is better to bake them in their jackets.

The fruit market is looking a little more colorful since the arrival of the citrus season. Clementines, tangerines and satsumas become available and oranges and lemons are brighter and juicier now. Choose thin-skinned varieties that feel heavy for their size to be sure of really juicy fruit. English apples and pears are well-priced and provide plenty of inspiration for puddings and desserts. Dried fruits and nuts appear on the market for those of us who like to make their own mincemeat and Christmas pudding (see page 195).

The fish market still has plenty of variety on offer. Cod is likely to be in good condition along with fresh haddock and pollock. Gray mullet can taste muddy during the summer months but improves considerably in the colder weather. Oily fish — mackerel, sea bass, herring, fresh sardines and sprats — seem to thrive in the cold weather and are often available at good prices. Flat fish are still plentiful although crabs and lobsters are no longer at their best. Scallops are never that cheap but their price will fall as the season continues. Other shellfish to look out for are oysters, mussels, cockles, winkles and whelks, with shrimp and prawns also in good supply.

The game season reaches its peak during November when both feathered and furred game are at their best. Now that the pheasant season is under way, prices should begin to fall. Partridge, snipe, teal and woodcock, still young and beautifully tender, make fine eating, providing they are not overcooked. The grouse season is nearing its end and most birds are now only suitable for slow cooking.

Wood pigeons are always a good buy at this time of the year and make a beefy tasting rich stew with red wine. Hare and wild rabbit are in good supply since farmers are concerned for their winter crops.

FRUIT & NUTS

British at their best:
Apples
Cooking Apples
Figs
Hazelnuts (Filberts)
Pears
Plums
Quinces
Rose Hips
Walnuts

Imported in season:
Almonds
Apricots
Bananas
Brazil Nuts
Chestnuts
Clementines
Cranberries
Dates
Grapefruit
Grapes
Kiwi Fruit
Lemons, Limes
Lychees (Litchis)
Mangoes
Melons
Oranges
Papaya
Passion Fruit
Pecans, Peanuts
Pineapples
Pistachio Nuts
Pomegranates
Satsumas

VEGETABLES & HERBS

British at their best:
Aubergines (Eggplant)
Beets
Brussels Sprouts
Cabbages
Carrots
Cauliflowers
Celeriac
Celery
Chicory (Belgian Endive)
Garlic
Kohlrabi
Leeks
Mustard and Cress
Onions
Parsley, Parsnips
Pickling (Pearl) Onions
Potatoes
Rosemary
Sage, Salsify
Savory
Shallots
Spring Greens
Spring Onions (Scallions)
Swedes (Rutabaga)Thyme
Thyme
Turnips
Watercress
Winter Squashes

Also available:
Broccoli
Corn
Cucumbers
Fennel
Globe Artichokes
Mange tout (Snow Peas)
Spinach

Imported in season:
Aubergines (Eggplant)
Avocados
Chicory (Belgian Endive)
Courgettes (Zucchini)
Garlic
Lettuce
Sweet Peppers
Tomatoes

FISH & SHELLFISH

British at their best:
Brill
Cockles
Cod, Coley (Pollock)
Crabs
Dabs
Dover Sole
Gray Mullet
Haddock, Hake
Halibut
Lemon Sole
Mussels
Monkfish
Oysters
Plaice
Red Mullet
Scallops
Sea Bass
Skate, Sprats
Trout
Turbot
Whiting
Winkles

Also available:
Conger Eel
Huss
Lobsters
Mackerel
Prawns
Salmon
Scampi (Langoustines)
Sea Trout
Shrimp
Torbay Sole

Imported in season:
Freshwater Crayfish
John Dory
Red Mullet
Sardines
Squid

POULTRY & GAME

British at their best:
Grouse
Hare
Partridge
Pheasant
Quail
Snipe
Venison
Wild Duck
Woodcock

Also available:
Chicken
Duck
Goose
Guinea Fowl
Pigeon
Rabbit
Turkey

MEAT

Beef
Lamb
Offal
Pork
Veal

Starters

CURRIED PEAR AND PARSNIP SOUP

*T*he pear and the parsnip have earned themselves a special reputation blended together with mild curry spices. The result is a perfect balance of flavors, each complementing the other in this fine soup.

ingredients

4tbsp butter
1 onion, chopped
2 bacon slices, chopped
¾lb parsnips, peeled and chopped
2 under-ripe pears, peeled, cored and chopped

1 celery stalk, chopped
2tsp mild curry powder
½tsp turmeric
1tbsp flour
3¾cups hot chicken bouillon
salt and pepper
4 watercress sprigs, for garnish

Melt the butter in a large saucepan, add the onion and bacon and soften over a gentle heat. Add the parsnips, pears and celery, cover and allow to cook in their own steam for 10 minutes. Stir in the curry powder, turmeric and flour until absorbed. Draw the saucepan away from the heat and stir in the hot chicken bouillon a little at a time until evenly mixed. Cover and simmer for 25-30 minutes or until the parsnips are tender.

Pour the soup through a vegetable mill or blend in a liquidizer until smooth. Adjust the seasoning with salt and pepper, garnish with watercress sprigs and serve.

PUMPKIN, LEEK AND POTATO SOUP

*A*t last the season for winter warming soups is upon us; thick and hearty, there is nothing like a good homemade soup after a brisk walk in the November air.

ingredients

2tbsp vegetable oil
2 bacon slices, roughly chopped
½lb white of leek, split, washed and sliced
1lb piece raw pumpkin, seeded, peeled and chopped
¾lb potatoes, chopped
1 pinch ground mace
2cups milk
2cups water
1 chicken bouillon cube

To finish
2tbsp butter
2 slices of white bread, crusts removed and cut into small fingers
2tbsp chopped parsley
¼cup heavy cream (optional)

Heat the oil in a large saucepan, add the bacon and leeks and soften without letting them color. Add the pumpkin, potatoes, mace, milk and water and the bouillon cube. Cover and simmer for 25-30 minutes or until the pumpkin has fallen apart.

The soup can be given a smooth finish in a liquidizer, although I prefer to leave it chunky. Heat the butter in a skillet, add the bread fingers and toss until crisp and golden. Serve to accompany the soup in bowls or mugs, sprinkled with parsley and with a little cream swirled into each serving if liked.

STILTON AND WALNUT PATÉ

It is not by chance that drums of Stilton (traditionally made with 17 gallons of creamy milk) should reach perfection as the weather turns colder. Stilton cheese is here to stay throughout our cold winter and is here blended with port wine and whipped up with walnuts in a savory pâté, a firm winter favorite.

 ingredients ....

3oz Stilton cheese
½cup packed pot cheese
½tsp rubbed sage
⅓cup ruby port wine
freshly ground black pepper
½cup whipping cream, softly
  whipped

½cup chopped walnuts, toasted

Garnish
24 walnut halves
4 sage sprigs

Blend the Stilton and pot cheese in a blender or food processor or mash together with a fork. Add the sage, stir in the port and season with pepper. Fold in the cream and the toasted walnuts. Turn into 4 ramekin dishes and chill for at least 1 hour before serving. Garnish with walnut halves and sage sprigs. Serve with melba toast or celery sticks.

CHEESE AND ZUCCHINI SOUFFLÉ

hen we are faced with bare cupboards and empty refrigerators the two great virtues of cooking, simplicity and originality, come to the fore. For this recipe 5 eggs, some milk, a lone zucchini and some scraps of cheese had to feed a family of 4. The result was an unforgettable soufflé. Once you have mastered the technique of the soufflé, you will find the basic recipe can be adapted to use up virtually anything. I have been able to use carrots, leeks, celery and broccoli with the addition of cheese or leftover chicken. Grated beets make a wonderfully pink surprise blended with the finely grated zest and juice of 2 oranges.

ingredients ....

3tbsp butter, softened
1 large zucchini, grated
3tbsp flour
1¼cups milk

¾oz grated Cheddar cheese
salt and pepper
5 eggs, separated

Preheat the oven to 400°F. Grease a 7inch soufflé dish with 1tbsp of the butter and set aside. Melt the remaining butter in a saucepan, add the grated zucchini and soften over a gentle heat. Stir in the flour, draw away from the heat and add the milk a little at a time until evenly blended. Add the grated cheese and seasoning and bring to a boil to thicken. Stir in the egg yolks and set aside. Beat the egg whites until they are smooth and hold a peak on the end of the beater. Stir about a quarter of the beaten egg whites into the cheese mixture, then fold in the remainder with a spatula or large metal spoon. Turn the mixture into the prepared soufflé dish and spread the top level.

   Bake in the center of the oven for about 25 minutes or until risen and golden and still slightly creamy in the center. Serve the soufflé straight from the oven accompanied by a mixed salad.

Main Courses

NORFOLK BAKED MUSSELS WITH GARLIC TRENCHERS

In days gone by, meat was often served at the English table on a trencher, a great piece of bread which would soften beneath the meat juices and was enjoyed as part of the meal. I have used this age-old principle to soak up the garlicky juices in this dish of baked mussels.

ingredients

5pints mussels
3 shallots or 1 onion, chopped
⅔cup dry white wine
2 parsley stems
4 very thick slices of bread
2 garlic cloves, minced
3tbsp chopped parsley
4tbsp butter, softened

parsley sprigs, for garnish

Sauce
4tbsp butter
¼cup flour
2cups milk
salt and pepper

Scrub the mussels well under cold running water and discard any that are open. Place the mussels in a large saucepan with the shallots or onion, wine and parsley stems. Cover and boil over a steady heat for 8 minutes. Drain the mussels in a colander set over a bowl. When the mussels are cool enough, remove them from their shells and set aside.

To prepare the trenchers, preheat the oven to 375°F. Cut the pieces of bread to fit into one large or four individual ovenproof dishes. Blend the garlic and the parsley into the butter and spread on both sides of the bread. Bake the trenchers in the oven for 10-15 minutes, turning them once.

Meanwhile, prepare the sauce: melt the butter in a saucepan, stir in the flour and cook briefly. Draw the saucepan away from the heat and stir in the milk a little at a time until smooth. Add the strained juices from the mussels and simmer to thicken.

When the trenchers are crisp, arrange them in a serving dish, place the mussels over the top, cover with the sauce and finish in the oven for 20-25 minutes. Decorate with parsley sprigs and serve as an informal lunch or supper dish.

SMOKED HADDOCK AND POTATO PIE WITH MUSHROOMS

When I was a lad my mother used to have great difficulty in getting me to eat proper fish. Fish sticks weren't a problem as I could put away up to five at one sitting. But as for real fish it wasn't until I first tried creamy fish and potato pie, that my love of fish was born and to this day it is still a great favorite of mine.

ingredients

Topping
2lb potatoes
salt and pepper
2tbsp butter
half-and-half
1 pinch finely grated nutmeg

Filling
1½lb smoked haddock (finnan haddie), cod or whiting
2cups milk

1 bay leaf
2tbsp butter
1 onion, chopped
3tbsp flour
½tsp dried thyme
¼lb button mushrooms, quartered
3 hard-cooked eggs (12 minutes), sliced
½cup grated Cheddar cheese

Bring the potatoes to a boil in plenty of salted water, simmer for 20 minutes or until tender, then drain and mash with the butter, half-and-half, nutmeg and pepper. Set aside.

To prepare the filling: season the fish with salt and pepper. Cover with the milk, add the bay leaf and simmer gently for 10-12 minutes. Lift the fish out of the milk and set aside. Melt the butter in a clean saucepan and soften the onion without letting it color. Stir in the flour and cook briefly. Remove the pan from the heat and gradually add the milk used to cook the fish, stirring until smooth. Add the thyme and mushrooms and simmer for 3-4 minutes. Preheat the oven to 400°F.

Flake the fish into the sauce, removing the skin and bones as you go. Taste for seasoning and turn into an ovenproof dish. Arrange the sliced egg over the fish and top with the mashed potato. Sprinkle the grated cheese over the top and bake in the oven for 20-25 minutes. Serve with carrots and broccoli.

ATLANTIC SEA BASS WITH SPINACH, MUSHROOMS AND THYME

A part from being one of the most attractive fish on the market, sea bass has a beautifully white flesh of an exceptional flavor. Understandably a fish with such qualities does command quite a price but by the time the fish is cooked and on the table in front of your guests, the sensation alone will be priceless.

ingredients . . . .

one 2lb sea bass (ask your fish
  monger to remove the
  backbone from the top of the
  fish leaving the belly intact)
watercress sprigs, for garnish

Stuffing
1lb/450g fresh bulk spinach
salt
2tbsp butter
1 onion, chopped
1 garlic clove, minced
1tbsp chopped thyme

¼lb open mushrooms, roughly
  chopped
1cup fresh bread crumbs
finely grated zest and juice of
  1 lemon

Sauce
3tbsp white wine vinegar
½tsp English mustard
2 egg yolks
10tbsp unsalted butter,
  softened

Wash the spinach and trim off any thick stems. Bring 1inch of water to a boil in a large saucepan, add a pinch of salt and cook the spinach for 3-4 minutes. Cool under running water and squeeze dry in the hands. Chop the spinach are finely as you can and set aside.

Melt the butter in a saucepan, add the onion and garlic and soften without allowing them to color. Add the thyme and mushrooms, cover and simmer for 3-4 minutes. Stir in the bread crumbs and add the lemon zest and juice. Season well.

Fill the interior cavity of the sea bass as loosely as possible with the stuffing. The most practical way of enclosing the stuffing is to push a wooden toothpick at intervals of about 2inches through the opening along the back of the fish. This done, wind fine string in an S fashion in between the picks as if you were lacing a shoe. When the fish is cooked, simply pull out the sticks to release the string. (Preparation so far can be done up to 24 hours in advance if you are planning ahead, and the fish kept in the refrigerator.)

To cook the bass: preheat the oven to 350°F. Wrap the whole fish in foil and lay it on its side on a baking sheet. Bake in the oven for 35-40 minutes. Garnish with watercress sprigs.

To prepare a delicious sauce to go with the bass: place the vinegar and mustard in a stainless steel saucepan and boil over a rapid heat until the liquid has reduced by half. Pour into a large heatproof bowl. Stand the bowl over a saucepan of simmering water, making sure the bowl does not touch the water, add the egg yolks and beat until pale and frothy. Remove the bowl from the saucepan and beat in pieces of soft butter until the sauce begins to thicken. Season with salt and pepper and serve immediately with the sea bass. This sauce is served warm rather than hot as it will curdle if heated too much.

A CHOWDER OF SEA FISH WITH POTATO AND OKRA

T here is nothing new about the idea of combining a variety of fish in a delicious stew. For centuries fishermen have used the odds and ends that arrive in their nets to provide a nutritious, warming supper in the form of a chowder. The best chowders are made up from whatever you can find at the fish market. This recipe is a basic structure to which you can add your own combination of fish.

ingredients . . . .

1lb cod, haddock or conger eel
  fillet
½lb squid or peeled and
  deveined raw shrimp
salt and pepper
2½pints mussels or clams
2 onions, sliced
6oz okra, trimmed
2tbsp butter
2cups fish bouillon or water

1¼cups milk
1½lb potatoes, peeled and diced
2 bay leaves
1 thyme sprig
1 pinch ground mace
⅔cup heavy cream (optional)
3tbsp chopped parsley

Prepare the fish of your choice by cutting it into equal sized pieces and seasoning with salt and pepper. If you are using mussels or clams they are best steamed open in a little bouillon or water. The mussels will need 8 minutes and clams 10-15 minutes depending on their size. Soften the onions and the okra in the butter without letting them color. Add the fish bouillon or water, milk, potatoes, bay leaves, thyme and mace. Simmer for 15-20 minutes or until the potatoes are nearly cooked. Add the fish and simmer for a further 8-10 minutes. Stir in the cream if used at the last minute, adjust the seasoning and serve the chowder in soup plates, sprinkled with freshly chopped parsley. Offer chunks of warm crusty bread to soak up the juices.

ROAST RIB OF BEEF WITH YORKSHIRE PUDDING

*N*o book of English cooking would be complete without a recipe for our most celebrated dish of Roast Beef and Yorkshire Pudding. Exactly how roast beef should be cooked has been a matter for debate among the English for generations, but when all is said and done, the truth must surely be in the eating. My grandfather, a hotelier for over thirty years, cooks beef that quite literally melts in the mouth. He tells me that the finest beef should be roasted quickly, at a high temperature, to start with and finished more gently to allow the fibers to relax and become beautifully tender. Easier said than done, I admit, but practice does make perfect.

ingredients . . . .

one 4-5lb rib roast of beef	Yorkshire Pudding
salt and pepper	3 eggs
⅓cup full-bodied red wine	salt and pepper
1¼cups beef bouillon	1¼cups milk
1tbsp cornstarch	¾cup flour

It is best to prepare the Yorkshire Pudding batter well in advance to ensure it has time to rest. Break the eggs into a measuring cup, add salt and pepper and beat with a fork. Add enough milk to measure 2cups. Sift the flour into the mixing bowl, make a well in the center, pour in half the liquid and stir to a smooth batter. Add the remaining liquid a little at a time and stir until evenly blended. Leave the batter to rest at room temperature until the beef is cooked.

To prepare the rib of beef for the oven, place it in a roasting pan, score the outer covering lightly in a criss-cross fashion and rub with salt and pepper.

The calculations that I find best when working out the cooking times are: 8 minutes per pound at 475°F followed by 15 minutes per pound at 325°F. The principle of this method is to subject the meat to severe heat to seal in the vital juices and then to reduce the heat to allow the meat to relax. It is important, however, not to open the oven door during cooking or the temperature inside the oven will not recover.

When the beef is cooked, transfer it to a plate, cover and keep

warm. Allow the roasting juices to settle in the pan and skim off the layer of fat. It is with this fat, or drippings, that the best Yorkshire puddings are made.

Increase the temperature of the oven to 450°F. Pour 2tbsp of the drippings into a 9inch roasting pan and heat it on the top shelf of the oven for 2-3 minutes or until it is beginning to smoke. Pour in the batter, return to the oven and cook for 20-25 minutes. Do not open the door until the pudding has risen and set.

To finish the gravy: heat the juices in the roasting pan on top of the stove, add the wine and stir to loosen the sediment. Add the bouillon and bring to a boil, then simmer. Classic beef gravy is served thin, but I like to thicken it just slightly with cornstarch, dissolved in 2tbsp water, to give a little body. Season to taste with salt and pepper, pour into a gravy boat and keep warm until ready to serve.

Divide the Yorkshire pudding into large pieces, carve the beef and serve with roast parsnips, carrots, Brussels sprouts and roast potatoes, with the gravy. Horseradish sauce and mustard are also traditional accompaniments.

BROWN LAMB STEW WITH PENNY ROYAL DUMPLINGS

❧

ingredients . . . .

2tbsp oil or drippings
2lb boned shoulder or leg of
  lamb, diced
1 medium-size onion, roughly
  chopped
1 celery stalk, roughly chopped
1 small carrot, roughly chopped
2tbsp flour
2tsp tomato paste
½tsp ground coriander

½tsp ground cumin
2½cups hot beef bouillon
salt and pepper

Penny Royal Dumplings
1⅔cups self-rising flour
½cup shredded beef suet
1tbsp chopped parsley
salt and pepper

Preheat the oven to 325°F.

Heat the oil or drippings in a heavy skillet and brown the lamb quickly to seal in the juices. Transfer to a casserole. Stir the onion, celery and carrot into the cooking juices and brown evenly. Add the flour, tomato paste and spices and cook briefly. Remove from the heat and stir in the beef bouillon a little at a time until absorbed by the flour. Pour the sauce over the lamb, cover and cook in the oven for 1¾ hours.

To make the dumplings: sift the flour into a mixing bowl. Add the suet, parsley and seasoning. Stir in about 4tbsp water and mix to an even dough. Sprinkle lightly with flour and shape into a thin sausage. Cut into even pieces no larger than a quarter.

When the lamb has been in the oven for 1¼ hours, add the dumplings, cover and cook for a further 15-20 minutes. Season the sauce to taste with salt and pepper and serve with buttered turnips, carrots and boiled potatoes.

RABBIT WITH MUSTARD AND CORIANDER

❧

efore you turn your nose up at the idea of rabbit for supper, let me remind you that the French, the Spanish and the Italians consider rabbit to be one of the finest meats available. The rest of us seem to have reached our opinion without even trying rabbit. Most butchers and game dealers in England stock fresh rabbit during the winter months. One of my favorite ways to cook rabbit is to spread the pieces with mustard and ground coriander and to braise them to perfection with a little wine.

ingredients . . . .

1 large rabbit, skinned, cleaned
  and cut up
flour for dusting
2tbsp vegetable oil
2 onions, sliced
1 garlic clove, minced
2 celery stalks, roughly chopped
2 carrots, roughly chopped
2tbsp flour

2tsp ground coriander
1tsp English mustard powder
2cups chicken bouillon
⅔cup dry white wine
1 thyme sprig
1 bay leaf
salt and pepper

Preheat the oven to 325°F.

Dry the rabbit pieces well and trim away any fine bones with kitchen scissors. Dust the pieces lightly with flour. Heat the oil in a heavy skillet and brown the rabbit pieces to seal in the juices, then transfer to a casserole.

Add the onions, garlic, celery and carrots to the cooking juices and soften over a low heat. Stir in the flour, coriander and mustard powder. Remove from the heat and gradually add the bouillon and the wine, stirring until evenly mixed. Pour the sauce over the rabbit, add the thyme, bay leaf and seasonings, cover and braise in the oven for 1-1½ hours, until tender. Younger rabbits usually take about an hour while older rabbits will take longer. Serve with boiled or baked potatoes, cabbage and carrots. If there is any sauce left over, it will make the basis for a fine soup with a few winter vegetables.

Cheese and Zucchini Soufflé; Roast Rib of Beef with Yorkshire Pudding;
Old English Apple Charlotte.

STEWED PIGEONS IN RED WINE FOR A COLD DAY

———— ❧ ————

*B*y the time the wild pigeons have finished gorging themselves through the best part of the grain harvest at the farmer's expense there can only be one good thing to say for them: they make a fine stew. To get the best flavor from pigeon, marinate it in red wine with a piece of stewing steak before cooking slowly in the oven.

ingredients ....

3 mature pigeons, each cut into
  4 pieces
¾lb chuck steak, diced
salt and pepper
2tbsp vegetable oil
2 bacon slices, cut into strips
1 onion, sliced

2 celery stalks, chopped
2tbsp flour
⅔cup red wine
2cups beef or game bouillon
1 thyme sprig
1 bay leaf

Season the pigeons and steak with salt and pepper. Heat the oil in a heavy skillet and brown the pigeons and beef quickly to seal in the juices, then transfer to a casserole. Fry the bacon together with the onion and celery until they begin to color. Stir in the flour and remove from the heat. Stir the wine and bouillon into the flour a little at a time until absorbed. Simmer briefly, then pour over the meat. Add the thyme and bay, cover and cook in the oven at 325°F for 2-2½ hours, until the pigeons and beef are tender.
Serve with creamed potatoes, cabbage and carrots.

ingredients ....

2 thyme sprigs
2 bay leaves
two 1½-2lb guinea fowl
salt and pepper
4 bacon slices
4tbsp butter, softened
2tbsp dry gin
2tbsp madeira or sherry
20 juniper berries

1 lemon, sliced
1 celery stalk, cut into large
  pieces
1 carrot, cut into large pieces
1cup hot chicken bouillon
1tbsp cornstarch
watercress sprigs, for garnish

Place the thyme and bay leaves inside the guinea fowl and season inside and out with salt and pepper, then cover the breasts with the bacon and truss with fine string.
Preheat the oven to 375°F.
Smear the butter over the birds, place them in a large flameproof casserole and roast uncovered for 55 minutes. Remove the birds and add the gin, madeira, juniper berries, lemon, celery and carrot to the casserole. Arrange the birds over the vegetables, add the bouillon, cover and cook for a further 45 minutes.
To finish the sauce, transfer the guinea fowl to a warmed serving dish, strain the cooking juices into a small saucepan and bring to a boil. Mix the cornstarch with 2tbsp cold water, stir into the sauce and simmer to thicken. Season the sauce with salt and pepper.
Carve the guinea fowl as you would chicken, garnish with watercress sprigs and serve with buttered savoy cabbage, carrots and rice, with the sauce handed separately.
For a special occasion, the rice can be mixed with a small quantity of wild rice, something of an expensive commodity in the west and much sought after by the gourmet for its delicate smoky flavor.

POT-ROASTED GUINEA FOWL WITH GIN AND JUNIPER

———— ❧ ————

*T*he guinea fowl is a rather handsome little bird with a profusion of black and white spotted feathers. Native of the jungles of West Africa, the guinea fowl has been popular at the English table since the time of Shakespeare and has recently made a come-back.

BAKED EGGS ON A BED OF CREAMY LEEKS AND POTATO

———— ❧ ————

*T*his is one of my favorite life-saving dishes that I often fall back on during the week when I have neither the time nor energy for anything more elaborate. The eggs may be baked topped with grated cheese if liked.

ingredients . . . .

2lb potatoes, peeled	3 bacon slices, chopped
salt and pepper	½tsp dried thyme
3tbsp butter	2tbsp flour
1cup milk	4 eggs
a little grated nutmeg	
2 large leeks, split, washed and	
sliced	

Cover the potatoes with cold water in a large saucepan, add a large pinch of salt and boil until they begin to fall apart. Drain and mash with 1tbsp butter, a little of the milk and nutmeg. Season with salt and pepper. Spread the potato into a shallow ovenproof dish and set aside.

Preheat the oven to 375°F.

Melt the remaining butter in a saucepan, add the leeks, bacon and thyme, cover and soften over a gentle heat for 3-4 minutes. Add the flour, remove from the heat and stir in the remaining milk a little at a time until smooth. Return to the heat to thicken. Season with salt and pepper and spread over the potato. Make four deep impressions, break an egg into each and bake for 15-20 minutes.

SPICED RED CABBAGE WITH APPLES AND BACON

*R*ed cabbage cooked slowly with apples, vinegar and spices is a classic combination which will improve with keeping, and can be stored in the refrigerator for up to 5 days.

ingredients . . . .

1 head red cabbage	zest and juice of ½ orange
2tbsp pork drippings or butter	¼cup wine vinegar
2 onions, sliced	2tbsp/30ml sugar
¼lb slab bacon, chopped	6 juniper berries
3 tart-sweet apples, peeled,	1 bay leaf
cored and chopped	salt and pepper

Preheat the oven to 325°F.

Cut the red cabbage into quarters with a large knife, remove the core and slice evenly. Cut the slices down the middle once or twice and wash in plenty of cold water. Melt the drippings or butter in a large flameproof casserole, add the onions and bacon and soften over a gentle heat without letting them brown.

Remove from the heat and add the apples. Add the orange zest and juice, the cabbage, vinegar, sugar, juniper berries and bay leaf and season with salt and pepper.

Cover the cabbage with a piece of parchment paper or foil, then with the lid, and cook in the oven for 1½-2 hours, until tender. The cabbage should not need any extra liquid during cooking but it is as well to check from time to time. Serve with roast pork or game dishes.

Puddings

BAKEWELL PEARS IN A CHOCOLATE AND ALMOND SPONGE

*T*he idea for this recipe came to me in a mad panic exactly one hour before my guests were due to arrive. Had I been more organized and planned properly in advance, this gorgeous dessert would never have seen the light of day.

the pears and simmer for 15 minutes.

Preheat the oven to 400°F.

Cream the butter and remaining sugar together in a mixing bowl until pale. Add the ground almonds, flour, eggs and almond extract and stir well to mix. Lift the poached pears out of the syrup and let them drain. Lightly grease a 9inch round baking dish with butter. Spoon half the creamed mixture into the dish in spaced out heaps. Stir the cocoa powder into the remaining mixture and spoon in between the other heaps to cover the bottom of the dish. Slice the pears so that they make a fan shape and lay them over the sponge mixture. Bake in the oven for 35-40 minutes or until springy to the touch.

To glaze the sponge, add 2tsp water to the apricot preserve, bring to a boil and brush over the top of the sponge. Serve warm or cold with fresh cream or custard sauce.

PROFITEROLES WITH A HOT CHOCOLATE SAUCE

*I*f you are cooking for a formal dinner party, deciding on a dessert that will please everyone can be a tricky business. An old favourite I keep up my sleeve for such occasions is a delicious bowl of cream-filled profiteroles with a hot chocolate sauce.

ingredients

1cup   caster sugar
thinly pared zest and juice of ½
   lemon
3 comice pears
10tbsp butter, softened
1cup ground almonds
6tbsp self-rising flour

2 eggs, beaten
½tsp almond extract
soft butter for greasing
1tbsp cocoa powder
3tbsp apricot preserve, to glaze

Measure 2½cups water into a saucepan, add 6tbsp of the sugar and bring to a boil with the lemon zest and juice. Peel the pears, halve them and remove the core with a melon baller. When the syrup is boiling add

ingredients

Choux pastry
1cup water
6tbsp butter
1cup flour
3 eggs
soft butter for greasing

Hot chocolate sauce
⅔cup light cream

1tbsp sugar
6oz semisweet plain chocolate

Filling .
¾pint whipping cream
2tbsp sugar
a few drops vanilla extract

Preheat the oven to 400°F. Bring the water and the butter to a boil in a heavy saucepan without allowing any of the water to boil away. Add the flour all at once and stir briskly over the heat until the mixture leaves the sides of the pan. Transfer the mixture to a mixing bowl or food processor and allow to cool slightly. Break the eggs into a bowl and beat lightly with a fork. Gradually add the eggs to the mixture beating all the time until smooth but firm.

Lightly grease a large baking sheet with butter. Pipe or spoon the choux pastry onto the sheet in little mounds no larger than a walnut, set 2 fingers apart. Bake in the oven for at least 35 minutes, until the buns are puffed up, browned and crisp. The most common mistake when making choux pastry is to take it out of the oven too soon.

To prepare the hot chocolate sauce: place the cream in a saucepan with the sugar and bring to a boil. Remove the pan from the heat and stir in the chocolate until melted. To keep the sauce warm, transfer to a small jug and stand in a saucepan of simmering water.

To finish the profiteroles: softly whip the cream with the sugar and add the vanilla. Spoon the cream into a bag fitted with a plain nozzle, poke a finger into the underside of each profiterole and fill generously. It is best to fill the profiteroles as near to serving time as possible so that the choux pastry is still crisp.

Pile the profiteroles in an attractive bowl. (I like to dust them with confectioners' sugar before bringing them to the table.) Hand the chocolate sauce separately.

Variation: for the discerning palate, profiteroles can be filled with vanilla ice cream. To do this, make a cut in the side of each profiterole and spoon in the ice cream. Keep in the freezer until you are to serve.

BAKED SOUFFLÉ PUDDING WITH ALMONDS AND A VANILLA SAUCE

Once bitten twice shy. There can be no greater fear for any cook than the fear of failure in front of invited guests. For this reason we often choose to play safe in the kitchen and will do anything to avoid repeat performances. Hot soufflés seem to create the most problems when after considerable commotion they fail to venture above the level of the dish and, if they do, often sink at a rate of knots. You will be pleased to hear that baked soufflé puddings can be prepared well in advance, unmolded and served as light as a feather with a delicious sauce. The secret of this soufflé, which uses no flour, is that it is very light and retains its shape after it has left the oven.

6tbsp soft unsalted butter
½cup sugar
½cup finely grated zest of ½ lemon
3 eggs, separated
1cup fresh brown bread crumbs
⅔cup ground almonds
⅓cup raisins, soaked overnight in dark rum (optional)

Vanilla sauce
2cups milk
½ vanilla pod or 2 drops vanilla extract
1tbsp/15ml cornstarch
3 egg yolks
2tbsp caster sugar

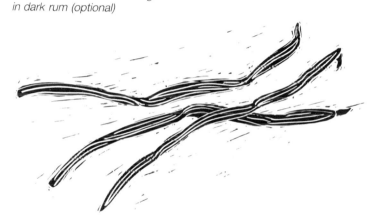

Preheat the oven to 400°F.

Lightly grease a 7inch soufflé dish with soft butter and put to one side. Cream the soft butter, half the sugar and the lemon zest together until smooth. Add the egg yolks and beat well. Beat the egg whites until firm with the remaining sugar. Fold in the bread crumbs, ground almonds and raisins (if using) by hand and in turn fold into the creamed mixture. Turn the mixture into the prepared soufflé dish, stand the dish in a roasting pan half-filled with boiling water and bake in the preheated oven for 25-30 minutes or until a skewer will come cleanly out of the center. At this stage the soufflé pudding may be kept in a warm oven for up to 2 hours without collapsing.

To prepare the vanilla sauce, bring the milk to a boil with the vanilla bean or extract. Soften the cornstarch with 2tbsp cold water, add the egg yolks and stir in the sugar. Pour the boiling milk over and stir with a wooden spoon. Strain the mixture back into the saucepan and stir to thicken. The consistency of the sauce should be that of light cream. If you are not yet ready to serve the soufflé, the sauce can be kept warm over a saucepan of simmering water, covered with a small plate. To serve the soufflé, unmold out onto an attractive dish and bring to the table with the sauce handed separately.

AN OLD ENGLISH APPLE CHARLOTTE

*A*pple Charlotte is as English as can be, despite its French sounding name. Serve it with plenty of hot custard sauce.

ingredients

1 large stale white loaf
4tbsp butter, softened
3tbsp confectioners' sugar

Filling
2tbsp butter

2lb firm, sweet apples, peeled, cored and chopped
finely grated zest and juice of 1 lemon
1 pinch ground cloves
3tbsp sugar

Slice half the loaf of bread and remove the crusts. Spread the slices with most of the butter, dredge with confectioners' sugar and toast on one side until golden. Lightly grease a 5-cup charlotte mold or round deep cake pan with the remaining butter and line with the slices of bread, arranging them overlapping with the toasted side outermost against the mold. Reserve enough bread slices for the lid. Set aside.

Make enough of the remaining bread into crumbs to fill 1cup. Pre-heat the oven to 400°F.

To prepare the filling: melt the butter in a large saucepan, add the apples, lemon and spice and soften over a steady heat. Continue to cook the apples uncovered until they are quite dry, then stir in the sugar to taste. Stir in the bread crumbs, pile the apple mixture into the prepared mold and cover the top with the remaining slices of buttered bread. Bake the charlotte in the center of the oven for 45-50 minutes. Unmold onto a serving dish and serve hot.

Bonfire Party

*O*n the night of November 5 hundreds of bonfires are lit up and down the country to commemorate the attempt by Guy Fawkes to blow up Parliament in 1605 (Guy is burned in effigy). Fireworks add to the excitement of the occasion and, of course. plenty of hot food is served. Since whoever is doing the cooking will probably want to enjoy the fireworks as well, I have suggested some dishes that can be prepared well in advance, all of which serve 8.

CHUNKY VEGETABLE SOUP

ingredients

2tbsp butter
1 onion, roughly chopped
1 large leek, split, washed and roughly chopped
1 garlic clove, minced
2 bacon slices, roughly chopped
2 carrots, peeled and sliced
2 celery stalks, sliced

¼lb turnip, peeled and sliced
¾lb potatoes, peeled and diced
5cups chicken bouillon
1 thyme sprig
1 bay leaf
salt and pepper

Melt the butter in a large saucepan and add the onion, leek, garlic, bacon, carrots and celery. Cover and soften over a gentle heat without letting the vegetables color. Add the turnip, potatoes and bouillon followed by the herbs. Allow to simmer for 30 minutes, then season to taste with salt and pepper and serve with hot crispy bread.

SPICY BANGERS WITH BACON AND BEANS

ingredients . . . .

1²⁄₃cups dried navy or pea
  beans, soaked for 8 hours and
  drained
2tbsp lard or vegetable oil
1lb pork small link sausages
½lb bacon slices, cut in half
2 onions, roughly chopped
1 garlic clove, minced

1 celery stalk, sliced
1 small carrot, peeled and
  sliced
2tsp garam masala
2tbsp plain flour
one 14oz can chopped tomatoes
2tsp tomato paste
1 chicken bouillon cube
salt and pepper

Place the soaked beans in a large saucepan, cover with cold water and simmer for 45 minutes. Meanwhile, heat the lard or oil in a large skillet and cook the sausages and the bacon until well browned. Add the sausages and bacon to the saucepan with the beans.

Soften the onions, garlic, celery and carrot in the remaining fat in the skillet without letting them color. Stir in the garam masala and the flour until absorbed into the fat. Draw the pan away from the heat and stir in the chopped tomatoes. Add the contents of the skillet to the beans and sausages and stir well. Add the tomato paste, bouillon cube and seasoning, cover and simmer over a gentle heat for 1-1½ hours or until the beans are tender.

If you already have the oven on, you may like to transfer the beans to a casserole and finish cooking at 325°F. Otherwise I find a low heat on top of the stove to be more economical. This dish will keep for up to 5 days in the refrigerator.

JACKET POTATOES BAKED IN CUMIN

ne of my favorite ways of preparing baked potatoes is to roll them first in a little vegetable oil before sprinkling them with cumin seeds and salt. The result is that the skins become crisp and spicy while the inside is soft. Baked potatoes usually take about an hour to cook in a 400°F oven. If you are planning ahead it is a good idea

to three-quarters cook the potatoes, then finish them off for 20 minutes or so before serving.

To serve: cut a cross in the top of each potato and push the edges of the potato down with the thumb and forefinger of each hand. Top each pot a to with a pat of butter, and offer a bowl of sour cream.

ROAST CHESTNUTS

oast chestnuts are always delicious when they are prepared over the open fire. Various methods can be employed, all of which seem to do the job. I use an old charred saucepan.

Before roasting the chestnuts it is necessary to pierce the soft skins with a small knife. The trick when roasting chestnuts over the fire is not to do them too quickly (unless of course you like them burnt to cinders). To roast them properly you should allow at least 20 minutes over the slow embers. If you do not have an open fire, chestnuts can be roasted in the oven at 400°F for 25-30 minutes.

KNOCK-OUT PUNCH

ingredients . . . .

5cups red wine
5cups orange juice
3tbsp brown sugar
2 oranges, quartered and sliced
1 lemon, quartered and sliced

2 apples, roughly chopped
3 cloves
1 cinnamon stick
1 bay leaf
2 star anise pods (optional)

Measure the red wine, orange juice and sugar into a large saucepan and add the fruit. Tie the spices in a piece of cheesecloth, add to the punch, simmer and infuse for 10-15 minutes. It is not a good idea to leave the spices in the punch for too long as it can become over-spiced.

Serves 8-10

BONFIRE CAKE

his cake, which is an old favorite of mine, is known in the north of England as parkin. It is traditionally eaten on Bonfire Night and is especially delicious in the cold November air.

ingredients . . . .

soft butter for greasing
1¼cups self-rising flour
1tbsp ground ginger
½tsp ground mace
2cups Scotch oats, ground in a
    food processor until quite fine

⅔cup golden raisins
1 stick butter or margarine
½cup treacle (light molasses) or
    golden syrup
2 eggs

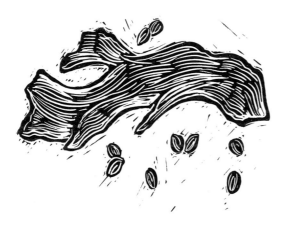

Preheat the oven to 350°F. Lightly grease an 8inch square cake pan and line with parchment paper. If you do not have an 8inch square pan, a 9inch round one will do instead. Sift the flour into a large mixing bowl with the ginger and mace. Add the oats and the raisins and set aside.

Measure the butter and treacle into a saucepan and warm over a gentle heat without letting the mixture boil. Stir the contents of the saucepan into the dry ingredients, add the eggs and stir until evenly mixed.

Turn the mixture into the prepared cake pan and bake in the center of the oven for 1¼ hours or until a skewer inserted into the center of the cake comes out clean. Cool in the pan, then unmold and cool completely on a wire rack.

The texture and flavor of Bonfire Cake will improve if kept in an air-tight container for 2-3 days.

Serves 8 or more

BAKED APPLES WITH AN APRICOT AND ALMOND STUFFING

ingredients . . . .

8 small baking apples
4tbsp butter, softened
¼cup sugar
⅔cup ground almonds

1 egg
2 drops almond extract
¾cup chopped dried apricots

Remove the cores from the apples with an apple corer or a small knife. Score the apples around their fattest part to prevent the skins from bursting. Arrange the apples on a baking sheet and set aside.

To prepare the filling: blend the butter and sugar together in a mixing bowl until pale. Add the ground almonds, egg and almond extract and stir until evenly mixed. Add the dried apricots and stuff the mixture into each of the apples. If you are planning ahead, the apples will keep up to 24 hours in the refrigerator covered with a damp cloth.

Bake the apples in the oven preheated to 375°F for 30-35 minutes. Serve the apples hot from the oven with cream or custard sauce.

Christmas Preparations

With less than 7 shopping weeks until Christmas, it is a good idea to make one or two preparations well ahead of the big rush. During November I like to find an afternoon when I can make the all-important Christmas pudding, mincemeat and cake, to give them time to mature. Most food stores are beginning by now to stock up on bulk quantities of dried fruit, often at competitive prices.

CHRISTMAS OR PLUM PUDDING

The ingredients that go into the perfect Christmas pudding have intrigued me since I was a lad when I would help my mother with the vital stirring. To this day I can remember the wonderful smells of the glistening fruits and spices to which Mum would add a generous measure of cooking brandy. Yet, delicious as the pudding was when it arrived at the table steaming with lashings of hot brandy custard, I knew that somehow it could always taste better and decided to devise a few improvements. The recipe I am giving you here is one that I have been perfecting for many years. The quantities are enough to fill 2 large pudding basins, each serving up to 8 people. If you do not need both, the other can be stored in a cool place until the following year. Some people have taken to keeping their Christmas puddings in the freezer, although I am not convinced that they mature as well as in a cool, dry, dark place.

ingredients..................

1½cups golden raisins	2½cups fresh white bread crumbs
1½cups raisins	1cup shredded beef suet
1½cups currants	¾cup Guinness or ale
⅔cup chopped pitted prunes	¼cup brandy
⅓cup chopped mixed candied peel	½tsp ground ginger
1 firm, sweet apple, grated	½tsp ground allspice
finely grated zest and juice of 1 orange	9tbsp flour
finely grated zest and juice of 1 lemon	1cup ground almonds
¾cup dark brown sugar	4 eggs
1tbsp black treacle (dark molasses)	olive oil for greasing

Wash the dried fruit, dusting it with a handful of flour before rinsing under cold water. Put all the dried fruit into a large mixing bowl. Add the remaining ingredients and stir well until thoroughly combined. Leave the mixture to stand overnight before filling the basins.

Lightly grease two 1½quart pudding basins with olive oil. (Butter is not suitable as it will tend to go rancid if the pudding is to be kept.) Divide the mixture between the basins, allowing an inch or so for the puddings to rise. Lightly grease two circles of parchment paper to fit into the basins. There are several methods of covering the puddings; the most effective is a large square of cheesecloth, secured with string, with the loose ends tied into a big granny knot. If you cannot find any cheesecloth, foil will do just as well, tucked securely around the rim of the basin.

Before the puddings are stored away they must be steamed for 5-6 hours. Stand them side by side in a large casserole, pour in boiling water to come halfway up the sides of the basins, cover and steam in the oven preheated to 300°F for 6 hours, adding more boiling water as necessary. On Christmas Day the puddings will need a further 2½-3 hours steaming before serving (see page 215 for serving instructions).

MINCEMEAT

※

incemeat is a useful addition to the pantry and can be added to apple pies, spread into tart cases and layered with an almond filling or used as a stuffing for baked apples and pears.

ingredients................................

1½cups golden raisins	1 carrot, grated
1½cups raisins	finely grated zest and juice of 2
1½cups currants	oranges
½lb firm, sweet apples, grated	finely grated zest and juice of 1
1¼cups dark brown sugar	lemon
⅔cup shredded beef suet	1¼cups Guinness or ale
1tsp ground ginger	¼cup brandy or dark rum
1tsp ground cinnamon	
½tsp ground mace	

To wash the dried fruits, rub them together with a handful of flour and rinse well under cold water. (The color of the water will tell you how effective this method is.) Combine the remaining ingredients and leave to macerate for 2-3 days. If you like a smoother mincemeat, as I do, grind or process about one third of the mixture and combine well with the remainder before sealing into clean jam jars.

Makes 3½-4lb

PIECES OF CANDIED QUINCE

※

hen the owl and the pussycat went to sea in their beautiful pea green boat they brought with them mince and slices of quince to eat beneath a silvery moon. To preserve the perfumed fragrance of the quince together with its magical color I find it most effective to saturate neat little slices in a heavy syrup and sprinkle them with fine sugar. Candied quince will keep almost indefinitely but it is unlikely that it will see the other side of Christmas.

ingredients................................

3 quinces
2cups sugar plus extra for
  finishing

Peel and quarter the quinces, remove the cores and cut into equal slices from top to bottom. Place the slices in a saucepan, cover with cold water, bring to a boil and simmer for 6-8 minutes. Discard the water and cool the slices under running water. This initial stage opens the natural pores in the fruit which will enable it to become saturated with sugar syrup. To prepare the syrup, measure ⅔cup water into a heavy saucepan with ½cup of the sugar, bring to a boil and stir until dissolved. Add the slices of quince, return to a boil and leave overnight. The remainder of the sugar is added in three ½cup intervals over as many days. Each day, bring the syrup to a boil, add the next measure of sugar, simmer briefly and allow to stand. When the slices have stood after their final addition of sugar, rinse them under cold water to remove any excess syrup and sprinkle them with extra sugar. Arrange the slices in small paper cases and store in a cool place.

DUNDEE CAKE

※

any people prefer Dundee cake to the traditional English iced Christmas cake because Dundee cake is less time-consuming to make and is not weighed down with excess calories.

ingredients................................

1cup raisins	1⅓cups ground almonds
1cup golden raisins	finely grated zest of 1 orange
½cup glacé cherries, halved	1tsp orange-flower water
2 sticks + 1tbsp butter, softened	(optional)
1½cups light brown sugar	1cup half blanced almonds
4 eggs, at room temperature	1 egg white
1⅓cups self-rising flour	

Preheat the oven to 375°F.

Wash the raisins and cherries well and leave to drain. Lightly grease an 8inch spring form cake pan with 1tbsp of the butter and line with parchment paper.

Cream the remaining butter with the sugar in a mixing bowl until pale. Break the eggs into a cup and beat lightly with a fork. Add the eggs a little at a time to the mixture, beating well. If the mixture begins to separate, add a little of the flour and continue mixing. To ensure that the fruit does not sink to the bottom of the cake, it is a good idea to dust it with a little of the flour. Add the fruit, flour, almonds, orange zest and orange-flower water to the mixture and stir well. Turn the mixture into the prepared cake pan and decorate the top with the halved almonds, then brush the almonds with egg white for an attractive glaze.

Bake in the center of the oven for 1 hour, then reduce the heat to 325°F, and bake for a further 1½ hours. Test the cake by inserting a skewer into the center; if it comes away clean, the cake is cooked. Allow to cool in the pan, then remove and store in an airtight container, or well wrapped in foil, until Christmas.

December

The month of December is really one big crescendo mounting up to the excitement of Christmas and the New Year. For those of us responsible for entertaining family and friends over Christmas, the arrival of the New Year can come as a relief.

December days can also be among the bleakest of the year. Farmers are restricted by the cold weather and grow what they can, while the markets depend on imports nearer Christmas to meet the ever-increasing demand for variety. English produce, although often limited, remains the best value for money with winter cabbages now at their best. Varieties include Savoy, red and white, with Savoy having the best flavor. Brussels sprouts are cheap and plentiful during December as are Brussels sprout tops or greens. Broccoli and cauliflower are in good condition although they can become expensive nearer Christmas time. Imported green beans, zucchini, snow peas, sweet peppers, fennel, eggplant and asparagus can be worth having providing you don't mind paying high prices. More down to earth are English root vegetables in great variety – celeriac, parsnips, turnips, carrots, ruta baga, salsify and Jerusalem artichokes – all at their best and full of flavor. Leeks, onions, shallots and garlic are also in good supply and will remain so throughout the winter months. Salad ingredients are all imported at the moment except English watercress, which will be in plentiful supply nearer Christmas to make a suitable garnish for the turkey, along with fresh cranberries for a tangy sauce. Celery is often good value during December and is good served as an accompanying vegetable with carrots and shredded cabbage. Parsley, sage and thyme, essential ingredients for homemade turkey stuffings, are usually available fresh at many greengrocers.

As we draw near to the festive season the varieties of exotic fruit include fresh litchis, mangoes, papayas, persimmons, guavas and passion fruits. A little more expensive but equally delicious are fresh pineapples imported from the Ivory Coast. As the citrus season comes into full swing, brightly colored oranges, grapefruits, lemons and limes are worth every penny for their wonderfully fresh flavor. An increasing variety of loose-skinned satsumas, tangerines and clementines floods the market and seems to adorn every fruit bowl in the land. Kumquats are the smallest of all the citrus fruits; no larger than a grape, they can be eaten whole, skin and all, and look attractive sliced into fruit salads or as a decoration for drinks. Grapes are usually in good supply for Christmas. English apples and pears are still available at competitive prices. Nuts always make an attractive display for the sideboard. Choose from brazils, pecans, almonds, walnuts and cobnuts, and chestnuts for the fire. Dried figs and dates are also traditional favorites at Christmas time.

Providing the weather is favourable, fishmongers are able to provide an attractive display of wet fish up until Christmas. The flat fish season continues with Dover and lemon soles, flounder, brill, turbot and halibut, all of which are still in good condition.

Fresh cod steaks cut from the tail end, haddock, pollock and whiting are worth having if you are looking for ideas for fast easy suppers. As the weather becomes colder, oily fish – mackerel, herring, sprats and fresh sardines – become plumper and fuller flavored. The king of the oily fish – with a price to match – is the sea bass with its delicate white flesh, ideal for stuffing and baking. There is usually a variety of smaller shellfish available during December, including native oysters, scallops, mussels, clams, cockles and winkles. Baby squid are imported throughout the winter months and are delicious combined with a seafood sauce. Smoked salmon is perhaps the most popular fish for the Christmas season, but if you are feeling the pinch and cannot manage it, smoked trout is an ideal alternative served on the bone with a salad or made into a delicious pâté with horseradish and walnuts.

Many fishmongers turn their attention to supplying game as well nearer Christmas and offer pheasant, partridge, teal, snipe and the ever popular goose. The grouse season finishes on 10 December, and the older birds are best suited to stewing or braising. Butcher's shop windows for the week before Christmas are literally crammed with fresh turkeys and roasting cuts of meat.

DECEMBER INGREDIENTS IN SEASON

FRUIT & NUTS

British at their best:
Apples
Figs
Hazelnuts (Filberts)
Pears
Plums
Quinces
Rose Hips
Walnuts

Imported in season:
Almonds
Apricots
Bananas
Brazil Nuts
Clementines
Cranberries
Dates
Grapefruit
Grapes
Kiwi Fruit
Lemons
Limes
Lychees (Litchis)
Mangoes
Melons
Oranges
Papaya
Passion Fruit
Peanuts
Pecans
Pineapples
Pistachio Nuts
Pomegranates
Satsumas
Walnuts

VEGETABLES & HERBS

British at their best:
Beets
Brussels Sprouts
Cabbages
Carrots
Cauliflowers
Celeriac
Celery
Chicory (Belgian Endive)
Kohlrabi
Leeks
Mustard and Cress
Onions
Parsley
Parsnips
Potatoes
Rosemary
Sage
Salsify
Savory
Shallots
Spring Greens
Spring Onions (Scallions)
Swedes (Rutabaga)
Thyme
Turnips
Watercress

Also available:
Broccoli
Cucumbers
Fennel
Globe Artichokes
Pickling (Pearl) Onions

Imported in season:
Aubergines (Eggplant)
Avocados
Chicory (Belgian Endive)
Courgettes (Zucchini)
French (Green) Beans
Garlic
Lettuce
Mange tout (Snow Peas)
Sweet Peppers
Tomatoes

FISH & SHELLFISH

British at their best:
Cod
Coley (Pollock)
Gray Mullet
Haddock
Hake
Herring
Monkfish
Mussels
Oysters
Sardines
Scallops
Sea Bass
Skate
Sprats
Trout
Whiting

Also available:
Brill
Cockles
Conger Eel
Crabs
Dover Sole
Halibut
Huss
Lemon Sole
Mackerel
Plaice
Prawns
Salmon
Scampi (Langoustines)
Sea Trout
Shrimp
Turbot
Winkles

Imported in season:
John Dory
Red Mullet
Sardines
Squid

POULTRY & GAME

British at their best:
Goose
Grouse until the 10th
Guinea Fowl
Hare
Partridge
Pheasant
Quail
Snipe
Turkey
Venison
Wild Duck
Woodcock

Also available:
Chicken
Duck
Pigeon
Rabbit

MEAT
Beef
Lamb
Offal
Pork
Veal

MUSHROOM SOUP WITH A HINT OF SHERRY

I often prepare this soup as a starter for the Christmas dinner. It makes use of fresh vegetables and is both light and easy to prepare.

ingredients...............................

2tbsp butter
1 onion, finely chopped
1 garlic clove, minced
½tsp thyme
6oz button mushrooms, sliced
3tbsp dry sherry
3¼cups chicken bouillon

⅓cup heavy cream
salt and pepper
2tbsp chopped parsley

Melt the butter in a non-aluminum saucepan, add the onion, garlic and thyme and soften over a gentle heat without letting them color. Add the mushrooms and sherry, cover and cook over a gentle heat for 3-4 minutes. Add the chicken bouillon and simmer for 15-20 minutes. If you are planning ahead the soup can be prepared to this stage and kept in the refrigerator for up to 3 days before finishing.

To finish the soup; stir a ladleful of the soup into the cream, add to the soup and heat through without letting the soup boil. Season with salt and pepper and serve sprinkled with chopped parsley.

If you are serving this soup for a casual lunch, provide a substantial accompaniment.

A CREAMY CHICKEN AND CELERY SOUP

Celery is full of flavor at the moment and is best appreciated in this delicious chicken soup, which is finished off with a generous measure of heavy cream.

ingredients...............................

2 chicken legs
4 stalks celery
1 small carrot, roughly chopped
½ small onion, roughly chopped
1 thyme sprig

2tbsp butter
3tbsp flour
⅓cup heavy cream
salt and pepper

Place the chicken legs in a large saucepan with one roughly chopped stalk of celery, the carrot, onion and thyme. Add 5cups of cold water, bring to a boil and simmer gently for 1 hour, removing any fat that comes to the surface. Strain the resulting bouillon into a large measuring cup. Discard the vegetables and set the chicken aside to cool until needed.

Melt the butter in a clean saucepan. Neatly slice the remainder of the celery and soften. Stir in the flour until absorbed by the cooking juices and remove from the heat. Stir in the chicken bouillon a little at a time until smooth and return to the heat to thicken.

Remove the chicken from the bone, chop roughly, add to the soup and simmer for 20-25 minutes. Season to taste with salt and pepper and finish with the cream. Serve as an informal lunch dish with a basket of hot crispy bread.

SMOKED SALMON WITH BROWN BREAD AND BUTTER

It saddens me when I read fancy recipes that attempt to improve on ingredients that are best left alone. When it comes to smoked salmon, I prefer to see it served as it is, thinly sliced, with buttered brown bread and a squeeze of lemon. Far be it from me to improve on perfection. When buying smoked salmon it is always worth spending a little extra on the best quality since inferior salmon is not worth having. Allow 2-3oz per person and enjoy yourself.

AVOCADO, CELERY AND SHRIMP COCKTAIL

Terrible things have happened to the shrimp cocktail since it has become so popular on the restaurant menu. For this homemade recipe I have bound ripe avocados, crisp celery and shrimp in a delicate sauce and presented them as a light salad served with fingers of hot toast.

ingredients . . . .

½lb cooked peeled shrimp
1 large avocado, quartered, peeled and diced
2 celery stalks, cut into 1inch strips
1 head attractive lettuce

Sauce
¼cup mayonnaise
¼cup light cream or half-and-half

3tbsp tomato catsup
2tsp grated horseradish
1tbsp Worcestershire sauce
3 shakes hot pepper sauce
1tbsp lemon juice

Garnish
2 tomatoes, cut into thin wedges
4 parsley sprigs

Combine the shrimp, avocado and celery in a bowl and set aside. To prepare the sauce; blend together all the ingredients until evenly mixed and combine with the shrimp mixture.

When you are ready to serve, arrange the lettuce on individual plates and spoon the shrimp mixture to one side. Decorate with thin wedges of tomato and parsley sprigs. Serve with fingers of hot toast as a starter or light main course. Mussels, crab, squid or scallops may be substituted for the shrimp.

AN EGGPLANT CHEESE DIP

One of the biggest problems I have when entertaining is keeping my guests out of the kitchen when I am busy with the last-minute preparations. The solution that I find most effective is to lure them into the next room with one of my tasty dips. For this recipe I have used a large aubergine.

ingredients . . . .

2tbsp sesame or olive oil
1 large eggplant, peeled and chopped
1 onion, roughly chopped
1 garlic clove, minced
½cup packed pot or cream cheese

2tbsp sesame seeds, toasted
2tbsp lemon juice
3 shakes hot pepper sauce
salt and pepper

Heat the oil in a small saucepan, add the eggplant, onion and garlic, cover and soften over a gentle heat for 10-12 minutes, stirring occasionally. Allow to cool, then blend together with the cheese, sesame seeds, lemon juice and seasonings until smooth.

Serve the dip with strips of raw carrot, celery and cucumber or toasted pitta bread cut into fingers.

Main Courses

TENDER MUSSELS IN A PUFF PASTRY CASE

Mussels are one of my favorite winter shellfish since they are full of flavor and always inspire me with new ideas for their preparation. Serve this as a starter or light main course.

ingredients

1lb puff pastry
1 egg, to glaze
5pints mussels
1 medium-size onion, sliced
¼cup sliced celery
¼cup sliced carrot
2 parsley stems
⅓cup dry white wine

Sauce
⅔cup fish bouillon

½ large carrot, cut into 1½inch matchsticks
½ celery stalk, cut into 1½inch matchsticks
1tbsp soft butter
1tbsp flour
¼cup whipping cream
salt and pepper
parsley sprigs, for garnish

To make the puff pastry cases, roll out the pastry on a floured work surface to a thickness of 1/8inch and cut out four 5inch squares. Fold each square from corner to corner into a triangle. With the point of the triangle facing away from you, cut a ¾inch border on each side to within ¾inch of the point. Open the squares out, brush the center with beaten egg and fold the two loose borders toward the center to form the sides of the case. Allow the puff pastry to rest for at least 1 hour before baking.

To prepare the mussels, scrub them well under cold running water to remove any beards and barnacles. Discard any that are open. Place the onion, celery, carrot, parsley stems and wine in a large saucepan. Add the mussels, cover and simmer for 6-8 minutes. Drain the mussels in a colander set over a bowl to collect the juices. Allow the mussels to cool, then remove from their shells. Discard any that have not opened. If you are planning ahead the mussels can be prepared to this stage and kept in the refrigerator for up to 12 hours before serving.

When the puff pastry cases have rested sufficiently, brush them with beaten egg again and bake in the oven preheated to 400°F for 35-40 minutes. Cut out the centers with a small knife and keep the pastry cases warm.

To finish the sauce: strain the cooking liquid from the mussels into a small saucepan. Add the bouillon together with the carrot and celery matchsticks and simmer for 2-3 minutes. Blend the butter with the flour and gradually beat into the sauce to thicken. Add the mussels and warm them through. Stir in the cream and season with salt and pepper. When you are ready to serve, spoon the mussels into the puff pastry cases and decorate with parsley sprigs.

CURRIED FISH WITH AN EGG SAUCE

ingredients

2lb cod or other white fish, skinned
1¼cups milk
2tbsp vegetable oil
1 onion, chopped
1 garlic clove, minced
1 celery stalk, chopped
½lb turnips, peeled and chopped

1inch piece ginger root, peeled and grated
2tsp mild curry paste
½tsp turmeric
1tbsp flour
4 fresh eggs, poached
4 parsley sprigs, for garnish

Place the fish and milk in a shallow saucepan and bring to a boil, then simmer gently for 6-8 minutes. Heat the oil in a non-stick skillet, add the onion, garlic, celery and turnips and soften over a gentle heat without letting them color. Add the ginger, curry paste, turmeric and flour and cook briefly to lift the flavor of the spices.

Remove the pan from the heat and gradually stir in the milk used to cook the fish until smooth. Return to the heat and simmer to thicken. Flake the cooked fish into the sauce, discarding any bones. Warm the fish briefly in the sauce, trying to keep the fish in large pieces.

Serve on a bed of rice with a lightly poached egg on each portion, garnished with parsley sprigs.

SEAFOOD SPAGHETTI WITH WINTER HERBS

*D*uring the winter months I like to put together a warming spaghetti dish making use of whatever I can find at the fishmonger's. At this time of the year mussels, cockles, clams and squid are good value for money and combine well with almost any white fish in a rich tomato sauce scented with garlic and herbs. The variety of fish that I have mentioned in the recipe is only a rough guide. If your supply of fish is limited to one or two varieties they should amount to 1½lb in weight.

ingredients

1lb cod, haddock or whiting fillet	one 14oz can chopped tomatoes
salt and pepper	½cup dry white wine
2½pints mussels or clams	1 bay leaf
3tbsp vegetable oil	1tsp chopped winter savory or
1 large onion, chopped	thyme
2 garlic cloves, minced	½lb squid, cleaned and cut into
1 celery stalk, sliced	rings
1 carrot, halved and sliced	½lb cooked peeled shrimp
1tbsp tomato paste	¾lb spaghetti
1tbsp flour	

Prepare the white fish of your choice by cutting it into equal-sized pieces and seasoning with salt and pepper. If you are using mussels or clams they are best steamed open in a little bouillon or water in a covered saucepan. The mussels will need 6-8 minutes and clams between 10-15 minutes, depending on their size. Clean well before cooking, discarding any that are open. When cooked, discard any that have not opened.

Heat the vegetable oil in a large skillet, add the onion, garlic, celery and carrot, cover and soften without letting them color. Stir in the tomato paste and the flour until absorbed. Then add the chopped tomatoes, the wine and the herbs. Stir in the white fish and the squid, cover and simmer for 10-12 minutes. Add the mussels and the shrimp at the last minute to warm them through.

Meanwhile, cook the spaghetti. Bring a large saucepan of water to the boil with a pinch of salt. Slide in the spaghetti, stir well to separate and boil, uncovered, for 10-12 minutes or until *al dente*, or firm to the bite. Drain and stir in the seafood sauce. Serve immediately.

FILLETS OF SOLE WITH PINK GRAPEFRUIT AND LIME

*S*ince the arrival of the cheap take-away and the frozen microwave dinner, most fast food has become a gourmet's nightmare. If I'm rushing off somewhere in the evening or arriving home late, I often resort to a simple fish dish that can be prepared with the minimum of fuss.

ingredients

2lb sole or other flatfish, filleted and skinned	3tbsp dry vermouth or white wine
salt and pepper	2tsp cornstarch
2 shallots or 1 small onion, finely chopped	¼cup heavy cream
2tbsp butter, diced	Garnish
finely grated zest and juice of 1 lime	1 pink grapefruit, segmented
	1 lime, thinly sliced

Preheat the oven to 350°F. Season the fish and fold the fillets in half, skinned sides innermost. Place the shallots or onion and the butter in an ovenproof dish and lay the fillets over the top. Add the lime zest and juice, the vermouth and ⅓cup water. Cover the dish with buttered paper or foil and cook in the oven for 10-12 minutes.

Lift the fillets out onto a warm plate and strain the cooking juices into a small saucepan. Mix the cornstarch with 2tbsp cold water, stir into the juices and simmer to thicken. Stir in the cream and adjust the seasoning. Arrange the fish onto 4 serving plates and cover with the sauce. Decorate with pink grapefruit segments and fresh lime twists. Serve with Basmati rice, broccoli and carrots.

STUFFED LOIN OF PORK WITH STILTON AND WALNUTS

One of the advantages of pork over other meats is that small cuts can be roasted without becoming dry. For this recipe I have chosen a loin of pork with the ribs attached since meat that is roasted on the bone has a better flavor. I have incorporated a stuffing of Stilton and walnuts with a hint of sage.

ingredients . . . .

one 3lb pork loin roast

Stuffing
1 small onion, chopped
½ celery stalk, chopped
2tbsp butter
¼cup chopped walnuts
1tsp rubbed sage
finely grated zest and juice of ½ lemon
¼cup crumbled Stilton cheese
½cup fresh bread crumbs

Gravy
½cup dry white wine or hard cider
⅔cup chicken bouillon
1tbsp cornstarch
salt and pepper

To prepare the pork for stuffing, make a single cut against the full length of the bones, leaving the meat intact at the base. Season the pork inside and out and set aside.

To prepare the stuffing: soften the onion and the celery in the butter without letting them color. Remove from the heat and stir in the walnuts and sage. Add the lemon zest and juice, Stilton and bread crumbs. Season well. Stuff the pork firmly and secure with fine string. If you are planning ahead, the pork can be prepared to this stage, then kept in the refrigerator for up to 2 days or frozen for up to 3 weeks.

To roast the pork: preheat the oven to 400°F.

Roast the pork without any additional fat in the center of the oven for 30 minutes, then reduce the oven temperature to 350°F and cook the pork for 1 further hour.

To prepare the gravy: transfer the pork to a carving board, cover and keep warm. Spoon off any visible fat from the cooking juices. Heat the juices on top of the stove, add the wine or cider and boil to reduce by half. Add the chicken bouillon, then thicken with the cornstarch mixed with 2tbsp water and season to taste.

Carve the pork off the bone and serve with roast potatoes and apple sauce, with the gravy handed separately.

POT-ROASTED PARTRIDGES IN A PEAR TREE

On the first day of Christmas my true love sent to me, 'A partridge in a pear tree.' And indeed young partridges, very much in season at the moment, make fine eating if they are pot-roasted with one or two of their native fruits.

ingredients . . . .

4 partridges, trussed
6tbsp butter
1 small carrot, roughly chopped
1 onion, roughly chopped
1 celery stalk, roughly chopped
¼cup mushroom trimmings
½cup full-bodied red wine
⅞cup game or chicken bouillon

4 small comice pears, peeled, quartered and cored
1 thyme sprig
2tbsp flour
2tsp red wine or raspberry vinegar
watercress sprigs, for garnish

Preheat the oven to 350°F.

Season the partridges well with salt and pepper. Heat 4tbsp of the butter in a flameproof casserole or a heavy roasting pan on top of the stove and brown the partridges two at a time on all sides. Place the carrot, onion and celery in the bottom of the casserole and place the birds on top. Add the mushroom trimmings together with the wine, bouillon, pears and thyme. Bring to a boil, then cover with a lid or foil and pot-roast in the center of the oven for 1¼ hours.

Transfer the partridges and the pears to a warm plate. Strain the cooking juices into a clean saucepan and spoon off any visible fat from the surface. To finish the sauce, soften the remaining butter with the flour to make a smooth paste and mix. Bring the cooking juices to a boil and beat in the paste a little at a time to thicken. Simmer briefly and taste for seasoning, adding the vinegar.

Garnish with watercress and serve.

ROAST GOOSE WITH APPLES, ONION AND SAGE

❧

f you are looking for a change from the over-celebrated Christmas turkey this year, why not settle for a fattened goose stuffed with apples, onions and sage? The goose was a popular centerpiece at the English table long before intensive turkey farming was even heard of. Lincolnshire, Norfolk and the Fens around Cambridge are the best-known breeding areas in England, providing the birds with a free-range environment in which they can feed. Roast goose not only looks splendid, it has a particularly fine flavor. Geese vary in weight from 6-12lb. Anything over 12lb is likely to be too tough for roasting. As a guide, a 10lb goose will feed between 6-8 people with enough meat left over for sandwiches on Boxing Day.

ingredients . . . .

one 10lb goose, with neck
  and giblets
salt
2 large baking apples
3 small bay leaves
3 cloves
watercress sprigs, for garnish

Giblet bouillon
1 small onion, chopped
1 small carrot, chopped
1 celery stalk, chopped
1 thyme sprig

Sage and onion stuffing
4tbsp butter

1 large onion, chopped
6 bacon slices, chopped
2tbsp rubbed sage
¼lb link pork sausages, skins
  removed
4cups fresh bread crumbs
⅔cup dry hard cider or chicken
  bouillon
salt and pepper

Gravy
⅔cup dry white wine
1tbsp cornstarch
2tsp white wine vinegar

Season the goose inside and out with salt and pierce the skin all over with a fork to allow the fat to flow. Core the apples, leaving their skins intact, and secure a bay leaf to each apple with a clove. Place the apples inside the goose and truss with string. When the goose is cooked the apples will make a delicious sauce.

To prepare a giblet bouillon: discard the liver from the giblets as it would dominate the flavor of the bouillon. Cover the giblets with cold water, add the onion, carrot, celery and thyme, bring to a boil and simmer for 1½-2 hours. Strain and reserve 1 cup stock; this will be the basis for a delicious gravy.

To prepare the stuffing: melt the butter in a saucepan and cook the onion and bacon without letting them color. Add the sage, sausagemeat and bread crumbs and stir in the cider or chicken bouillon. Season the stuffing well and stuff the front cavity of the goose, securing it underneath with wooden toothpicks. If you are planning ahead, the goose can be prepared to this stage up to 2 days in advance, providing it is kept in a cool place.

To roast a 10lb goose you need to allow 3-3½ hours cooking, then 30 minutes standing before carving. Preheat the oven to 425°F, place the goose on a trivet and stand in a deep roasting pan to collect the fat. Roast the goose in the center of the oven for 1 hour, then reduce the heat to 325°F and continue roasting for a further 2-2½ hours until cooked through, basting occasionally. If the goose is coloring too quickly, cover it with foil.

When the goose is cooked, transfer to a carving board and allow to rest in a warm place. Resting the bird before carving will allow the juices to absorb into the meat, keeping it moist and tender, and will also give you plenty of time to finish the gravy. Tilt the roasting pan to one side and spoon off the layer of fat. It is worth saving the fat since it has an excellent flavor.

Heat the cooking juices in the pan on top of the stove, add the wine and loosen the sediment with a wooden spoon. Reduce by half, then add the strained giblet bouillon and thicken with the cornstarch mixed with 2 tbsp water. Taste for seasoning and add the vinegar. Pour into a sauce-boat and keep warm.

To finish the apple sauce: remove the apples from inside the goose and scrape the soft flesh into a serving dish. (1tsp horseradish may be added if liked to the sauce to give it an extra lift.) Serve the goose, garnished with watercress, with roast potatoes, buttered carrots, broccoli and celeriac finished in a parsley cream sauce with a hint of garlic, with the gravy and apple sauce handed separately.

SAVORY RICE WITH CHICKEN, CHESTNUTS AND BACON

❧

hen I arrive home late, exhausted and hungry after a late night shopping spree, I often put together an all-in-one dish of savory rice, which can be prepared from start to finish in 30 minutes. An added bonus is that there is only one saucepan to wash afterwards.

ingredients ....

2tbsp   olive oil
2   boneless chicken breast
    halves, skinned and cut into
    strips
4   bacon slices, chopped
1   onion, chopped
½tsp   oregano or marjoram

1⅓cups   long-grain rice
2½cups   hot chicken bouillon
¾lb   dried chestnuts, soaked
½lb   Brussels sprouts, trimmed
    and quartered

ingredients ....

1lb   link pork sausages
2tbsp   drippings or lard

Batter
3   eggs
1   large pinch salt and pepper
1¼cups   milk
¼⁄¾cup   flour

Mushroom and onion gravy
2tbsp   drippings
1   onion, sliced
1tbsp   flour
1cup   brown beef bouillon
2oz   open mushrooms, sliced

Heat the oil in a heavy saucepan and brown the chicken and the bacon over a fast heat. Lower the heat and soften the onion together with the herbs. Add the rice, stirring to coat all the grains in the cooking juices. Add the bouillon together with the chestnuts and simmer uncovered for 10 minutes, then add the Brussels sprouts and simmer for a further 5-10 minutes. Season with freshly ground black pepper and serve.

Savoury rice dishes can be made up from almost anything you can find in the refrigerator. Variations on this recipe could make use of lef-tover turkey or ham together with a number of winter vegetables. A little white wine can be added with the bouillon for a special flavor.

Preheat the oven to 425°F. Pierce the sausages all over with a fork. Place the drippings in a roasting pan and brown the sausages in the preheated oven for 10-15 minutes.

While the sausages are cooking, make the batter: break the eggs into a measuring cup, add the seasoning and beat with a fork. Add the milk to measure 2cups. Sift the flour into a mixing bowl, make a well in the center, pour in half of the liquid and stir to make a lump-free batter. When the batter is smooth, add the remaining liquid and stir until evenly mixed. If you have time, it is a good idea to leave the batter to rest for an hour or so before using it. When the sausages have browned evenly, pour in the batter and bake in the center of the oven for 35-40 minutes.

To prepare the mushroom and onion gravy: heat the drippings in a skillet and brown the onion evenly. Stir in the flour and remove from the heat. Add the bouillon a little at a time until it is absorbed. Return to the heat, add the mushrooms and simmer for 2-3 minutes. Serve the toad-in-the-hole with buttered cabbage and carrots, with the gravy served separately.

TOAD-IN-THE-HOLE WITH A MUSHROOM AND ONION GRAVY

*G*ood food often evokes memories of childhood. Along with pro-cessions of toasted Marmite soldiers, sponge puddings and second helpings of custard comes the magnificent toad-in-the-hole. To this day it remains a mystery to me how such a simple batter can transform itself so dramatically into an enormous fluffy toad. The secret, as all lovers of toad-in-the-hole will tell you, is to cook it in a blazing hot oven with the door firmly closed.

Puddings

ENGLISH APPLE CRÊPES

One of the secrets of successful dessert making, as of all good cooking, is to choose only the finest ingredients. During my stay at the Connaught Hotel in London, my pastry chef Wally Ladd, now retired after an incredible forty-six years service, used to say, "You can't make a silk purse out of a sow's ear." Even the most humble desserts rely on the finest ingredients of the season. At this time of the year English apples are full of flavor and make a delicious filling for crêpes, rolled up and served hot with brandy custard. If you are planning ahead for Christmas, the filled crêpes can be frozen for up to 6 weeks.

ingredients

Batter
⅓cup flour
1tbsp sugar
2 eggs
1cup milk
1tbsp butter

Filling
2tbsp butter

2lb firm, sweet apples, peeled, cored and chopped
¼cup dry white wine
finely grated zest of ½ orange
1 pinch ground allspice or cinnamon
1tbsp sugar (optional)

To make the crêpe batter, sift the flour and sugar into a mixing bowl and make a well in the center. Beat the eggs into the milk with a fork, pour into the well and stir to make a smooth batter. Heat the butter in a 7inch crêpe pan over a fast heat until it begins to brown. Allow to cool a little, then stir into the batter and leave to rest while you prepare the filling. Set the pan aside.

Melt the butter in a large skillet, add the apples, wine, orange zest and spices, cover and simmer for 6-8 minutes. If the apples seem a little moist, remove the lid and allow some of the liquid to evaporate. Taste the apple filling and sweeten if necessary.

To make the crêpes: heat the crêpe pan, brush with a little extra melted butter, pour in enough crêpe batter to coat the bottom of the pan and cook for 20-30 seconds. Lift the edge of the crêpe with a palette knife, turn over and allow to color briefly before turning out onto a clean dish towel. Continue until you have 12 crêpes.

Spoon a little of the apple filling onto each crêpe and roll into cigar shapes. Arrange the crêpes in a lightly greased ovenproof dish and cover with foil. Warm the crêpes in the oven preheated to 350°F for 25-30 minutes. Serve hot with Brandy Custard Sauce (see page 215).

Makes 12 crêpes

A CHOCOLATE ROULADE WITH A GINGER AND ORANGE CREAM

ingredients

Chocolate sponge cake
3 eggs
6tbsp caster sugar
¼cup ground almonds
2tbsp flour
2tbsp cocoa powder

Filling
3 eggs, separated

1¼cups milk
¼cup flour
2tbsp marmalade
2tbsp Grand Marnier (optional)
⅓cup chopped preserved stem ginger
3tbsp sugar
confectioners' sugar to decorate

Preheat the oven to 425°F. Line a 15×12inch jelly roll pan with parchment paper.

Place the eggs and sugar in a mixing bowl and beat for 10-12 minutes until a thick ribbon of the mixture can be drawn across the surface. Sift the ground almonds, flour and cocoa powder over the beaten egg and fold in with a large metal spoon.

Spread the mixture in the lined pan and bake near the top of the oven for 10-12 minutes or until the surface is springy to the touch. Turn the cake upside-down onto a clean dish towel to keep it moist.

To prepare the filling: place the egg yolks in a mixing bowl, add 2tbsp of the milk and stir in the flour until smooth. Bring the remaining milk to a boil, pour over the egg mixture and beat until evenly mixed. Return the mixture to the saucepan and stir back to a boil to thicken. Remove from the heat and stir in the marmalade, Grand Marnier and ginger.

Beat the egg whites together with the sugar until soft peaks form, then fold into the hot filling.

To finish: remove the lining paper from the cake, spread the filling over the surface and roll up from a short edge. The roulade will keep overnight at room temperature. To finish, dust with confectioners' sugar and wrap in wax paper.

CHOCOLATE MARQUISE

❧

 f I had to explain to an admirer of chocolate the meaning of the word sumptuous, a slice of chocolate marquise would say it all. Use semisweet chocolate chips to cover.

ingredients . . . .

Chocolate sponge cake
2 eggs
¼cups sugar
3tbsp flour
1tbsp cocoa powder
3tbsp dark rum

Filling
7oz semisweet chocolate
3 egg whites

3tbsp sugar
1¼cups heavy cream, softly
   whipped

Decoration
1¼cups semisweet chocolate
   chips
confectioners' sugar

To prepare the chocolate sponge cake: preheat the oven to 400°F. Lightly grease an 8inch springform cake pan, cut a circle of parchment paper to fit into the bottom and dust the inside of the pan with flour.

Place the eggs and sugar in a mixing bowl and beat for 10-12 minutes until a thick ribbon of the mixture can be drawn across the surface. Sift the flour and cocoa powder over the beaten egg and fold into with a large metal spoon. Turn the mixture into the prepared cake pan and bake in the center of the oven for 25-30 minutes or until the cake is springy to the touch. Unmold the cake onto a wire rack and leave to cool, then peel off the lining paper and moisten with the rum. Line the sides of the cake pan with parchment paper and place the cake back in the pan.

To prepare the filling: break the chocolate into small pieces and melt in a bowl over a saucepan of boiling water. Beat the egg whites together with the sugar to make a firm meringue. Add the melted chocolate and fold in with a rubber spatula. Fold in the whipped cream evenly, then spread over the cake and chill.

To decorate the marquise: melt the chocolate over a saucepan of boiling water and spread evenly on a smooth work surface. Release the marquise from the cake pan ready to cover. Before the melted chocolate has set completely, scrape it into long strips with a metal scraper and wrap around the sides of the cake. Cover the top in thin layers starting from the outside and working toward the center.

Dust with sifted confectioners' sugar before serving.

ICED ORANGE AND LEMON SOUFFLE

❧

ingredients . . . .

3 eggs
⅔cup sugar
2tsp unflavored gelatin
finely grated zest and juice of 1
   orange
finely grated zest and juice of 1
   lemon

3tbsp Grand Marnier
1¼cups heavy cream, whipped

Decoration
1 orange, peeled and segmented
1cup black grapes, halved

Cut a piece of cardboard to fit around the side of a 6inch soufflé dish to raise the edge by 2inches. Secure the cardboard with freezer tape. Place the eggs and the sugar in a mixing bowl and beat for 10-12 minutes until a thick ribbon of mixture can be drawn across the surface.

Soften the gelatin in 2tbsp cold water in a small heatproof bowl and melt by standing directly in a saucepan of boiling water. Whisk the liquid gelatin into the beaten egg mixture together with the orange and lemon zest and juice. Add the Grand Marnier and fold in the cream with a large metal spoon.

Turn the mixture into the prepared soufflé dish and freeze for at least 3 hours before serving. Decorate with orange segments and grapes.

A SHERRY TRIFLE OF EXOTIC FRUITS

A visit to the greengrocer's at this time of the year can be quite an education since there are so many unusual and exotic fruits imported from abroad for the Christmas season. On a recent visit I came home with a papaya, a prickly pear, a persimmon and a bag of fresh litchis, all of which were delicious. I turned some of them into an unusual trifle with a cardamom custard and an inviting topping of yogurt instead of cream. My guests haven't stopped talking about it since.

ingredients . . . .

4-6 slices plain sponge cake
3tbsp marmalade
¼cup medium sherry
1 papaya, peeled, seeded and
   diced
1 prickly pear, peeled and sliced
1 persimmon, peeled and sliced
½lb fresh litchis, peeled and
   seeded

Cardamom Custard
2½cups milk

2tbsp cornstarch
3 egg yolks
2tbsp sugar
5 cardamom pods, split
1cup thick plain yogurt

Decoration
2 bananas, peeled and sliced
   diagonally
candied angelica, cut into strips
¼cup sliced almonds, toasted

Arrange the cake slices in the bottom of an 8inch glass serving bowl. Measure the marmalade and sherry into a measuring cup and add ⅔cup water. Stir to dissolve. Scatter the prepared fruits over the cake and moisten with the liquid.

To prepare the custard: measure 2tbsp of the milk into a bowl, add the cornstarch and stir in the egg yolks and sugar until smooth. Bring the remaining milk to a boil with the cardamom pods and strain over the other ingredients. Return to the saucepan and simmer to thicken.

Pour the custard over the cake and fruit and leave to cool.

To finish: spread the yogurt over the custard and decorate with slices of banana and angelica. Sprinkle the toasted sliced almonds in the center.

ICE CREAM FRITTERS WITH AN APRICOT SAUCE

If you are looking for something completely different to surprise your guests why not see how they get on with fried ice cream; I guarantee they will have experienced nothing like it.

ingredients . . . .

1¼cups flour
2cups milk
3 eggs
oil for frying
1quart vanilla ice cream

2 egg whites
3tbsp sugar

Apricot sauce
one 7oz can apricots in syrup

To prepare the sauce, place the apricots together with their juices in a food processor and blend until smooth.

To prepare the batter, sift the flour into a mixing bowl and make a well in the center. Add one third of the milk and stir into a lump-free paste. Add the remaining milk, followed by the whole eggs and make a smooth batter. Heat a little of the oil in a skillet. Pour just enough batter into the pan to coat the bottom, tilting evenly. Allow 30 seconds for the crêpe to brown on the underside, turn over and cook briefly until lightly colored. Make 8 crêpes and pile them up between pieces of paper towel to cool. Set the remaining crêpe batter aside. Cut the ice cream into eight pieces and wrap in the crêpes. Store in the freezer until required.

For the enrobing batter, beat the egg whites until firm, adding the sugar a little at a time until smooth. Fold the beaten egg white into the remaining crêpe batter. To finish, half fill a deep fat fryer with oil and heat to 360°F. Dip the ice cream parcels in the batter and deep fry for 40-50 seconds, turning once. Drain, sprinkle with sugar and serve immediately in a folded napkin.

Mushroom Soup with a Hint of Sherry; Roast Goose with Apples, Onion and Sage;
Chocolate Roulade with a Ginger and Orange Cream.

CHRISTMAS DINNER

Once a year comes the daunting task of preparing Christmas dinner for what can seem like an army of visiting relatives and friends. It was the Victorians who started us off eating such enormous amounts of food at Christmas-time with the idea of sleeping it off afterwards over brandy in front of the fire. I must say I quite look forward to the idea since having prepared the meal, I am usually let off the dish washing.

When I am deciding what to cook for Christmas dinner, I usually settle for dishes that I can prepare well in advance, making best use of the freezer. To start the meal I like to choose something light and easy such as Mushroom Soup with a Hint of Sherry, a seafood cocktail or Smoked Trout and Walnut Pâté with Horseradish, all of which can be made a day or so beforehand.

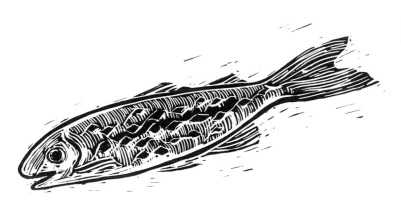

Turkey seems to be the most popular bird to roast at Christmas time, although goose is a festive alternative and duck, pheasant and partridge are worth considering for smaller gatherings. Getting away from poultry and game, I often settle for a large roast of beef or pork with the idea of serving the leftovers cold. As for vegetables, it is a good idea to half-cook them and refresh in cold water, then when ready to serve, they can be immersed briefly in boiling water.

The Christmas pudding should be put onto boil 2½-3 hours before the meal, while Brandy Custard Sauce can be kept warm by standing over a saucepan of simmering water. The pudding is usually followed by one or two cheeses to assist the port wine, while the younger members of the family fight over the nut-crackers. To conclude there might even be room for a homemade beaty truffle and a cup of coffee.

SMOKED TROUT AND WALNUT PÂTÉ WITH HORSERADISH

This is the perfect starter for Christmas dinner – light, delicious and easy to prepare. It will keep in the refrigerator for 3-4 days or can be frozen for up to 6 weeks. The pâté can also be served as an informal lunch on another occasion with a salad, and accompanied by whole-grain bread or toast.

ingredients........................

10oz smoked trout fillets, skinned	juice of 1 lemon
⅔cup cream cheese	½cup roughly chopped walnuts, toasted
3 scallions, chopped	salt and pepper
1tbsp horseradish cream	6tbsp unsalted butter
1tbsp Worcestershire sauce	

Place the smoked trout and the cream cheese in a blender or food processor with the scallions, horseradish, Worcestershire sauce and lemon juice. Blend together until smooth. Stir the walnuts in by hand and season to taste with salt and pepper.

Pack the pâté into 4 small ramekin dishes or one large dish. To finish: melt the butter over a gentle heat, pour a thin layer over the surface of the pâté and leave to set. Serve with fingers of hot toast.

CHRISTMAS ROAST TURKEY WITH APPLE AND CELERY STUFFING

For a good many people the Christmas celebrations would be incomplete without an enormous turkey. Fresh turkeys make the best eating, properly hung before they are dressed. When choosing your bird, look for a plump white breast, avoiding any signs of a blue or purple tinge. To calculate the weight of the bird, you can expect 1lb of dressed turkey to feed one person with enough meat left over. Thus a 10lb bird will feed 10 people. If you have settled for a frozen

turkey do remember to take the bird out of the freezer in plenty of time for it to thaw.

I have chosen an apple and celery stuffing to fill the turkey breast cavity since a good stuffing will always complement the sometimes bland flavor of the meat. There are several methods of roasting turkey to ensure that the flesh is both tender and moist. I prefer the traditional way of starting the bird off in a hot oven (425°F) for the first quarter of the calculated cooking time, after which the temperature is reduced to 350°F for the remainder. Allow 20 minutes per pound dressed weight.

It always pays to be well organized before you start cooking the Christmas dinner since even the most experienced cooks can run into problems. Before I begin, I need to know exactly how long the dishes I have chosen will take to cook and how many of them can be prepared in advance. The Christmas pudding, for instance, can be put onto steam at roughly the same time as the turkey goes into the oven. Potatoes and vegetables can be prepared and half cooked well in advance together with any other trimmings such as cranberry sauce, sausage and bacon rolls and stuffings.

The wine should be chosen well in advance to allow it to reach the correct serving temperature. Cheeses should also be taken out of the refrigerator, unwrapped and allowed to settle before serving. With everything so finely balanced in the kitchen, it is often best to be left to your own devices, although it may be helpful to make someone responsible for looking after the guests.

pings in a saucepan, add the onion, turkey liver, apples and celery and soften over a gentle heat. Add the sage and bread crumbs, stir in the eggs to bind and season well with salt and pepper. Fill the neck cavity of the turkey with the stuffing and secure the neckflap underneath with a metal skewer. If there is any stuffing left over, it can be roasted separately in a small pan. I tend not to stuff the main cavity of the bird since doing so can upset the cooking time calculations, leaving the meat undercooked.

Before the turkey goes into the oven it is worth making a simple bouillon from the giblets (not the liver), a handful of chicken wings, onion, carrot and a bay leaf. Cover with cold water, bring to a boil and simmer for as long as the turkey takes to roast.

To calculate the cooking time you should allow 20 minutes per pound of turkey excluding the stuffing. If you have chosen a 10lb bird, the cooking time works out at 3 hours and 20 minutes. Start the bird off in the oven preheated to 425°F for a quarter of the cooking time, i.e. 50 minutes for a 10lb bird, then lower the temperature to 350°F for the remaining 2½ hours. To test whether the bird is cooked, pierce its thigh with a skewer: if the juices run clear and only slightly rosy the bird is ready. It should then be lifted out onto a carving board and allowed to rest for 20 minutes before carving. If the juices are more red than pink, the bird will need longer in the oven.

To prepare the gravy: pour off the layer of fat from the roasting juices, saving the fat for roasting potatoes on another occasion. Heat the juices in the roasting pan on top of the stove, add the wine or sherry and loosen the sediment with a wooden spoon. Add the strained bouillon and transfer to a small saucepan. Dissolve the cornstarch with 2tbsp cold water and stir into the gravy to thicken. Add the vinegar and season with salt and pepper.

ingredients . . . .

one 10lb turkey
6tbsp soft butter or drippings

Apple and celery stuffing
2tbsp butter or drippings
1 onion, chopped
1 turkey liver, chopped
3 firm, sweet apples, peeled, cored and chopped
2 celery stalks, chopped
2tsp rubbed sage
4cups fresh bread crumbs

2 eggs, beaten

Gravy
turkey giblets, excluding the liver
½lb chicken wings
1 small onion, quartered
1 small carrot, roughly chopped
1 bay leaf
1 glass white wine or ½ glass dry sherry
1tbsp cornstarch
1tsp wine vinegar

SAUSAGE AND BACON ROLLS

ingredients . . . .

½lb sliced bacon
½lb cocktail sausages

Pierce the turkey all over with a fork, rub the skin with the butter or drippings and set aside.

To prepare the stuffing for the breast cavity: melt the butter or drip-

Cut the slices in half, wrap each sausage in a piece of bacon and secure with a wooden toothpick. Roast the sausages and bacon rolls together with the potatoes or around the bird for 45-50 minutes.

CRANBERRY AND ORANGE SAUCE

ingredients . . . .

½lb fresh or frozen cranberries   6tbsp sugar
¼cup concentrated orange juice

Place the cranberries in a non-aluminum saucepan together with the orange juice, cover and cook for 7 minutes or until the berries have burst. Remove from the heat and stir in the sugar until dissolved. Allow to cool completely before serving.

BRUSSELS SPROUTS WITH CRISPY BACON AND CHESTNUTS

russels sprouts have become a popular addition to the Christmas dinner, although it is difficult to understand why when they are so often overcooked. One of my favorite ways of preparing sprouts is to cook them briefly, then toss them together with crispy bacon and smooth chestnuts.

ingredients . . . .

1lb Brussels sprouts, trimmed   2tbsp lard or drippings
    and crosses cut in the base   ¼lb Canadian bacon, cut into
¼lb dried chestnuts, soaked, or   strips
    ½lb fresh chestnuts, blanched in
    boiling water for 20 minutes,
    then peeled

Half-cook the Brussels sprouts well in advance, then refresh them in cold water. Simmer the soaked or blanched chestnuts in a saucepan of boiling water until tender.
    Place the sprouts in a saucepan of boiling water together with the chestnuts and cook briefly. Meanwhile, melt the lard or drippings in a large skillet and crisp the bacon. Drain the sprouts thoroughly, toss with the bacon, season with freshly, ground black pepper and serve.

GLAZED CARROTS WITH GINGER

lazed carrots make a colorful contribution to the Christmas dinner and are delicious cooked with a little ginger. Allow ¼lb carrots per person.

ingredients . . . .

1lb carrots, peeled and cut into   1inch piece ginger root, bruised
    short fingers   1tbsp sugar
2tbsp butter   1 pinch salt

Place the carrots in a saucepan with the butter, ginger, sugar and salt. Cover with cold water, bring to a boil and simmer for 15-20 minutes until the liquid has reduced to a glaze. Remove the ginger and serve.

CRISPY ROAST POTATOES

ingredients . . . .

2lb firm potatoes   salt
2tbsp duck or goose fat or
    drippings

Peel the potatoes and cut them into equal-sized pieces. If you are planning ahead, the potatoes can be kept in cold water for up to 2 days.
    Drain the potatoes and pat them dry with a dish towel. Melt the fat or

drippings in a roasting pan and toss the potatoes to coat them evenly. Sprinkle with salt and roast near the top of a hot oven for 1-1¼ hours, turning them occasionally, until crisp and golden.

SERVING THE CHRISTMAS PUDDING WITH BRANDY CUSTARD SAUCE

tand the pudding in a large saucepan of boiling water, cover and simmer for 2½-3 hours, topping up from time to time with more boiling water to prevent it boiling dry. The custard sauce can be made before serving and kept warm by standing over a saucepan of simmering water. Unmold the pudding onto a plate, warm a ladleful of brandy and pour over the pudding. Ignite and serve in a darkened room.

ingredients ....

Brandy Custard Sauce
2½cups milk
2tbsp cornstarch

3 egg yolks
3tbsp brandy
2tbsp sugar

Measure 3tbsp of the milk into a mixing bowl and stir in the cornstarch, egg yolks, brandy and sugar until smooth. Bring the remaining milk to a boil and whisk into the cornstarch mixture. Return the custard to the saucepan and simmer briefly to thicken. The cornstarch in the recipe will prevent the custard from curdling.

MELT-IN-THE-MOUTH MINCE PIES

ne of the secrets of successful mince pies is to use a pastry that is made with more butter than is strictly good for us! But, after all, Christmas and mince pies come only once a year. . . .

ingredients ....

2cups flour
1½ sticks cool unsalted butter, diced
6tbsp caster sugar
1 egg
a little soft butter for greasing

1lb mincemeat (page 196)

Glaze
a little milk
a little sugar

To make the pastry: sift the flour into a mixing bowl or food processor. Add the butter and sugar and rub in with the fingertips or process until the mixture resembles large bread crumbs. Add the egg and mix to a smooth dough. Dust the pastry lightly with flour, shape into a sausage, wrap in plastic wrap or foil and chill in the refrigerator for 30 minutes before using. Lightly grease 18 mince pie pans and set aside.
    Preheat the oven to 400°F.
    Reserve one-third of the pastry and roll out the remainder on a floured work surface. Cut out 18 rounds with a fluted cookie cutter and line the pans. Fill the cases about half full with mincemeat and moisten the edges with water. Roll out the remaining pastry together with any scraps and cut out the lids. Brush the edges with water and place the tops on the mincemeat, pressing to seal the edges. Brush with milk and sprinkle with sugar.
    Bake the mince pies in the oven for 25-30 minutes or until golden, then cool on a wire rack. Serve warm with cream.

Makes 18

AN ENGLISH CHEESEBOARD

y the time the Christmas pudding has been served, most of us have just about had enough to eat, but one or two people may have been saving room for a taste of cheese. English cheeses are best suited to the occasion since they make way for a glass of vintage port wine perfectly. As it is unlikely that your guests will eat very much cheese, settle for quality rather than quantity.
    When you are choosing cheeses, try to maintain a good balance of flavor and texture. Serve one blue cheese: a Stilton, Shropshire Blue or Beenleigh Blue; a semi-hard cheese: Red Leicester, Caerphilly or a good Cheddar, and a soft goat's cheese.

215

EDIBLE DECORATIONS AND CHRISTMAS PRESENTS

*W*hen I was a child, my sister and I used to spend hours in the kitchen making fancy cookies to hang from the Christmas tree and qresents and decorations that can be eaten.

STORK'S NEST COOKIES

ingredients . . . .

¾cup flour
2tbsp ground almonds
1tbsp confectioners' sugar

1 egg, beaten
½tsp almond extract
oil for deep frying

Sift the flour, ground almonds and sugar into a mixing bowl. Add the egg and almond extract and stir to a firm dough. Cover and rest in the refrigerator for 30 minutes.

Take a piece of dough no bigger than the end of your thumb and roll it out as thinly as possible in a dusting of flour. Make a series of cuts in the dough ¼inch apart to within the same distance of the edge.

To cook the stork's nests, open an empty can at both ends and stand in the bottom of a deep-fat fryer. Heat oil to 375°F, drop pieces of dough into the can one at a time and cook for 1½-2 minutes or until golden. Remove from the oil, allow to cool on a napkin, then dust with confectioners' sugar.

Makes 12

SPICED COOKIES FOR THE CHRISTMAS TREE

*T*his recipe for spiced cookies is easy to prepare and will provide hours of fun for children who enjoy cutting out and decorating pretty shapes ready for baking.

ingredients . . . .

2½cups flour
2tsp apple pie spice
¾cup light brown sugar
10tbsp butter, diced
2 eggs
milk to glaze

candied fruit, nuts and sugar decorations

Sugar frosting
¾cup confectioners' sugar, sifted
1tbsp lemon juice or water

Sift the flour together with the spice into a mixing bowl or food processor. Add the sugar and butter. Rub together with the fingertips or process until the mixture resembles large bread crumbs. Add the eggs and mix to a smooth dough. Chill for 30 minutes.

Preheat the oven to 350°F.

Roll the pastry out in small batches on a floured work surface and cut out various shapes with cookie cutters or a sharp knife. Lay the shapes on a baking sheet, brush with milk and decorate to taste. Before baking make a small hole at the top of each cookie with a toothpick ready to attach a length of thread or ribbon.

Bake the cookies in the oven for 20-25 minutes. Leave to cool on a wire rack. To frost, mix the sifted sugar with the lemon juice or water and brush onto the cookies.

Makes 18

VODKA CLEMENTINES

*I*f you are looking for a present for someone who enjoys a fruit liqueur after their meal, this idea of macerating fresh clementines in spiced vodka will have special appeal.

ingredients . . . .

1lb clementines or other
tangerines, peeled
finely pared zest of 1 clementine
1inch cinnamon stick

2 whole cloves
5 allspice berries
¼cup sugar
⅓cup vodka

Arrange the peeled clementines in a 2lb canning jar, halving them if necessary. Cut the clementine zest into neat little strips and tuck them down the side of the jar. Add the spices and the sugar. Cover the fruit with vodka and seal. Cover the top of the jar with a piece of pretty fabric and label.

Allow the clementines to macerate for at least 3 weeks to allow the spices to mingle. Spiced vodka clementines will keep for up to 6 months prior to opening.

A variation of this recipe can be made with kumquats instead of clementines. ½lb kumquats will fill a 1lb jar. Pierce the kumquats several times with a skewer and cover with cold water in a saucepan. Bring to a boil, then simmer for 10-12 minutes. Drain the kumquats and place in the jar with the spices and the sugar. Cover with vodka and leave for 3 weeks.

WHISKY TRUFFLES

ingredients . . . .

3tbsp heavy cream
9oz semisweet chocolate,
   chopped

3tbsp beaty
¾cup semisweet chocolate
   chips, for coating

Measure the cream into a small saucepan and bring to a boil. Remove from the heat, add the chopped chocolate and stir until completely melted. Add the rum and stir until evenly mixed. Leave the mixture to cool at room temperature for 10-15 minutes until it begins to firm.

Line a baking sheet with wax paper. Spoon the chocolate mixture onto the sheet in little heaps no bigger than a hazelnut. Refrigerate for 30 minutes until firm, then shape into balls ready for coating. Do not overhandle the chocolate mixture.

Place the chocolate chips in a heatproof bowl and stand over a saucepan of boiling water until melted. The most effective way to cover the truffles happens to be one of the messiest! Spread a little of the cooled, melted chocolate onto the palm of one (clean) hand and roll the truffles in it to coat evenly. Leave the truffles to set on wax paper.

Place in dark paper bonbon cases and pack into pretty boxes.

Makes about 36

CHOCOLATE CREAM FUDGE

ingredients . . . .

a little soft butter for greasing
2¼cups sugar
½cup water

1¼cups condensed milk
5oz semisweet chocolate

Lightly grease a 7inch square pan with butter and set aside. Measure the sugar into a heavy saucepan. Stir in the water and bring to a boil slowly, stirring until the sugar has dissolved. Add the condensed milk and boil the mixture steadily until the ingredients reach 475°F on a candy thermometer. This will usually take about 30 minutes.

Remove the pan from the heat and stir in the chocolate until melted. Pour the fudge into the prepared pan and leave to cool. Turn the fudge out onto a wooden board, cut into 1inch squares and arrange in paper bonbon cases.

CHOCOLATE-COVERED GINGER

These sweets are the perfect accompaniment to after-dinner coffee. At the same time, you may like to dip a few brazil nuts and strips of candied orange peel.

ingredients . . . .

6 pieces of preserved stem
  ginger, quartered
6oz semisweet chocolate chips

Rinse the stem ginger in warm water and dry well to remove excess syrup. Place the chocolate chips in a heatproof bowl and melt by standing over a saucepan of boiling water. Dip the pieces of ginger using a fork and leave to set on wax paper.

Almonds
and Plum Shuttle, 173
Salted, Cocktail, 100

Apple
and Apricot Crumble with an Almond
    Topping, 52
and Blackberry Pudding, Steamed, 172
and Chicken Liver and Walnut Pâté, 14
and Hazelnut Tart, 172
and Plum Tart, 154
and Rosehip Jelly, 157
Baked, with an Apricot and Almond
    Stuffing, 194
Charlotte, Old English, 192
Sponge Cake, Upside Down, 20
Toddy, Spiced, 176
Wafer, Caramelized, 32

Apricot
and Apple Crumble, 52
and Gooseberry Tart, 97

Artichokes
Warm salad of, with New Potatoes and
    Bacon, 112
with Mushroom Stuffing, 162, *166*

Asparagus
with a Beautiful Egg Sauce, 80
and Chicken Soup, Homemade, 78
and Mushroom Tartlets, 80-81
and Pink Salmon Pillow Cases, 80
season, 78

Atlantic Sea Bass with Spinach,
    Mushrooms and Thyme, 184

Avocado
and Bacon Salad, with a Sharp Tomato
    Dressing, 126-7
and Chicken, Bacon and Potato Gratin,
    Hot, 30
and Smoked Haddock Crumble, 59
and Walnut Terrine, 163
Celery and Shrimp Cocktail, 202
-stuffed Tomatoes in a Simple Green
    Salad, 74

Bacon
and Avocado Salad with a Sharp Tomato
    Dressing, 126-7
and Broad Beans, 134
and Sausage Rolls, 213

Baked
Apples, with an Apricot and Almond
    Stuffing, 194
Caramel Custards Scented with Orange,
    33
Eggs on a Bed of Creamy Leeks and
    Potato, 188
Mackerel with Gooseberry Mayonnaise,
    92
Soufflé Pudding with Almonds and a
    Vanilla Sauce, 191

Banana
Cake, Sticky, 69
Custard Creams, 53

Barbecue
party, recipes for, 112-114, 116
Sauce, Special, 112

Barbecued Fish Kabobs with Fennel and
    Herbs, 113

Basic Crêpes with Sugar and Lemon,
    34-5

Beans
and Pork Stew, English-Style, 48
Broad, and Bacon, 134
Flageolet, and Tuna Fish Salad, 57
Green, Buttered, with Young Parsnips,
    135
recipes, 134-6
Green, Sliced, with Butter and Black
    Pepper, 131
Green, with Toasted Almonds, 136

Beef
Casserole, Cooked with Guinness, 17
Olives, with Mustard and Herb Stuffing,
    45
Oxtail Stew with Flageolet Beans, 46
Roast Rib of, with Yorkshire Pudding, 185
Steak and Kidney Pudding with
    Mushrooms, 29

Beets and Baby Turnips, Spiced, in a
    Cheese Sauce, 94

Black Olive Straws, 100

Blackberry
and Apple Pudding, Steamed, 172
and Pear Mousses, 173
Wild, with Melon, Iced, 147

Black Currant Yogurt Ice, 118

Blueberry
and Lavender Tartlets, 117
Pancakes with Vanilla Ice Cream, 117

Bombe, Red Currant and Passion
    Fruit, 139

Boned Shoulder of Lamb with Marjorie
    Pryor's Tomato Crumble, 150

Bonfire Cake, 194

Bonfire party, recipes for, 192-4

Braised Squabs with Little Onions,
    Mushrooms and Peas, 169

Brandied Peaches in a Burnt Custard
    Cream, 155

Bread and Butter Pudding, Toasted, 68

Broad Beans and Bacon, 134

Brown Lamb Stew with Penny Royal
    Dumplings, 186

Brûlée of Soft English Fruits, 119

Brussels Sprouts with Crispy Bacon and
    Chestnuts, 214

Butter-Glazed Carrots, 52

Buttered
Flatfish with a Sauce of Vermouth and
    Orange, 129
Green Beans with Young Parsnips, 136
Oyster Mushrooms with Lemon Thyme,
    170

Butterfly Lamb Chops with a Red Currant
    Sauce, 130

Butterscotch
Meringue Tart, 21
Pecan Pie, *167*, 174

Cabbage
Red, Spiced, with Apples and Bacon,
    189
Savoy, Stuffed, 28

Cake, *see also* Desserts
Banana, Sticky, 69
Bonfire, 194
Chocolate, Wickedly Gooey, 177
Dundee, 196
Simnel, 65
Strawberry Layer, 98
Tea, Gooseberry and Red Currant, 118

Caramel
Custard Scented with Orange, Baked, 33
with Easy Oranges, 34

Caramelized Apple Wafer, 32-3

Carrot
and Hazelnut Soufflé, 14
Butter-Glazed, 52
Glazed, with Ginger, 214
Soup, with Tender Tops, 73

Casseroles
Beef, Slow, Cooked with Guinness, 17
Chicken, with Lemon, Ginger and Yogurt,
    48
Chicken, with Mussels and Root
    Vegetables, 30
Chicken, with Port Wine and Green Figs,
    166
Hare, with Sour Cream and Capers, 29

Cauliflower
and Watercress Soup, 161
Twenty-Minute, with Stilton and Walnut
    Sauce, 169

Celery
and Chicken Soup, Creamy, 201
and Stilton Soufflé, 16

Charcoal-Baked Mackerel with Lemon
    and Garden Herbs, 113
Grilled Salmon Steaks with Vermouth and
    Ginger, 114

Cheese
and Zucchini Soufflé, 182, *187*
Cream Cheese, Shrimp and Bacon Pâté,
    56
English, 82, 215
Goat's, Soufflé with Leeks and Walnuts,
    42
Goat's, with Late Summer Figs, 147
Red Windsor Salad, 107
Stilton and Celery Soufflé, 16

Cheesecake
Orange and Lemon, 21
White Chocolate and Chestnut, 175

Chestnut and White Chocolate
Cheesecake, 175

Chestnuts, Roast, 193

Chicken
and Asparagus Soup, Homemade, 78
and Celery Soup, Creamy, 201
and Hot Avocado, Bacon and Potato
Gratin, 30
and Parsley Soup, Fifteen-Minute, 145
Breast, Poached with Broccoli Cream
Sauce, 93
Breast, Sliced, with a Lavender Sauce,
131
Breast, Stir-Fried, with Crispy Vegetables,
111
Casserole, with Lemon, Ginger and
Yogurt, 40
Casserole, with Port Wine and Green
Figs, 166
Drumsticks, Deviled, 176
Leek and Mushroom Cobbler, 63
Liver, Apple and Walnut Pâté, 14
Pot-Roasted, with Fennel, Garlic and
Mustard, 62
Roast, at Scarborough Fair, 153
Spatchcock, in a Piquant Sauce,
114
Warm, in a Salad of Autumn Leaves,
166

Chinese-Style Pork Balls, 100

Chocolate
and Orange-Scented Flummery, 50
and Rum Trifle with a Coffee Custard
Topping, 84
Cake, Wickedly Gooey, 177
-covered Ginger, 217
Cream Fudge, 217
Marquise, 209
Roulade, with a Ginger and Orange
Cream, 208, 211

Chowder of Sea Fish with Potato and
Okra, 184

Christmas
Dinner, 212-215
or Plum Pudding, 195
recipes for, 195-7
Roast Turkey with Apple and Celery
Stuffing, 212-213
Serving the Christmas Pudding with
Brandy Custard Sauce, 215

Chunky Vegetable Soup, 192

Cider-Baked Mackerel with a Yogurt and
Mustard Dressing, 165

Cockles
East End, with Bacon and Samphire,
109
Cakes, Norfolk, 126

Cocktails (drinks)
Leave It To Me, 99
Prince of Wales, 99
Silver Fizz, 99
Tequila Sunrise, 99

Cocktails
Avocado, Celery and Shrimp, 202
Curried Shrimp and Melon, 90
nibbles, 99-101

Cod
Fillets, Flaky, in a Mild Curry Sauce, 45
Roe, Smoked, Pâté of, 41
steaks, 44

Coddled Eggs on a Bed of Spinach,
Potato and Mushroom, 43

Cold Salmon and Cucumber Soup, 89

Cookies
Spiced, for Christmas tree, 216
Stork's Nest, 216

Corn-on-the-Cob, Golden, with Melted
Butter, 116

Crab
and Potted Shrimp Salad, 90
Potted, 106
Ragout of, with Egg Noodles, 59

Cranberry and Orange Sauce, 214

Cream of Leek and Potato Soup, 51

Creamy
Chicken and Celery Soup, 201
Leek and Mushroom Tartlets, 26
Rice, Apricot and Almond Mousse,
84

Crêpes
Apple, English, 208
Basic, with Sugar and Lemon, 34
North Atlantic (Seafood) in a White Wine
and Mushroom Sauce, 28
Parcels with Fresh Pineapple and Orange
Custard, 35

Rolled, with Moist Almond and Orange
Filling, 35
Crispy
Duck Breast with a Plum Sauce, 132
Fish Cakes with Parsley and Lemon
Sauce, 27
Roast Potatoes, 214
Whitebait with Fried Parsley and Lemon,
109

Crumble
Apple and Apricot, 52
Smoked Haddock and Avocado, 39
Wild Blackberry, Apple and Almond, 155

Cucumber
and Melon Soup, Iced, 123
and Salmon Soup, Cold, 89

Curried
Fish with an Egg Sauce, 203
Pear and Parsnip Soup, 181
Shrimp and Melon Cocktail, 90

Custard
and Rhubarb Tart, 49
Baked Caramel, Scented with Orange, 33

Dark Chocolate Mousse, 65

Deep Sea Scallops in a Forest of Wild
Mushrooms, 164

Desserts and Puddings, see also
separate entries, Tart, Mousse, etc
Apple Wafer, Caramelized, 32
Baked Caramel Custards, 33
Blackberry and Apple Pudding, Steamed,
172-3
Bread and Butter Pudding, Toasted, 68
Brûlée of Soft Fruits, 119
Easy Orange with Dark Caramel, 34
English Summer Pudding, 138
Flummery, Chocolate, Orange Scented,
50
Fruit Salad, Exotic, 49
Fruits, soft summer, 117-121
Gooseberry and Elderflower Huff, 139
Gooseberries, Poached in Elderflower
and Orange, 97
Harvest Fruit, 155
Jellied Raspberry Shapes, 141
Lemon Possets, Old English, 54
Manchester Pudding with Bananas and
Lime, 20
Orange and Lemon Cheesecake, 21
Oranges with Dark Caramel, 34
Peaches and Raspberries in Beaujolais
Wine, 120

Desserts and Puddings (contd)
Raspberry Extravaganza, 140
Raspberry Sorbet, 140
Rhubarb and Ginger Sponge, 32
Red Currant and Passion Fruit Bombe,
139
Strawberries and Cream, 83
Syllabub, Old English, 50
Upside Down Apple Sponge Cake, 20
Upside Down Summer Fruit Cake, 135,
138

Deviled Chicken Drumsticks, 176

Dip
Avocado, Tangy, 101
Eggplant Cheese, 202

Duck
Breast, Crispy, with a Plum Sauce, 132
Breast, Sliced, with a Black Currant
Sauce, 111
Roast, with Cardamom and Orange, 18
Roast, with Kumquats and Lime, 77
Wild, Roast, with Sharp Plum Sauce,
168

Duckling, Roast, with Cherries and Ginger
Wine, 93

Dundee Cake, 196

East End Cockles with Bacon and
Samphire, 109

Easter recipes, 64, 66

Easy Oranges with Dark Caramel at the
Drop of a Hat, 34

Edible Decorations and Presents,
Christmas, 216

Eel, Smoked, Salad of, with Crisp Pears,
145

Eggplant Cheese Dip, 202

Eggs
Braised, on a Bed of Creamy Leeks and
Potato, 188
Coddled, on a Bed of Spinach, Potato
and Mushroom, 43
Goose, Omelette of, with Mushrooms
and Sorrel, 94
Noodles and Ragout of Crab, 59
Scrambled, with Chanterelles, 170

Elderflower and Gooseberry Huff, 139

English
Apple Crêpes, 208
asparagus season, 78-80
Cheeses, 82, 215
cookery, 7-8
Fish Stew with Parsley Dumplings, 15
Flapjacks, 69
Onion Soup with a Toasted Cheese
    Topping, 25
Style Pork and Bean Stew, 48
Summer Pudding, 138

Eton Mess, 139

Exotic Fruit Salad, 49

Fava Beans and Bacon, 134

Fifteen-Minute Chicken and Parsley
    Soup, 145

Fig Jam, 157

Figs, Late Summer, with Goat's Cheese,
    147

Fillets
Flatfish with a Spicy Shrimp
    Stuffing, 75
Pink Trout with a Tarragon Cream Sauce,
    76
Red Mullet with Nasturtium Leaf Salad,
    107
Sole with a Delicate Green Sauce, 108-
    109
Sole with Pink Grapefruit and Lime, 204

Fish, see also separate entries Cod,
    Haddock etc
Cakes, Crisp, with Parsley and Lemon
    Sauce, 27
Chowder of Sea Fish with Potato and
    Okra, 184
Curried, with an Egg Sauce, 203
Kabobs, Barbecued, with Fennel and
    Herbs, 113
North Atlantic Crêpes in a White Wine
    and Mushroom Sauce, 28
White, Gratin with Young Vegetables,
    75
White, Stew with Leeks and Mushrooms,
    165

Flaky Cod Fillets in a Mild Curry Sauce,
    45

Flapjacks, English, 69

Flummery, Chocolate, 50

Fondant Potatoes, 169

Fresh Raspberry Sauce, 140

Fresh Sardines with Rhubarb, Ginger and
    Soy, 27

Fresh Tomato Salad Scented with Basil,
    146

Freshwater Crayfish in a Nest of Zucchini,
    130, 135

Frozen Mousse of Gooseberries and
    Cardamom, 118-9

Fruit, see also separate entries
Eton Mess, 139
Harvest, in a Muscat Jelly, 155
Salad, Exotic, 49
Soft summer, recipes, 117-21

Fudge, Chocolate Cream, 217

Game, see also separate entries
Soup, Old English, 13

Garlic-Stuffed Mushrooms in their Buttery
    Juices, 43

Ginger
and Rhubarb Sponge Pudding, 32
Chocolate-covered, 217
Stem, and Orange Marmalade, 36

Glazed Carrots with Ginger, 214

Goose, Roast, with Apple, Onion and
    Sage, 206

Gooseberries
and Apricot Tart, 97
and Elderflower Huff, 139
and Red Currant Tea Cake, 118
Poached, with Elderflower and Orange,
    97

Grandad's Gudgeons of Sole with
    Bananas and Almonds, 15

Grapefruit and Campari Sorbet Slices, 99

Gratin of Haddock with Creamy Leeks
    and Mushrooms, 44-5

Gratin of White Fish with Young
    Vegetables, 75

Green Tomato Chutney, 137

Greens, Simmered, with Toasted Cashew
    Nuts, 52

Grouse, Roast, with all the Trimmings,
    133

Gudgeons of Sole, Grandad's, with
    Bananas and Almonds, 15

Guinea Fowl, Pot-Roasted, with Gin and
    Juniper, 188

Haddock
Gratin of, with Creamy Leeks and
    Mushrooms, 44
Smoked, and Avocado Crumble, 59
Smoked, and Potato Pie, 183
Smoked, in Parsley Sauce, 161

Halibut Steaks with a Sauce of Leeks and
    Pears, 44

Halloween party, recipes for, 176-7

Ham
Country, Boiled with Parsley Dumplings,
    51
and Pea Soup, Winter, 13

Hare Casserole with Sour Cream and
    Capers, 29

Harvest Fruits in a Muscat Jelly, 151, 155

Hazelnut
and Apple Tart, 172
and Carrot Soufflé, 14
Meringue Cake with Flaked Chocolate, 175

Herbs, for winter keeping, 171

Herring
Home-Soused, with Sour Cream and
    Chives, 128-9
North Sea, with Mustard and Oatmeal,
    149

Hot Avocado Chicken, Bacon and Potato
    Gratin, 30

Hot Blueberry Pancakes with Vanilla Ice
    Cream, 117

Hot Pots
Lancashire, of Lamb, 17
Seafood, Little, 25

Ice Cream Fritters with an Apricot Sauce,
    210

Iced
Beet and Orange Soup, 89
Cucumber and Melon Soup, 125
Melon and Raspberry Soup, 105, 115
Melon with Wild Blackberries, 147
Orange and Lemon Soufflé, 209

Jam
Fig, 157
Plum, 157
Raspberry, 14
Strawberry, Homemade, 120-121

Jelly
Apple and Rose Hip, 157

John Dory, Steamed fillets of, with
    Tarragon and Orange, 110

Kabobs, Fish, Barbecued, with Fennel
    and Herbs, 113

Kedgeree of Salmon with Smoked
    Haddock and Cucumber, 164

Kentish Cherry Pie, 98

Kipper Pâté, with Lemon and Parsley,
    26

Knock-out Punch, 193

Lamb
Boned Shoulder of, with Marjorie Pryor's
    Tomato Crumble, 150
Burgers in Buns, 176
Butterfly Chops with a Red Currant
    Sauce, 130
Chops, Pan-Fried, with Garlic and
    Rosemary, 62
Lancashire Hot Pot, 17
Liver, with Fresh Coriander and Orange,
    46
Loin of, in the Style of Wellington, 76
Roast Leg of, with Garlic and Rosemary,
    66
Stew, Brown, with Penny Royal
    Dumplings, 186
Stew, White Lamb, with Collage of Spring
    Vegetables, 61
Stuffed, with Parsley, Lemon and Thyme,
    92

Lancashire Hot Pot of Lamb, 17

Late Summer Figs with Goat's Cheese,
    147

Leek and Mushroom Tartlets, Creamy, 26

Lemon
and Orange Cheesecake, 21
and Orange Soufflé, 209
Possets, Old English, 64

Lentil and Mushroom Pâté, with Garlic
and Thyme, 42

Light Vegetable Stew, 127

Light Onion Tartlets with New Garlic and
Fresh Herbs, 57

Little Seafood Hot Pots, 28

Liver
Calves', Sliced, with Capers and Cream,
133
Lamb's, with Fresh Coriander and
Orange, 46

Lobster for Two in a Sea of Green
Noodles, 110

Loin of Lamb in the Style of Wellington,
76

Mackerel
Baked, with Gooseberry Mayonnaise, 92
Charcoal Baked, with Lemon and Garden
Herbs, 119
Cider-Baked, with a Yogurt and Mustard
Dressing, 165

Manchester Pudding with Bananas and
Lime, 20

Marmalade
Seville Orange, 36
Stem Ginger and Orange, 36
Three-Fruit, 37
Valencia Orange Curd, 37

Melon
and Cucumber Soup, Iced, 125
and Raspberry Soup, Iced, 105, 115
with Wild Blackberries, Iced, 147

Meringue
in a Custard, 49
Red Currant Tart, 119
Soufflé, Passion Fruit, 33

Mincemeat, 196
Mincepies, Melt-in-the-Mouth, 215

Mother's Day, recipes for, 51, 65

Mousse
Blackberry and Pear, 173
Creamy Rice, Apricot and Almond, 84
Dark Chocolate, 65
Gooseberry and Cardamom, Frozen, 118

Mushrooms
and Lentil Pâté with Garlic and Thyme, 42
and Spinach Soufflé, 73
Garlic Stuffed, in their Buttery Juices, 43
gathering of, 170
Oyster, Buttered, with Lemon Thyme, 170
Soup with a Hint of Sherry, 201, 211
Wild, Pancakes, with Coddled Eggs, 170
Wild, Stuffed, with Chicken, Bacon and
Herbs, 153

Mussels
Norfolk Baked, with Garlic Trenchers,
183
Tender, in a Puff Pastry Case, 203
with White Wine and Parsley, 148

Nasturtium Leaf Salad with Warm Fillets
of Red Mullet, 107, 115

New Potato Salad with Chives, 81

New Potato Truffles, 101

Norfolk Baked Mussels with Garlic
Trenchers, 183

Norfolk Cockle Cakes, 126

North Atlantic Crêpes in a White Wine
and Mushroom Sauce, 28

North Sea Herring with Mustard and
Oatmeal, 149

Old English
Apple Charlotte, 187, 192
Game Soup, 13
Lemon Possets, 64
Syllabubs in Pretty Stem Glasses, 50

Old-Fashioned Duck Broth, 162

Omelette of Goose Eggs, with
Mushrooms and Sorrel, 94

Onion
Pickled, 156
Soup, English, with Toasted Cheese
Topping, 25
Tartlets, with New Garlic and Fresh
Herbs, 57

Orange
and Cranberry Sauce, 214
and Lemon Cheesecake, 21
and Lemon Soufflé, 209
and Stem Ginger Marmalade, 36
Curd, Valencia, 37
Marmalade, Seville, 36
with Dark Caramel, 34

Oxtail Stew with Flageolet Beans, 46

Oysters, on the Half Shell, with Black
Pepper and Lemon, 146

Pancakes
Blueberry, Hot, with Vanilla Ice Cream,
117
Wild Mushroom, with Coddled Eggs, 170

Pan-fried
Lamb Chops with Garlic and Rosemary,
62
Pork with Peaches and Green
Peppercorns, 151, 152
Salmon Steaks with a Sauce of
Cucumber and Tarragon, 129

Parsley
and Chicken Soup, Fifteen-Minute, 145
and Pear Soup, Curried, 181

Parsnips, Young, with Buttered Green
Beans, 136

Passion Fruit
and Red Currant Bombe, 130
Meringue Soufflé for You and Your
Valentine, 33

Pâté
Chicken Liver, Apple and Walnut, 14
Cream Cheese, Shrimp and Bacon,
66
Kipper, with Lemon and Parsley, 26
Lentil and Mushroom, with Garlic and
Thyme, 42
Smoked Cod Roe, 41
Smoked Trout and Walnut, with
Horseradish, 212
Stilton and Walnut, 182

Pea and Ham Soup, Winter, 13

Peaches
and Raspberries in a Fluffy Egg Custard,
140
and Raspberries in Beaujolais Wine, 120
Brandied, in a Burnt Custard Cream, 150
Pickled, 156-7

Pear
and Blackberry Mousses, 173
and Parsnip Soup, Curried, 181

Pheasant, Roast, with Pomegranates,
167, 168

Piccalilli, 156

Pickled
Mixed Vegetables, 156
Onions, 156
Peaches, 156-7

Picnics, recipes for, 81-2

Pieces of Candied Quince, 196

Pies
Butterscotch Pecan, 174
Cherry, Kentish, 96
Spiced, Pumpkin, 174

Pigeons
Braised Squabs with Little Onions,
Mushrooms and Peas, 169
Stewed in Red Wine, 188

Pink Salmon and Asparagus Pillow
Cases, 80

Pink Trout with Cucumber, Shrimp and
Tomato Cream, 150

Plum
and Almond Shuttle, 173
and Almond Tart, 154
Jam, 157

Poached
Breast of Chicken with Broccoli Cream
Sauce, 93
Gooseberries with Elderflower and
Orange, 97
River Trout with Cucumber and Fennel, 91

Pork
and Bean Stew, English-Style, 48
Balls, Chinese-Style, 101
Chops, with Apple Slices and Sage, 166
Chops, Sweet and Sour, with Crab Apple
and Orange, 152
Spareribs of, with Spiced Apricot Sauce,
77
Stir-fried, with Fresh Figs and Raspberry
Vinegar, 131
Stuffed Loin of, with Orange, Lemon and
Thyme, 60

Possets, Lemon, Old English, 54

Potatoes
and Leek Soup, Cream of, 51
and Smoked Haddock Pie, with
   Mushrooms, 183
Baked with Cumin, 193
New, Salad with Chives, 81
Roast, Crispy, 214
Scalloped, with Garlic and Herbs, 52
Smoky Baked, with Sour Cream and
   Chives, 116
Truffles, 101

Pot-Roasted
Chicken with Fennel, Garlic and Mustard,
   62
Guinea Fowl with Gin and Juniper, 188
Partridges in a Pear Tree, 205

Potted
Crab, 106
Salmon with Toasted Walnuts, 162
Trout with Lemon and Toasted Almonds,
   41

Poultry, see separate entries, Chicken,
   etc.

Preserves, 120, 121, 141, 156, 157

Puff Pastry Butterflies, 100

Pumpkin
and Walnut Tea Bread, 174-5
Leek and Potato Soup, 181
Pie, Spiced, 174

Punch, Knock-Out, 193

Quail, Spatchcock, Scented with English
   Wine, 132

Quiche, Zuchinni and Tomato made
   without Pastry, 127

Quince, Candied, Pieces of, 196

Rabbit with Mustard and Coriander,
   186

Ragout of Crab with Egg Noodles, 59

Raspberry
and Melon Soup, Iced, 105, 115
   and Peaches in Beaujolais Wine, 120
Extravaganza, 140
in a Fluffy Egg Custard, 140
Jam, 141
Jellied Shapes, 141

Raspberry (contd)
Sauce, Fresh, 140
Sorbet, 140
Vinegar, 121

Raw Tomato, Cucumber and Garlic
   Soup, 74

Red Windsor Salad, 107

Red Currant
and Gooseberry Tea Cake, 118
and Passion Fruit Bombe, 139
and Tomato Soup, 125
Jelly, 121
Meringue, 115, 119

Rhubard
and Custard Tart, 49
and Ginger Sponge Pudding, 32

Rice, Savory, with Chicken and Bacon,
   206

Roast
Chestnuts, 193
Chicken at Scarborough Fair, 153
Duck with Cardamom and Orange,
   18
Duck with Kumquats and Lime, 77
Duckling with Cherries and Ginger Wine,
   93
Goose, with Apples, Onion and Sage,
   206, 211
Grouse, with all the Trimmings, 133
Leg of Spring Lamb with Garlic and
   Rosemary, 66
Pheasant with Pomegranates, 167, 168
Potatoes, Crispy, 214
Rib of Beef with Yorkshire Pudding, 185
Stuffed Loin of Pork with Orange, Lemon
   and Thyme, 60
Turkey, Christmas, with Apple and Celery
   Stuffing, 212
Wild Duck with a Sharp Plum Sauce,
   168

Rolled Fillets of Sole on a Bed of Creamy
   Leeks, 149

Rolled Crêpes with a Moist Almond and
   Orange Filling, 85

Rose Hip and Apple Jelly, 157

Roulade, Spinach and Taramasalata,
   82

St Valentine's Day, recipe for, 33

Salads
Artichokes, New Potato and Bacon,
   Warm, 112
Bacon and Avocado, with a Sharp
   Tomato Dressing, 126
Bacon, Lettuce and Tomato, 146
Crab and Potted Shrimp, 90
Dandelion, with Bacon and Fresh
   Spinach, Warm, 90
Nasturtium Leaf, with Warm Fillets of Red
   Mullet, 107, 115
New Potato, with Chives, 81
Red Windsor, 107
Smoked Eel with Crisp Pears, 145, 151
Smoked Trout with Fresh Horseradish,
   108
Spinach, with Crispy Bacon and Hard-
   Cooked Egg, 58
Tomato, Fresh, Scented with Basil, 196
Tomatoes, Avocado-Stuffed, in Green
   Salad, 74
Tuna Fish and Flageolet Beans, 57

Salmon
and Cucumber Soup, Cold 89
Kedgereee of, with Smoked Haddock
   and Cucumber, 164
Potted, with Toasted Walnuts, 162
Smoked, with Brown Bread and Butter,
   202
Steaks, Broiled, with a Tomato
   Vinaigrette, 91
Steaks, Charcoal-Grilled, with Vermouth
   and Ginger, 114
Steaks, Pan-Fried, with a Sauce of
   Cucumber and Tarragon, 129

Salted Cocktail Almonds, 100

Sardines, Fresh, with Rhubarb, Ginger
   and Soy, 27

Sauce, Cranberry and Orange, 214

Sausage
and Bacon Rolls, 213
Bacon and Mushroom Crust, 81
Spicy Bangers with Bacon and Beans, 193
Toad-in-the-Hole, with a Mushroom and
   Onion Gravy, 207

Savory Nuts and Seeds, 196

Savory Rice with Chicken, Chestnuts and
   Bacon, 206

Scallops, Deep Sea, in Mushrooms, 64

Scalloped Potatoes with Garlic and
   Herbs, 22

Scrambled Eggs with Chanterelles, 170

Sea Bass, Atlantic, with Spinach,
   Mushroom and Thyme, 184

Seafood
Cockle Cakes, Norfolk, 126
Cockles, East End, with Bacon and
   Samphire, 109
Crab, Potted, 106
Crayfish, Freshwater, in a Nest of
   Zucchini, 130
Crêpes, North Atlantic, with White Wine
   and Mushroom Sauce, 28
Hot Pots, Little, 25
Lobster for Two in a Sea of Green
   Noodles, 110
Mussels and Chicken Casserole, with
   Root Vegetables, 30
Mussels, with White Wine and Parsley,
   148
Scallops, Deep Sea, in Mushrooms, 164
Seafood Spaghetti with Winter Herbs,
   204
Shrimp, Avocado and Celery Cocktail,
   202

Seasonal ingredients, 7-8, 11, 12, 23, 24,
   39, 40, 55, 56, 71, 72, 87, 88, 103,
   104, 123, 124, 143, 144, 159, 160, 179,
   180, 199, 200

Serving the Christmas Pudding with
   Brandy Custard Sauce, 215

Seville Orange Marmalade, 36

Sherry Trifle of Exotic Fruits, 210

Shrimp, Avocado and Celery Cocktail,
   202

Shuttle, Plum and Almond, 173

Simmered Greens with Toasted Cashew
   Nuts, 52

Simnel Cake, 65

Skate, Wings of, with Nut Brown Butter
   and Capers, 16

Sliced
Calves' Liver with Capers and Cream, 133
Chicken Breast with a Lavender Sauce,
   131, 135
Duck Breast, with a Black Currant Sauce,
   111
Green Beans, with Butter and Black
   Pepper, 134

Slow Beef Casserole Cooked with Guinness, 17

Smoked
Cod roe, Pâté of, 41
Haddock and Avocado Crumble, 59
Haddock and Potato Pie, with Mushrooms, 183
Trout and Walnut Pâté with Horseradish, 212
Trout Salad with Fresh Horseradish, 108

Smoky Baked Potatoes with Sour Cream and Chives, 116

Sole
Fillets of, with Pink Grapefruit and Lime, 204
Fillets of, with a Delicate Green Sauce, 118
Fillets of, Steamed in Green Jackets, 126
Rolled Fillets of, on a Bed of Creamy Leeks, 149
Turbans of, with a Mushroom Filling, 60

Soufflé
Carrot and Hazelnut, 14
Cheese and Zucchini, 182
Goat's Cheese, with Leeks and Walnuts, 42
Orange and Lemon, 209
Passion Fruit Meringue, 33
Pudding, Baked, with Almonds and a Vanilla Sauce, 191
Spinach and Mushroom, Scented with New Garlic, 75
Stilton and Celery, 16

Soups
Baby Carrots with their Tender Tops, 73
Beet and Orange, Iced, 89
Cauliflower and Watercress, 161
Chunky Vegetable, 192
Cream of Leek and Potato, 51
Creamy Chicken and Celery, 120
Chicken and Asparagus, Homemade, 78
Chicken and Parsley, Fifteen-Minute, 145
Cucumber and Melon, Iced, 125
Curried Pear and Parsnip, 181
Duck Broth, Old-Fashioned, with Port Wine, 162
Game, Old English, 13
Melon and Raspberry, Iced, 105
Mushroom with a Hint of Sherry, 201
Onion, with Toasted Cheese Topping, English, 25
Pea and Ham, Winter, 13
Pumpkin, Leek and Potato, 181
Salmon and Cucumber, Cold, 89
Squash and Tomato, 105
Tomato and Red Currant, 125

Spareribs of Pork with Spiced Apricot Sauce, 77

Spatchcock Chicken in a Piquant Sauce, 114

Spatchcock Quail, Scented with English Wine, 132

Special Barbecue Sauce, 112-113

Spiced
Apple Toddy, 176
Baby Turnips and Beets in a Cheese Sauce, 94,
Cookies for the Christmas Tree, 216
Ginger Pears with a Chocolate Interior, 154
Pumpkin Pie, 174
Red Cabbage with Apples and Bacon, 189

Spicy Bangers with Bacon and Beans, 193

Spinach
and Mushroom Soufflé, Scented with New Garlic, 73
and Taramasalata Roulade, 82
Salad with Crispy Bacon and Hard-Cooked Eggs, 58

Squash
Flowers, Stuffed, 96
Patty pan, Stuffed, 106
and Tomato Soup, 105
Zucchini, see Zucchini

Squid, with Tomatoes and Fresh Herbs, 148

Starters, 13-14, 25-6, 41-3, 57-8, 73-4, 89-90, 105-7, 125-7, 145-7, 161-3, 181-4, 201-2

Steak and Kidney Pudding, with Mushrooms, 29

Steamed
Blackberry and Apple Pudding, 172
Fillets of John Dory with Tarragon and Orange, 110-111
Fillets of Sole in Green Jackets, 128

Stem Ginger and Orange Marmalade, 36

Stewed Pigeons in Red Wine, for a Cold Day, 188

Stews
Fish, with Parsley Dumplings, 15

Stews contd)
Oxtail, with Flageolet Beans, 46
Pork and Bean, English-Style, 48
Vegetable, Light, 127
White Lamb, with a Collage of Spring Vegetables, 61
Sticky Banana Cake, 69

Stilton
and Celery Soufflé, 16
and Walnut Pâté, 182

Stir-Fried
Chicken Breast with Crispy Vegetables, 111
Pork with Fresh Figs and Raspberry Vinegar, 131

Stork's Nest Cookies, 216

Strawberries
and Cream, 83
Floating in Port Wine and Grand Marnier, 83
Layer Cake, 95, 98
Spectacular, 83

Straws, Black, Olive, 100

Stuffed
Loin of Pork with Orange, Lemon and Thyme, 60-61
Rib of Pork with Stilton and Walnuts, 205
Pattypan Squash, 106-7
Savoy Cabbage, 23
Squash Flowers, 96
Wild Mushrooms with Chicken, Bacon and Herbs, 153

Sweet and Sour Pork Chops with Crab Apple and Orange, 152

Syllabub, Old English, in Pretty Stem Glasses, 50

Tangy Avocado Dip, 101

Tartlets
Blueberry and Lavender, 117
Leek and Mushroom, Creamy, 26
Onion, Little, with New Garlic and Fresh Herbs, 57

Tarts
Apple and Hazelnut, 172
Apricot and Gooseberry, 97
Butterscotch Meringue, 21
Plum and Almond, 154
Red Currant Meringue, 119
Rhubarb and Custard, 49

Tarts (contd)
Treacle, with Lemon and Bitter Almonds, 64

Tea Bread, Pumpkin and Walnut, 174

Tender Mussels in a Puff Pastry Case, 203
Three-Fruit Marmalade, 37

Toad-in-the-Hole with a Mushroom and Onion Gravy, 207

Toasted Bread and Butter Pudding, 68

Tomato
and Red Currant Soup, 125
and Squash Soup, 105
and Zucchini Quiche, Made without Pastry, 127
Green, Chutney, 136, 137
Relish, 136
Sauce, 137

Treacle Tart with Lemon and Bitter Almonds, 64

Trifle
Chocolate and Rum, with Coffee Custard Topping, 84
Sherry, of Exotic Fruits, 210

Trout
Pink, with Cucumber, Shrimp and Tomato Cream, 150
Potted with Lemon and Toasted Almonds, 41
River, Poached, with Cucumber and Fennel, 91
Sea, Whiskey-Cured, with Fresh Sage and Lemon, 58
Shrimp and Tomato Cream, 150
Smoked, and Walnut Pâté with Horseradish, 212
Smoked, Salad of, with Fresh Horseradish, 108

Truffles
Potato, New, 101
Whisky, 217

Tuna Fish and Flageolet Bean Salad, 57

Turbans of Sole with a Mushroom Filling,

Turkey, Gratin, with Leeks and Garlic, 18

Turnips, Baby, and Beets, Spiced in a Cheese Sauce, 94

Twenty-Minute Cauliflower with a Stilton and Walnut Sauce, 169

Upside Down Apple Sponge Cake, 20
Upside Down Summer Fruit Cake, *135*, 138

Valencia Orange Curd, 37

Vegetables
Pickled, Mixed, 156
Stew, Light, 127
Summer, Combination, 96

Vodka Clementines, 216-7

Wafer, Apple, Caramelized, 38

Walnut
and Avocado Terrine, 163
and Pumpkin Tea Bread, 174
and Stilton Pâté, 182

Warm Chicken in a Salad of Autumn Leaves, 166
Warm Dandelion Salad with Bacon and Fresh Spinach, 90, *95*

Warm Salad of Artichokes, New Potatoes, and Bacon, 112

Watercress and Cauliflower Soup, 181

Whisky Truffles, 217

Whisky-Cured Sea Trout with Fresh Sage and Lemon, 58

White Chocolate and Chestnut Cheesecake, 175

White Fish
Gratin with Young Vegetable, 75
Stew with Leeks and Mushrooms, 165
White Lamb Stew with a Collage of Spring Vegetables, 61

Whitebait, Crispy, with Fried Parsley and Lemon, 109

Wickedly Gooey Chocolate Cake, 177

Wild Blackberry, Apple and Almond Crumble, 155

Wild Duck, Roast, with a Sharp Plum Sauce, 168

Wild Mushroom Pancakes with Coddled Eggs, 170-171

Wings of Skate with Nut Butter and Capers, 16

Winter Pea and Ham Soup, 13

Zucchini
and Cheese Soufflé, 182
and Tomato Quiche, Made Without Pastry, 127
Tomato and Onion Layer, 68

ACKNOWLEDGEMENTS

Photographs; *Simon Wheeler*
Stylist: *Rebecca Gillies*
Painted Effects: *Tabby Riley*
Illustrations: *Lorraine Harrison*